"In *Growing With*, Kara and Steve approach the topic of parenting with sound biblical wisdom and valuable practical tools. As a mother of two, I will be applying these insights to my own parenting in these rapidly changing times."

**Christine Caine**, bestselling author;
founder of A21 and Propel Women

"There is no joy or challenge or burden like that of parenthood. We're drowning in information; we crave wisdom. *Growing With* has both. It is an outstanding book."

**John Ortberg**, senior pastor of Menlo Church;
author of *I'd Like You More If You Were More Like Me*

"As a dad of two teenagers, I couldn't wait for this book! The mix of real research and real families makes it a valuable addition to any parent's toolbox."

**Jon Acuff**, *New York Times* bestselling author of *Finish*

"*Growing With* is bursting with good news for all parents of teenagers and young adults: you don't have to feel alone, and you don't have to guess what to do next. Through groundbreaking research on families like yours, this book gives you the best answers to your toughest questions about your maturing child's relationship with you, God, and our world."

**Neil Clark Warren**, chairman and cofounder of eHarmony.com

"At a time when the generation gap feels wider and the parenting journey more confusing, *Growing With* offers a way forward through practical resources, thought-provoking questions, and real-life stories. This is a must-read guide for those wanting to grow and to see their children thrive."

**Tom Lin**, president and CEO of InterVarsity
Christian Fellowship

"Kara and Steve's research is helping a generation of parents know how to raise kids who are healthy, loved, and ready to face the challenges of this world. This book is a must-read for parents everywhere."

Margaret Feinberg, author of *Taste and See*

"We all sense that everything's changing, especially when it comes to parenting and raising the next generation. That's why I'm so thankful for *Growing With*. Kara Powell and Steve Argue combine top-notch clinical research, their personal parenting journeys, and a wealth of experience gleaned from helping thousands of parents into an incredible book that will guide parents as they navigate the journey ahead. If you're looking for expert guidance at a critical time because the stakes are high, you'll find it here."

Carey Nieuwhof, founding pastor of Connexus Church; author of *Didn't See It Coming*

"What an incredible book! With one teenager and one twenty-something, we feel like Kara and Steve wrote it just for us—and we couldn't be more grateful. *Growing With* is chock full of compelling, inspiring, and practical help. We'll be recommending this book to every parent we know."

Drs. Les and Leslie Parrott, #1 *New York Times* bestselling authors of *Saving Your Marriage Before It Starts*

"As pastors, my colleagues and I have countless counseling sessions with parents and their adulting children in which both generations have to learn fresh ways to engage each other. I couldn't be happier that Kara Powell and Steve Argue have given leaders and parents a map to navigate this critical space!"

Bryan Loritts, pastor of Abundant Life; author of *Insider/Outsider*

"If you are looking for a fresh perspective on parenting, this is the book. Kara and Steve offer a paradigm-shifting approach that feels both empowering and practical. If you want to connect with your kids in more meaningful ways, are curious about the changing landscape of adolescence, or want revolutionary ideas for how to help raise empowered adults who are connected to their family and faith, *Growing With* is the resource you have been searching for."

**Mandy Arioto**, president and CEO of MOPS International

"Every parent I know (including me) feels overwhelmed and underprepared! I'm so grateful that this well-researched and easy-to-read book offers parents a lifeline. *Growing With* is deep enough to help you adjust to your maturing child, authentic enough to fill you with the courage you crave, and practical enough to guide your next conversation with your teenager or young adult. Not just you but your whole family will be glad you've read this book."

**Doug Fields**, author of *Intentional Parenting*; cofounder of Downloadyouthministry.com

"*Growing With* thoroughly arms parents by providing heartfelt and necessary insights regarding strategies for the holistic development of youth. As a parent of two young adults and a trainer of youth workers, I found *Growing With* to be a welcome addition to my training tool kit. This guide will rescue many parents as they navigate through difficult spaces and will bring new supports to the needs of the ever-changing family."

**Virginia Ward**, assistant dean of the Boston campus and assistant professor of youth ministry and leadership, Gordon-Conwell Theological Seminary

"In *Growing With*, Kara and Steve help parents, teachers, pastors, leaders, and mentors understand the power of walking alongside their adolescent and young adult children and friends. Their focused research and practical advice provide knowledgeable and actionable steps that each of us can take as we enter into the lives of young people in hopes of being a blessing to them and seeking God's best for them as they move toward adulthood."

**Newt Crenshaw**, president of Young Life

"No two families are alike, no two parents are alike, and no two phases are alike. Kara and Steve give you all you need to know and do to have a winning relationship with your ever-changing teenager or twentysomething. If you're like me, you're going to recommend this book to every parent you know."

Reggie Joiner, founder and CEO of Orange

"As a parent, I'm always looking and listening to people I trust. I trust Kara Powell and Steve Argue because I've known them both as people and as leaders. Their hearts to raise up godly young people are on display in *Growing With*. Parents, we need this research and insight because the culture our children are growing up in changes daily. I'm so thankful for this great project!"

Tyler Reagin, president of Catalyst;
author of *The Life-Giving Leader*

# GROWING
## WITH

To Nathan, Krista, and Jessica Powell;
and Kara, Elise, and Lauren Argue.
Growing with you is one of our greatest joys and privileges.
Your love, laughter, and perspectives
animate these pages and our lives.

# GROWING

# WITH

EVERY PARENT'S GUIDE TO HELPING
TEENAGERS AND YOUNG ADULTS THRIVE
IN THEIR FAITH, FAMILY, AND FUTURE

## KARA POWELL AND STEVEN ARGUE

**BakerBooks**
*a division of Baker Publishing Group*
Grand Rapids, Michigan

© 2019 by Kara Powell and Steven Argue

Published by Baker Books
a division of Baker Publishing Group
P.O. Box 6287, Grand Rapids, MI 49516-6287
www.bakerbooks.com

Printed in the United States of America

Library of Congress Cataloging-in-Publication Data
Names: Powell, Kara Eckmann, 1970– author. | Argue, Steven, author.
Title: Growing with : every parent's guide to helping teenagers and young adults thrive in their faith, family, and future / Kara Powell and Steven Argue.
Description: Grand Rapids, MI : Baker Books, [2019] | Includes bibliographical references.
Identifiers: LCCN 2018030386 | ISBN 9780801019265 (cloth)
Subjects: LCSH: Parenting—Religious aspects—Christianity. | Parent and teenager—Religious aspects—Christianity. | Teenagers—Religious life. | Christian education of teenagers.
Classification: LCC BV4529 .P69 2019 | DDC 248.8/45—dc23
LC record available at https://lccn.loc.gov/2018030386

ISBN 978-0-8010-9450-7 (ITPE)

Authors are represented by WordServe Literary Group (www.wordserveliterary.com).

19  20  21  22  23  24  25      7  6  5  4  3  2  1

In keeping with biblical principles of creation stewardship, Baker Publishing Group advocates the responsible use of our natural resources. As a member of the Green Press Initiative, our company uses recycled paper when possible. The text paper of this book is composed in part of post-consumer waste.

# Contents

# Acknowledgments

A mutual journey.

Those are the first three words of our definition of Growing With parenting.

That's not just how we try to parent. It's also how we try to live as scholars, leaders, colleagues, and followers of Jesus.

And it's definitely what made this book possible.

That journey is far better thanks to three teammates at the Fuller Youth Institute—Brad Griffin, Jake Mulder, and Tyler Greenway—who lent their best insights, editing, and research savvy to this book.

We also love sharing this Fuller Youth Institute adventure with the rest of our team, who we brag about at every chance: Jennifer Guerra Aldana, Irene Cho, Macy Davis, Rachel Dodd, Matthew Deprez, Nica Halula, Jen Hananouchi, Cass McCarthy, Giovanny Panginda, Caleb Roose, and Daisy Rosales.

Our research on young people and families is always sharpened by our amazing colleagues at Fuller Seminary, especially Tod Bolsinger, Chap Clark, Scott Cormode, Cynthia Eriksson, Miyoung Yoon Hammer, Ben Houltberg, and Pam King, all of whom offered insights during the development of this project. We also are grateful to the Fuller faculty and deans who provide ongoing guidance to our work, including Justin Barrett, Mari Clements, Joel Green, Dave Scott, Scott Sunquist, Marianne Meye Thompson, and Jude Tiersma Watson.

Every step of our ministry and parenting trek is better (and often faster) thanks to our Advisory Council: Mary Andringa, Jim Bergman, Judy Bergman, April Diaz, Cindy Go, Wally Hawley, Megan Hutchinson, Ken Knipp, Janet Labberton, Jeff Mattesich, June Michealsen, Russ Michealsen, Christa Peitzman, Linda Prinn, Judi Shupper, Albert Tate, Jeremy Taylor, and Jeff Wright. A special thank-you to Advisory Council member Tim Galleher for his herculean work in interviewing and leading focus groups of parents during his sabbatical.

Our Growing With path has been smoothed by a host of sharp leaders, researchers, and parents who gave crucial feedback to our thinking and writing: Jeanelle Austin, Marcos Canales, Annamarie Hamilton, Hal Hamilton, Kristen Ivy, Patrick Jacques, Reggie Joiner, Danny Kwon, Dave Livermore, Linda Livermore, Angel Ruiz, Drea Ruiz, Colleen Sonderman, Steve Sonderman, Shirleen Thorpe, and Virginia Ward.

This book's journey has been fueled by the entire Baker Books team, the vision and editing of Mark Rice and Brian Thomasson, along with Greg Johnson at WordServe Literary Group, who continues to strengthen our collaborative partnership with Baker Books.

To our spouses—Dave and Jen—we can't imagine parenting without you. For every parenting freak-out moment and late-night conversation, every moment of laughter and tears, and every time you stepped in when we've been wiped out: thank you. You have not only made us better parents but better people.

To our kids, not only do we love you, we like you. Thanks for loving and liking us too. When we have fallen short in our parenting, thank you for showing grace and extending forgiveness.

Growing with you is a daily adventure, a perpetual gift, and an indescribable joy. We love seeing each of you uniquely respond to Jesus's invitation to love God and love others. May your lives continue to make this world a better place. We are cheering for you every step of the way.

# PART 1

# GROWING WITH PARENTING

**Growing With parenting:** *a mutual journey of intentional growth for both ourselves and our children that trusts God to transform us all.*

As parents and caring adults, we often feel the gap between us and our kids widening as they become teenagers and young adults. Maybe it's just that they're growing up. But we fear the gap is also a symptom that we're growing *apart*.

Growing With is an attempt to close this family gap.

Growing With requires new lenses so we can see more clearly the world our teens and twentysomethings encounter. In chapter 1, we explore the new cultural, relational, and sociological landscapes that today's young people navigate. Building on this new understanding of our kids, in chapter 2 we propose three new paradigms for parenting that take into account what's worked before but provide your family with a better map to move forward.

Once we are equipped with a new understanding of our kids' world and new parenting paradigms, chapters 3–9 will then offer you a menu of practical ideas to grow with your child both now and in the future.

*A prayer as you begin your Growing With journey:*
*Jesus, our kids are growing up and we are growing older. These truths weigh heavily on us, some days more than others. There are moments when it feels like we're growing together and other times when we fear we're growing apart. By your grace, please grant us faith to trust you with our kids as well as courage to grow with them through our parenting. Spark in us a more expansive vision for this journey—a vision not only about who they might become, but also about who we might become.*

# 1. Growing Up Today

*How Our Kids' Paths Are Different from Ours*

#HowToConfuseAMillennial

Launched recently, this social media hashtag pokes fun at Millennials, meaning those born between 1980 and 2000. The Twitter floodgates opened as users posted their humorous ideas for "How to confuse a Millennial."

*Show them a phone book. #HowToConfuseAMillennial*

*Turn off their autocorrect. #HowToConfuseAMillennial*

*Hand them a job application form. #HowToConfuseAMillennial*

But then young people turned the tables. Teenagers and young adults shared online what they find confusing, and even condemning, about the choices they face.

*Destroy the housing market. Replace grad jobs with unpaid internships. Tell them to buy a house. #HowToConfuseAMillennial*

*Crash their economy and then condescendingly ask why so many of them are living with their parents. #HowToConfuseAMillennial*

*Tell them to follow their passions! As long as they aren't passionate about art, writing, or anything creative. #HowToConfuseAMillennial*

*Baby Boomers will tweet #HowToConfuseAMillennial then call us to fix their internet problems 30 seconds later.*

Ouch.

These #HowToConfuseAMillennial posts highlight pressures that pulsate through our homes, workplaces, churches, and anywhere else those under and over age 30 share life together. The hashtags for iGen, the label for those born after 2000 (including two of the six kids in our two families), are likely to echo these same intergenerational tensions.

Today's teenagers and young adults feel unappreciated, while adults feel like young people are unappreciative.

The younger generation feels belittled; parents often find their children bewildering.

We know. We have been there. We are there. Together with our spouses, Dave and Jen, we each parent three children whom we love more fully than we ever thought possible. Kara's three are now teenagers or college students. Steve's three are a few years ahead of Kara's. Steve's older two daughters are in their early and middle twenties, and his youngest is midway through college. None of our kids are perfect, but we couldn't be prouder of them—foibles and all.

We are crazy about our kids.

And in certain moments, if we are really honest, they drive us crazy. (For the record, we both read this sentence to our kids to make sure they were okay with it. They were, and yes, they feel the same.)

Just last week my (Steve's) oldest daughter (who is also named Kara, not that that's ever confusing) decided that after saving up money from freelance jobs and securing a job with a steady paycheck in a city without great public transportation, it was time to stop borrowing one of our family cars and instead buy her own used car. After she conducted a month's worth of research to figure out her purchasing priorities, I joined her in

## "Millennial" and "iGen"

You've likely seen the term *Millennial* used to describe today's young people. Generational theorists William Strauss and Neil Howe are credited with designating Millennials as those generally born between 1980 and 2000.[1] Like Boomers (those born from 1946 to 1964) and Gen Xers (those born from 1965 to 1980) before them, Millennials are a sociological group who carry certain distinctions influenced by corresponding cultural events (e.g., Millennials were alive during the 9/11 terrorist attack in 2001); significant relationships (with their Gen X parents and Boomer grandparents as well as with more diverse peers than previous generations); and technological shifts (they are the first generation born into the internet age). Now that the Millennial population has reached 83.1 million, they make up over 25 percent of the population and officially outnumber Baby Boomers.[2]

As Millennials age, increasing numbers of our teenage and young adult children will represent Gen Z, sometimes called iGen. iGen is the post-Millennial generational cohort who grew up embedded in the digital age of the internet and social media, which radically impacts how they communicate, relate with others, and learn.[3]

1. Neil Howe and William Strauss, *Millennials Rising: The Next Great Generation* (New York: Vintage, 2000). Other birth year designations for Millennials have been developed, but they tend to overlap heavily with the birth years of 1980–2000.

2. "Millennials Outnumber Baby Boomers and Are Far More Diverse, Census Bureau Reports," United States Census Bureau, June 2015, https://www.census.gov/newsroom/press-releases/2015/cb15-113.html.

3. Jean M. Twenge, *iGen: Why Today's Super-Connected Kids Are Growing Up Less Rebellious, More Tolerant, Less Happy—and Completely Unprepared for Adulthood (and What This Means for the Rest of Us)* (New York: Atria Books, 2017), 1–10.

visiting a local used car lot to check out a few options she'd seen online.

Despite all I say and believe about empowering young people, I was nonetheless surprised by how hard it was for me to let her take the steering wheel in this process. From the moment we drove onto the lot, I felt myself going into "Dad mode"—wanting to speak to the agent for her, guiding her to look at cars she didn't care about. Early on, Kara muttered in my direction, "Dad, I've got this," which was her not-so-subtle cue that I needed to tone down my dad dial a few notches.

I had a host of opinions about the car she should get. I wanted her to have a thousand-airbag, brightly colored behemoth so that all drivers within a mile could see her on the road. She wanted a small, silver economy car that blended in and had the two features most important to her: Bluetooth and a sunroof.

I made a test-drive suggestion; she ignored me.

She pointed out a car; I had to hold my tongue.

I'm certain the agent was amused! In the end, we both got what we wanted. My eldest got the car *she* preferred, and I watched her grow into a woman who knows how to make *her own* thoughtful decisions.

We both grew that day.

## Growing With Parenting

Steve's car lot experience with his daughter, along with a host of studies that would fill your nearest library, suggest that as our kids approach and inhabit their third decade of life, they still need us but in different ways.[1] Some of the core principles of our parenting that worked in the preschool and elementary years are just as important now, but others need to be retired and replaced with new parenting imagination and intuition. To grow our relationship with our 13- to 29-year-olds—and to grow *period*—requires a new strategy we call "Growing With parenting."

We define Growing With parenting as *a mutual journey of intentional growth for both ourselves and our children that trusts God to transform us all.*

Let's unpack this sentence. Growing With parenting is

For additional research and resources to help you embrace and apply our Growing With parenting strategy, please visit fulleryouthinstitute.org/growingwith.

. . . *a mutual journey*, meaning a relational odyssey with our kids that changes over time. Though our kids may *move away* as they grow up, it does not mean that we have to *grow apart* from them. We are always the parent and our child is always our child, but we can parent in a way that keeps closing the relational distance between us and our kids and keeps strengthening our relational muscles. That means Growing With parenting

values relationship and responsiveness over tasks and techniques; pursues our kids rather than waiting for them to go first; and accepts the kid we have, not the kid we wish we had.

. . . *of intentional growth* in that as we watch our kids gain more autonomy and make more decisions on their own, we are not rendered irrelevant (even when we feel so). Instead, our kids need us in crucial new ways. We can address unfamiliar parenting situations with strategic approaches and resources. That means Growing With parenting

works toward solutions rather than only identifying problems; seeks new resources instead of defaulting to old patterns; and catches our kids doing things right rather than only naming the things they do wrong.

. . . *for both ourselves and our children*, meaning we shift focus from getting our kids to do or change something to how we change *with* our kids. That means Growing With parenting pays attention without obsessively controlling;

considers new relational challenges as opportunities for our
own growth; and

celebrates our parenting wins and admits our parenting fails.

*. . . that trusts God to transform us all*, so while we can pursue
relational, intentional, and personal parenting goals, we acknowledge that there are no parenting formulas. The only sure thing
is that God loves our kids and us and has entrusted us to each
other. Let's be faithful parents who commit to develop alongside
our kids, while trusting God's commitment to transform us all.[2]
Accordingly, Growing With parenting

believes that God is working *in* us as much as *through* us;

nurtures our kids to grow in God's image not ours; and

believes that no parenting situation is a "lost cause," because
with God there's always hope.

## Why Do Today's Families Need This New Parenting Posture?

As we highlight the need for Growing With parenting as well as
contrasts among generations (like those that emerged on the used
car lot), we're often asked, "Why do we need a new parenting
strategy now? Hasn't there always been a generation gap?"

Yes. Absolutely. If we turn back the clock 25 years to when I
(Kara) was on a used car lot with my mom and stepdad to buy
my first used car, my story is not all that different from Steve's.
All I cared about was the color (it had to be teal green), while my
stepdad looked under the hood and quizzed the salesperson about
gas mileage and repair records.

But as scholars, pastors, and parents of young people, part of
our advocacy for Growing With parenting stems from our belief
that today's generation gap is often wider. This gap—as well as

the innovative parenting bridges required to cross it—became apparent during a recent four-year study conducted by our team at the Fuller Youth Institute at Fuller Theological Seminary. In the

While there is ongoing debate in the academic and ministry communities about the best terms to describe various age groups before 30, we opt for the following phrases throughout this book:

*Teenagers* and *adolescents* refer to 13- to 18-year-olds.
*Emerging adults* and *young adults* indicate 18- to 29-year-olds.[1]

The term *emerging adult* was first coined by psychologist Jeffrey Arnett, a leading scholar on emerging adults, who identified five main features of the time period between ages 18 and 29:[2]

1. Identity exploration, meaning young people try out various possibilities—especially in love and work
2. Instability
3. Self-focus
4. Feeling in between, in transition, and neither adolescent nor adult
5. Full of possibilities, with flourishing hopes and unparalleled opportunities for transformation

*Young people* is an umbrella term that includes everyone from age 13 to 29.

1. We intentionally leave an overlap between the end of the teenage stage and the beginning of the emerging adult stage as 18-year-olds often straddle the two. Jeffrey Arnett believes that emerging adulthood and young adulthood are two separate phases, with the former most closely associated with the late teens and early twenties, and the latter a more appropriate label for those in their thirties. Jeffrey J. Arnett, *Emerging Adulthood* (New York: Oxford University Press, 2014), 16–17. Yet the majority of parents and practitioners use the two terms interchangeably. While we appreciate the rationale behind Arnett's distinction, given the audience of this book is primarily parents and leaders, we use the terms interchangeably.

2. Jeffrey Jensen Arnett, "Emerging Adulthood: A Theory of Development from the Late Teens Through the Twenties," *American Psychologist* 55, no. 5 (May 2000): 469. Some scholars actually prefer the term *extended adolescence* to *emerging adulthood*. We find *extended adolescence* well describes the delay in transition to adulthood, but as a general rule, we will use the more common term of *emerging adulthood*.

For more on churches that are growing young, including a host of free resources proven to help churches like yours, please visit fulleryouthinstitute.org/growingyoung.

midst of so many churches and denominations aging and shrinking, we wanted to study congregations beating these trends. So we surveyed 250 Protestant and Roman Catholic churches that are "growing young" and pinpointed the six core commitments that make them so appealing and transformative for 15- to 29-year-olds.

During the course of our 10,000 hours of Growing Young research, we immersed ourselves in the last two decades of world-class scholarship on teenagers and young adults. More importantly, we convened focus groups and interviews with over 1,300 people of all generations—including hundreds with teenagers and young adults like your kids as well as with parents like you. To flesh out our understanding of Growing With parenting, we subsequently conducted interviews and focus groups with an additional 79 parents from across the US.

Nominated by church leaders, these parents, who help bring our Growing With parenting definition to life, stem from different geographical regions and denominations, diverse ages and ethnicities, and various marital situations. As you'll see from their quotes and stories, these moms, dads, stepmoms, and stepdads are far from flawless.[3] But they have welcomed you and me to lace up our shoes and trek through the highs and lows of their own family's Growing With journey.

## Why 14 Is the New 24

What we've seen in our research and around our own kitchen tables, and what has fueled our commitment to Growing With parenting, is that the young people of today feel like a new breed. Sixth and seventh graders have just barely put away the stuffed animals of their childhood, but their journey toward adulthood has

Our hope with the 79 additional parents we interviewed was to mirror the ethnic and racial diversity of our nation.

### Our Interviewees and US Census Data[1]

| Ethnic category | Percentage of parents interviewed by FYI | Percentage of all US individuals |
|---|---|---|
| African American | 12.7 percent | 13.3 percent |
| Asian or Pacific Islander | 13.9 percent | 5.7 percent |
| Hispanic or Latino | 8.9 percent | 17.8 percent |
| White | 64.5 percent | 76.9 percent |

To more specifically address parenting dynamics unique to particular cultures, ethnicities, and races, we have sprinkled sidebars throughout our chapters to help you and others apply our principles and practices to your own context. For more resources addressing the realities of multicultural families and communities, see fulleryouthinstitute.org/multicultural.

Our commitment to intentionally pay attention to different cultures stems from our growing awareness of our social location. We are both white, highly educated, upper middle-class Protestant Christians. Throughout our research and our ministry, we have been deeply shaped by diverse young people and parents, and we look forward to continuing to learn with and from our brothers and sisters from different social locations.

For more about the research methodologies we followed as we interviewed 79 amazing Growing With parents of teenagers and young adults, see the appendix.

1. The "Percentage of all US individuals" data is derived from the 2016 US census. While our sample underrepresented white and Hispanic/Latino parents, and overrepresented Asian and Pacific Islander families, we are overall fairly pleased with the ethnic diversity of our interviewees. Note that the total of the percentages for US individuals exceeds 100 percent because some individuals are included in multiple categories and because census questions explore both race and ethnicity.

already started. Teenagers today in the US are facing life choices that many of us didn't experience until our midtwenties. Growing With is important because for the teenagers in your family and community, 14 is the new 24.

The onset of puberty, marked by the average age of first menstruation in girls, has dropped three years—from age 16 to somewhere between ages 12 and 13.[4] While that biological shift is noteworthy, we are more concerned with the cultural and experiential pressures that leave adolescents with too many burdens and too few resources.

## MORE TIME-DEMANDING ACTIVITIES AND LESS FAMILY TIME TOGETHER

Often in our formal and informal discussions with youth pastors and parents, we ask them to name the biggest struggle of teenagers. Their number one response? Busyness. By far. In one study, 13- to 17-year-olds were more likely to report feeling "extreme stress" than adults.[5]

Even more appalling is the gap between teenagers' anxiety and parents' recognition of their kids' stress. Approximately 20 percent of teenagers confess that they worry "a great deal" about current and future life events. But only 8 percent of the parents of these same teenagers are aware that their child is experiencing such stress.[6]

Once adolescents obtain their driver's license, today's parents install apps that keep them updated of their child's whereabouts. Such apps may assuage parental fears for their safety but not fears that their teenagers are drifting emotionally.

Once a source of love and support, the family has become the vehicle (pun intended) that drives teenagers from one activity to the next. Our good friend and former colleague, Chap Clark, has conducted ethnographic adolescent research on church and school campuses and concluded that parents "have evolved to the point where we believe driving is support, being active is love, and providing any and every opportunity is selfless nurture. We are a culture that has forgotten to be together. We have lost the ability to spend unstructured down time."[7] Of course, there are times when the sacrifices we make (e.g., missing out on rest, work, or time with our own friends) are a reflection of our love, but Growing With parents realize that loving our kids often requires something different.

## MORE SUPERFICIALLY CONNECTED BUT LESS DEEPLY SUPPORTED

Our kids' use of devices opens them to new and unfamiliar worldviews and perspectives with just a few taps. When you and I were their age, that same exposure required plane trips or visits to the local public library.

What we needed cars to do, our kids can do on their phones. Without leaving their rooms.

We had to check out encyclopedias. Our kids click on Wikipedia.

We talked with our friends on analog phones, with long cords connected to walls, from inside our homes. Our kids message their friends using apps on smartphones—ever-connected minicomputers—from anywhere.

Our teenagers can't imagine not being able to google questions about a map and "YouTube" questions about math. While that's helpful when we don't know how to help them with their homework, our teenagers' connections with others expose them to adult waters you and I probably didn't dive into until college or beyond.

Here are some quick facts to help you understand how your teenager uses digital technology to connect with others:

- Ninety-two percent of teenagers report going online at least once per day. Almost one in four teenagers confess going online "almost constantly."[8] This continual access to the world is often an expected—or required—part of the school day and homework load.

- Teens who own a smartphone spend an average of 4.38 hours per day using it.[9]

- Three-quarters (78 percent) of higher-income teens have their own smartphones, compared with 51 percent of lower-income teens.[10]

- A majority of teenagers—approximately 71 percent—use multiple social media platforms to stay in touch with friends.[11]

- The median number of texts a teenager sends and receives per day is 60. That number increases significantly for 15- to 17-year-old girls.[12]

As you pursue Growing With parenting, keep in mind that the devices, apps, and social media platforms used by our relationship-hungry kids have become a double-edged sword—simultaneously making them feel both more connected and more alienated. Pictures and social media posts about Tuesday afternoon ice cream runs and Saturday night parties can make your teenager feel like "everyone else" has more friends and a more exciting life.[13] Your child posts something humorous or heartfelt and is crushed when no one "likes" or comments on their pictures or words. Technology lets your child put themselves out there, but often their disappointment in feeling excluded or unaffirmed leaves them feeling like a trapeze artist floating through the air, unsure whether a friend ahead will grasp their hand before they fall.

### Why 28 Is the New 18

While our kids' journey toward adolescence has accelerated, the inverse is also true. We need Growing With parenting to help bridge the generation gap between us and our kids because for the typical twentysomething in the US, the process of becoming an adult has slowed down. Way down.

Take Jordan, a smart, put-together 25-year-old at my (Steve's) church who seems to love his life. He's single, sets his own schedule, has good friends, and is trying to live in an urban center with other peers.

From the outside, Jordan's life seems charmed. But in a recent conversation, he confessed that he just lost his job, which made him realize that he does not love his career trajectory. Further, the amount of debt he accrued to get his degree leaves him overwhelmed with school loan payments. With a specialized degree, it's not easy to break into a relatively new field, so Jordan feels vocationally stuck. The competitive job market leaves him few options beyond an hour-long commute, inadequate pay, and slim benefits.

Most adults tell Jordan to "move" or "just get another job," but this feels insensitive. He has worked to develop a meaningful friend group, wants to grow his relationship with his girlfriend, and attends a church he cares about. Moving away for the sake of a better job means Jordan loses almost everything and everyone valuable to him. Like so many of his peers, Jordan feels behind in his life goals and sees little hope of catching up.

Our young adult children typically trend older when they finally achieve many of the markers usually associated with full adulthood. A Growing With parenting posture helps us appreciate and empathize with our kids' extended trek to adulthood.

The median age for first marriage is now five years later than 50 years ago, hovering at around 26.5 for women and 28.7 for men.[14] Only 20 percent of 18- to 29-year-olds were married in 2010, in comparison with 59 percent in 1960.[15] Despite this shift, both young men and young women still feel an "age 30 deadline" by which they hope to find their soul mate and tie the knot.[16]

The average age for women bearing their first child is 25 years, almost five years later than women in 1970.[17] The average birthrate has declined steeply in the US, from 3.5 children per woman in 1960 to 2.0 in 2010.[18]

Given the uncertainties of today's economic climate and the increased assumption that a college degree is a nearly universal requirement for the middle-class job market, more of our young adult kids are pursuing more higher education. Two-thirds of high school graduates now enter college, a higher proportion than previously in American history. Yet only 28 percent of young adults have secured a four-year college degree by age 25.[19]

When they eventually plunge into the workforce, the average young adult holds six different jobs between the ages of 18 to 26. Whether because of job dissatisfaction, better opportunities, or a young person's changing immigration status, two-thirds of these job shifts occur between ages 18 and 22.[20]

Partly because of our young adults' lengthening career and educational odysseys, they take longer to become financially

## Why Are Young Adults Getting Married Later Than Previous Generations?

In answering the question of why young adults seem to meander toward marriage, practical theologians David P. Setran and Chris A. Kiesling highlight two types of reasons, the first of which are "objective" and represent broad sociocultural changes such as:[1]

- More education is now required to secure preferred jobs, which delays the financial security generally desired before marriage.
- Women have more educational and career opportunities, so they may feel less dependent on marriage for financial and social status.
- While the biological clock is a reality, reproductive technology opens options for later childbearing not possible for previous generations.
- The widespread availability of birth control and the cultural tolerance for premarital sex means individu-

independent. In comparison with fifty years ago, parents today provide 11 percent more financial help to young adult children.[21] Forty percent of young adults in their twenties move back home with their parents at least once.[22] In some cases, twentysomethings are pouring their paychecks into their extended family, which provides needed help for their parents, grandparents, and siblings but also prohibits them from saving or investing.

As a result of these shifts, sociologists monitoring the five key "adult" events of leaving home, finishing school, becoming financially independent, getting married, and having children report a dip in the number of 30-year-olds who have attained all five of these markers. In 1960, more than two-thirds of young adults could check all five of these boxes. In 2000, this was true of less than half of females and less than a third of males.[23]

als feel freer to engage in a sexual relationship prior to marriage.

In addition, Setran and Kiesling point to more "subjective" individual reasons, including:

- Many young adults have grown up in the shadow of divorce and shy away from lasting commitments before investing extra time to ensure the relationship will work.
- Some would rather explore, travel, experience life on their own, and develop a strong personal identity instead of getting married.
- Many young adults do not see marriage as part of the pathway to adult maturity, but rather as the endpoint of that pathway—a relationship to enter once their individual accomplishments are complete. This makes marriage the ultimate "merit badge" when the time is right—which is likely "not right now."

1. David P. Setran and Chris A. Kiesling, *Spiritual Formation in Emerging Adulthood: A Practical Theology for College and Young Adult Ministry* (Grand Rapids: Baker Academic, 2013), 166.

In fact, today's young adults choose different markers to define adulthood. According to Arnett, they believe adulthood arrives when they are able to accept responsibility for their actions, make independent decisions, and become financially stable.[24]

It's just that those three markers are occurring later and later. Growing With parenting helps us journey with our kids, not judge them, especially when our 28-year-olds sometimes seem like 18-year-olds.

## Are Today's Young People as Entitled as They're Labeled?

No, they aren't. We wince when we see young people characterized as entitled simply because they are taking longer to achieve our cultural markers of adulthood. Having said that, today's teenagers and young adults have logged experiences that make them more prone to attitudes and actions that can be easily misperceived.

Current teenagers and emerging adults are not as loyal to employers as previous generations, in part because they have seen their parents and peers experience layoffs and the pensions of older generations evaporate.[25] In addition, despite being told they will get a well-paying job after college, it's often the youngest in our society who are hardest hit during our nation's economic downturns. Fearful and financially strapped young adults are quick to jump ship to new (and hopefully more secure) job possibilities when they emerge.[26] What might look flighty may actually be a reasoned response to a new employment reality.

In addition, our culture promises this generation instant results. They can take online classes, binge-watch Netflix when they want, and receive online orders in less than 24 hours.

Your kids are also used to giving feedback on Yelp and posting about themselves and others on social media, instilling a sometimes-inflated sense of others' interest in their opinions.[27]

They've also come to expect that things will generally go their way. Holding up the mirror to examine our own parenting, we see today's young people are used to their parents stepping in to change the rules in their favor. If teachers are too strict, supervisors are unfair, or coaches are blind to their talent, many (especially middle- and upper-class) parents, stepparents, and grandparents have inserted themselves to fix what was "wrong."[28]

Add this together and we end up with a current generation that approaches vocational and other major choices more like dating relationships they can exit when desired.[29] On the surface this may seem like entitlement or disloyalty, but often underneath hide the foundations of parenting strategies and cultural expectations that previous generations have instilled and passed on.

### Why 30 Can't Be the New 20

Given the earlier starting line and later finish line in the journey toward adulthood, it's tempting for twentysomethings to conclude that it's acceptable—and maybe desirable—to drift from job to job and relationship to relationship. Meg Jay, a clinical psychologist specializing in adult development and twentysomethings, recalls being told by one of her clients that the twenties were supposed to be "the time of her life." After all, this young person quipped, "30 is the new 20."[30]

What's at risk when young people begin to see 30 as the new 20?

Having watched far too many young adults roam romantically and vocationally, Jay warns that as young adults approach age 30, "a spotty resume that used to reflect twentysomething freedom suddenly seems suspect and embarrassing. A good first date leads not so much to romantic fantasies about 'The One' as to calculations about the soonest possible time marriage and a baby might happen."[31]

Far from being a decade to coast, the twenties are a developmental sweet spot not to be wasted. Growing With parents grasp that while kids can make important decisions and even change their trajectory after age 30, the twenties are an important inflection point for investment as young adults make some of their most significant choices about life, love, work, and worldview. Your twentysomething young adult will benefit from preparation, a plan, and people who nudge them toward God's best for them not only now but also for decades to come. This third decade in life is a time not just to drift toward adulthood but instead to take deliberate, intentional steps toward specific adult-like goals.

## Growing With in Faith, Family, and World: Three Dynamic Verbs

As you've gathered by now, the need for us to learn and grow with our children has emerged in large part because their twenty-first-century expedition is different than ours was at their age. On the one hand, our kids' sophistication has accelerated and it seems like they are getting older earlier; but on the other hand, they feel less mature as the typical markers of adulthood are now delayed. In the midst of this jumble of both hurry and waiting, Growing With parenting integrates our children's developmental shifts into a cohesive family strategy that brings out the best both in us and in our kids.

As we work toward a mutual journey of intentional growth that trusts God to transform us all, we need to pay special attention to three key areas of our child's exploration: *family*, *faith*, and *future*.[32] In all three areas, they need us to learn from parenting strategies that have worked for us when they were younger while simultaneously adjusting those strategies to the contours of their current trail.

Because Growing With parenting is an evolving pilgrimage, our research and experiences compel us to suggest three verbs that reflect the primary goal in a child's trek with family, faith, and the future. We call these "dynamic verbs" because a young person's experience of them is constantly changing, so we have to keep paying attention and keep responding with agility. Since these three dynamic verbs—*withing, faithing,* and *adulting*— comprise the essence of the Growing With parenting strategy we showcase in the rest of this book, we conclude this chapter with illustrative stories of three different families, each learning to grow with their children.

## Withing: A New Relational Support

By *withing,* we mean *a family's growth in supporting each other as children grow more independent.* At any life stage, we are either growing or stagnating. In any family's journey, we are relationally either growing together or growing apart. Activities done on behalf of our kids or near our kids do not necessarily mean connection. As we will dive into further in chapters 3 and 4, Growing With seeks more.

Nineteen-year-old TJ and his parents, Cedric and Kimberly, are a Growing With family seeking more. They have been active in a Growing Young church (included in our research) since TJ was a toddler. Six years ago, Cedric, who is a football coach, wanted his middle school son to play a sport. It didn't have to be football; Cedric just wanted TJ to stay active. So TJ chose golf.

While not the sport Cedric envisioned for his son, it quickly became obvious to TJ's family that TJ had a knack for golf. And he loved it. Both in middle school and high school, TJ played as much golf as his homework schedule allowed. TJ's hard work paid off with multiple regional and state championships. TJ's parents were at every tournament, cheering him on.

Thanks to his golf prowess, TJ was recruited by 12 major universities during his senior year in high school. Even though Cedric and Kimberly cared deeply about TJ's success in college and beyond, they knew they faced a parental fork in the road. While they both had strong opinions and wanted God's best for TJ, they recognized that college was a life-orienting decision they could not and should not make on his behalf. As they later explained to us, "Our guiding principle was that we weren't going to make the decision *for* him, but we wanted to walk *with* him."

Kimberly asked TJ to make a list of questions to investigate at each school. As he got answers to those questions, TJ crossed six schools off the list where playing golf would preclude him from exploring his interest in debate and his passion for playing guitar.

With four months left to make his college decision, TJ visited the remaining six schools. Cedric and Kimberly accompanied him on some of the trips when they felt like they needed to see and taste a particular college's culture. They wanted to experience the military flavor of Annapolis. They wanted to imagine with their son how his ethnicity might affect his college experience. As a biracial teenager growing up in a multicultural urban neighborhood, TJ quickly realized that he felt most at home on ethnically diverse college campuses.

Whether or not they were at each campus with TJ, Cedric and Kimberly helped TJ list what he liked and disliked about each college. Oriented by their conviction that this was TJ's decision to make, they never told him what they thought he should do. Instead, in the spirit of Growing With, they helped him pinpoint the aspects of each college that matched his emerging vision for his life.

One evening TJ came into the living room and announced that he had just emailed coaches at two of the schools to withdraw himself from their recruitment pool—without first talking to Cedric and Kimberly. Kimberly's first internal reaction was, "Oh no, you didn't talk to us about this first." But within a few moments, as she later recalled, "I knew I needed to put my money where my mouth was and support him as he figured this out himself."

In the end, TJ narrowed down his choice to two great—but very different—schools. With two days left before the NCAA deadline, he chose a small private college close to home that would give him plenty of time to pursue debate and leading worship in addition to playing golf.

Cedric and Kimberly could have tried to make TJ's decision *for* him. Instead, they wisely chose to journey *with* him. Not once did his parents tell him what they thought he should do; the decision was his to make.

### Faithing: A New Spiritual Openness

We tend to think of *faith* as a noun. We assume faith is something we have. That's true, but theologically faith is also a verb; it is something we exercise so that it continues to grow. By *faithing*, we mean *a child's growth in owning and embodying their own journey with God as they encounter new experiences and information.*[33]

For some of our adolescents, those early encounters with new experiences and information initially cause their faith to cool. As we will further explore in chapters 5 and 6, Growing With parents who hope that their teenagers' transition into the next life stage will bring about more encouraging faith news often end up disappointed. Whether it's because college-age young adults want to party, they are differentiating from the family and faith cultures of their adolescence, or they simply stayed up too late the night before, being involved in a faith community often feels counter to a young person's quest for autonomy. As Christian Smith, a sociologist and lead researcher for the National Study of Youth and Religion (NSYR), describes, college-aged adults "aren't asking their parents for a weekly allowance anymore, so why should they keep going to their church or keep practicing their faith in the same old way?"[34]

While there are some indicators (and finger crossing) that young adults will find their way back to church, the migration often doesn't happen until after they get married or have children of their own. Given the trend toward emerging adults waiting longer to become spouses and/or parents, this means that their church attendance gap could be 10 years or more.[35] The absence of religious input during the period when young people are making crucial life decisions may significantly impact their future spiritual trajectories.[36]

In the midst of our kids' faithing highs and lows, our faith as parents also continues to evolve and grow. This was certainly the case with the McKay family. College was not in 17-year-old Colin McKay's plans. Instead, he had set his sights on becoming a microbrewer.

One comprehensive study of the faith of over 2,000 young people, the National Study of Youth and Religion (NSYR), identified the dominant, de facto religious belief system of teenagers today as *moralistic therapeutic deism*.

It is *moralistic*, meaning that religious young people equate faith with being a good, moral person (often this boils down to "being nice").

It is *therapeutic*, meaning that faith becomes a mechanism to feel better about oneself.

And it is *deistic*, meaning that God exists but is not involved in human affairs with any regularity.[1]

Teenagers are not devising this lackluster faith on their own. They are not *substituting* moralistic therapeutic deism for the messages they hear and the modeling they see in churches and families. Instead, they are *mimicking* the tame faith that permeates their faith communities and homes. Dr. Kenda Creasy Dean, a frequent advisor for FYI's research and a member of the NSYR research team, concludes,

> Who can blame churches, really, for earnestly ladling this stew into teenagers, filling them with an agreeable porridge about the importance of being nice, feeling good about yourself, and saving God for emergencies? We have convinced ourselves that this is the gospel, but in fact it is much closer to another mess of pottage, an unacknowledged but widely held religious outlook among American teenagers that is primarily dedicated, not to loving God, but to avoiding interpersonal friction.[2]

1. Christian Smith and Melinda Lundquist Denton, *Soul Searching* (New York: Oxford University Press, 2005), 162–65.
2. Kenda Creasy Dean, *Almost Christian* (New York: Oxford University Press, 2010), 10.

While his mom and stepdad, Deanne and Ray, had a hard time imagining microbrewing as a career, they tried to hold their tongues. They were glad they did so, because eight years later, the midtwenties version of Colin was recognized in his field for his diverse creations and unique flavors.

While Colin's career was soaring, his faith was not. Though he had been raised in the church, Colin told his mom and stepdad that he was now agnostic. As devout Christians, Deanne and Ray tried to be patient with their son's journey, but that patience turned to panic when Colin started dating Mindy, a young woman who made it very clear that she was an atheist.

Desperate for help, Deanne and Ray sought advice from others in their church. Some in their congregation admonished them to "cut off" their son. Others challenged them to "take a stand for Jesus" by evangelizing Mindy. Still others said their son would return to Christ if they would simply pray more.

None of this well-intended counsel sat right with Deanne and Ray, so they chose to keep loving their son and welcomed Mindy into their occasional family gatherings. After a few months, Mindy pulled Deanne aside and with tears in her eyes said, "I don't understand why you welcome me the way you do. I've told you I'm an atheist, yet you show me so much kindness. Thank you."

Now 27, Colin is still brewing beer and still dating Mindy. While Deanne and Ray remain authentic in their faith and Colin and Mindy still keep faith largely at bay, they all seem to be experiencing a more profound sense of grace and love.

While Deanne and Ray wish—and pray—that Colin and Mindy would reorient their lives toward Jesus, they cherish their relationship with these two young adults and the sparks of openness to faith that flicker in them here and there. Instead of Colin and Mindy distancing themselves from God and family, they have been drawn to the faithing of Colin's parents who, admittedly, are still figuring it out as they go.

## Adulting: A New Capacity to Shape the World

The verb *adulting*, with origins traced back as far as 2008 on Twitter (usually as a hashtag), captures the ups and downs a young person experiences as they do the hard work of growing up. By *adulting*, we mean *a child's growth in agency as they embrace opportunities to shape the world around them.*

Our daughter, Krista, gave me (Kara) and my husband a front-row seat to her adulting process when she started high school. Midway through her eighth-grade year, she and I met with her new high school counselor to choose her classes. When it was time to specify her foreign language requirement, Spanish was the obvious option. While she didn't think she was very good at foreign languages like Spanish, Krista already had a few years of Spanish under her belt from middle school. We live in Southern California. More and more of our neighbors locally, nationally, and globally speak Spanish. I took AP Spanish in high school. My husband and I met on a mission trip to Mexico. Krista's older brother loves Spanish. In short, this was an easy choice.

Until a few weeks later when she started taking American Sign Language (ASL) during her last quarter of eighth grade. She came home every day and enthusiastically showed us what she had learned that day in ASL. She never did that in Spanish (or any other class for that matter).

She watched videos online to learn more signs—working ahead of the rest of the class. (For the record, she never did that in any other classes either.)

With high school still a few months off, Krista asked if she could replace Spanish with ASL. Dave and I told her we wanted to think about it for a few days. That night in our bedroom, it took only a few minutes for Dave and me to make a decision that seemed pretty simple to us—Spanish offered our eighth grader more future job prospects, more opportunities for conversation and to build relationships in our neighborhood and church, and was more likely to be used by God in cross-cultural friendships.

Krista decided to convince us to change our minds. She decided to take some first steps toward adulting.

She prepared a presentation about sign language for Dave and me—accompanied by a multimedia show she designed on her laptop—expounding on the top 10 reasons she should take ASL.

She called the admissions offices at not one but two colleges she was interested in attending to see if taking ASL would affect her acceptance.

In her 14 years, she had never done extra work to try to change our minds. So we prayed, did our own research, talked to other parents and her teacher, and worked through some of our control issues as well as our pseudo-obsession with this decision. We eventually granted her permission to substitute ASL for Spanish.

Three years later, part of me still wishes she was taking Spanish. In many ways, Spanish is the "safer" choice for her future. Letting her choose sign language was a Growing With baby step for Dave and me in letting go of the reins of control and letting her race forward.

## All-In Parenting

These three Growing With verbs remind us and our kids that we are all in-process, and as parents, we must keep reimagining our roles. More specifically:

While *withing* is about our relationship with our children, we generally take the lead in laying the relational bridges that keep us connected. Our role focuses on building new ways to connect with them as they (and we) grow older.

While both we and our children are *faithing*, we are more likely than they are to keep our radar tuned to both our and their faith journeys. Our role is to engage them creatively as they explore their faith journeys while recognizing that our own journeys must unfold as well.

While our children are the primary ones in the family who are *adulting*, it's usually up to us to thoughtfully respond to the relational and vocational challenges they encounter. Our role thus shifts, requiring us to be more patient, less controlling, and more attentive to their values.

We think of this interplay of withing, faithing, and adulting as a journey that you take with your child along a Growing With path.

We will add more details to this path in chapter 2, but for now, note that it is not a linear path. It is not a completely clear or straight path. Like navigating a complex trail or a city subway system, there are curves, stops, and at times confusing intersections that require help and support. As you know from parenting thus far, every day with your child is an (often unpredictable) adventure—one that keeps you on your toes and wondering what to do next.

So while this book offers all sorts of ideas and suggestions for your child, we offer even more for you as the parent. Parenting in this stage isn't about meeting your kid halfway. Parenting is more about being all-in.

## Our Prayer-Filled Hope for You and Your Family

Name any error that could be made in trying to journey with your kids' withing, faithing, and adulting. The two of us have probably made any error you can think of. And we've felt the struggles and tensions that seem almost inherent in parenting today.

We know the feelings of peer pressure that emerge as parents compare their kids' achievements and watch their kids compete for coveted slots on the court, in the classroom, in the concert hall, and eventually maybe on the college campus.

We know how it feels to be bombarded by articles, books, and posts that remind us that we aren't giving our kids enough attention and one-on-one time. Or maybe too much attention and too much one-on-one time.

We have felt the force of the unreachable standard that tells us we're not preparing our teenagers and young adults for future tech jobs. Simultaneously, we are also accused of allowing them to become addicted to technology.

We have aspired to raise strong and compassionate girls and boys in the midst of the plethora of voices that caution us not to make them too masculine or feminine.

We have wrestled with the tension of pushing our kids too hard while preparing them for a competitive world.

We have encountered the excitement and lament of navigating a world that fails to see what we see in our kids while still demanding so much from them.

In the midst of these tensions and contradictions we navigate, here is our invitation for all of us parents: Let's be honest with ourselves. Let's admit that we are not perfect. Let's accept that we are not meant to be perfect. And neither are our kids.

Our hope-filled prayer is that this book helps you avoid the outright lie that it's too late to adjust your parenting. That the ship has sailed. That you've missed the boat. (And any other nautical phrases that make you feel anchored—get it?—to parenting-as-you've-always-done-it.)

To swap metaphors, as your child hits adolescence and young adulthood, the ruts of your family's routines and patterns are deeper than when your child was younger. It takes more energy to exit those ruts and forge a new Growing With path.

But both of us are optimistic that you can forge that path.

Our optimism for you and your Growing With parenting is fueled by how we've seen the God of the universe change families and young people alike.

Like the 28-year-old pastor's daughter who wanted nothing to do with faith or church during college who is now blogging about how Jesus has changed her life.

Or the 23-year-old who chose drugs over relationship with his parents but has now done an about-face and is taking baby steps toward home.

Or the 17-year-old who used to "hate" her dad and stepmom but now seems to tolerate—and sometimes even enjoy—them.

But forging new paths means we need to forge a new parenting strategy. As Albert Einstein reportedly claimed, "Insanity is doing the same thing over and over again and expecting different results."[37] So in the rest of this book, we continue to dream with you about a Growing With parenting method that helps your teenagers and emerging adults grow with God, your family, and our world. And that helps you do the same.

## Practical Questions to Grow With My Child

1. If you are a parent of a teenager, how does your child's experience confirm that 14 is the new 24? What in your child's life counters this saying?

2. If you are a parent of a twentysomething, how does your child's life confirm that 28 is the new 18? How, if at all, is your child perhaps also embracing the myth that 30 is the new 20?

3. Which of the three Growing With dynamic verbs—withing, faithing, and adulting—is easiest for you to embrace?

4. Which of the three Growing With verbs is toughest for you and your child to embody? What makes it difficult for you?

5. What do you hope happens in your family as a result of reading this book? How about in your own attitudes or behaviors?

# 2. Pursuing the Growing With Posture

*Parenting in Real Time*

The Argue family has photographs everywhere.

That's because my (Steve's) wife, Jen, loves taking pictures. Over the decades her photos have chronicled our marriage, friendships, vacations, and kids' growth.

At each photo opportunity, the Argue family dialogue is predictable. Jen urges, "Oh, here's a great shot. Get together!" The other four Argues roll our eyes, take a deep breath, and assume the photo-shoot pose. While we complain in the moment, inevitably we end up thanking her for each great snapshot when we pore over pictures that spark memories and feelings.

Honestly, it's sometimes hard for me to look at these old photos. We seem so happy and carefree. But then I remember that the snapshots never tell the whole story. Over the years we have been committed to growing with our daughters, but this commitment is not always easy. Our photos rarely capture how exhausted we were as young parents; how overwhelmed we were trying to balance grad school, jobs, and work; or how anxious we were about moving, parenting, kids' sicknesses, or extended family challenges.

Not only are we tempted to selectively forget certain past family seasons, we also are tempted to try to preselect ideal future scenarios for our kids. These "future snapshots" are laced with our hopes, dreams, and expectations and are reflected in the language we use about our kids' futures.

"When Trey gets his driver's license . . ."

"When Jasmine goes to college . . ."

"When Valentina takes over the family business . . ."

"When Zach comes home this summer . . ."

"When George gets married . . ."

These future aspirations for our children are completely normal, but they can be just as unrealistic as the snapshots remembered from the past. They are selective and likely have more to do with us as parents than with what may actually be best for our teenagers and young adults.

The reality is that our kids are growing into their own persons. Their interests, aspirations, and skill sets may be different from ours. Growing alongside our withing, faithing, and adulting kids requires holding our future snapshots loosely, because our dreams may not end up being theirs.

You want your son to get his driver's license, but he isn't interested.

Instead of going to college, your daughter chooses to take a gap year.

You're mentoring your stepdaughter into the family business, but her interests are in a different field altogether.

You love his girlfriend and envision wedding bells, but they announce they're going to live together first.

You're encouraged by his steps toward independence, but then he gets arrested for drug possession and needs rehab.

You couldn't wait for your new grandchild to take on the family name, but they named her after a flower with a strange spelling.

You assumed that she would secure a full-time job after graduation, but she moved home and is still looking.

You're excited that he finally got married, but then his wife wants a divorce and you feel caught in the middle.

You were so proud when she told you that she made the dean's list, but then she admitted she was pregnant.

You sacrificed so much to see the first person in your family go to college, but you worry that her ethnic identity and sense of responsibility to the family are eroding.

You raised him to be Christian, but he just told you that he's not sure he believes in God anymore.

Growing With parenting means putting aside our selective past memories or attempts to control our kids' future dreams. Instead, our kids need us most in the present. And that requires a new parenting vision.

## From Snapshots to Live Cams: Parenting in Motion

In contrast to snapshots, let's consider live cameras (or "live cams") as a better Growing With parenting metaphor. The campus where my (Steve's) daughter attends college has live cams that let viewers see new buildings being constructed in real time or a moment-by-moment view of the local beach. In fact, whatever your hobby, there's probably an online live cam for you. For climbing enthusiasts, there are Mount Everest cams, and for budding zoologists, there are panda cams!

While it may be adorable to watch a panda feed her young, we are not advocating "live cam" parenting as a new method to track our adolescent or young adult 24/7. Unlike snapshots, the live cam metaphor reminds us that since our kids' lives are in motion, what we see in them is constantly changing. Growing With parenting isn't about preserving the past or predicting the future (as if either of those were even possible) as much as it is about cultivating our relationships with our kids where they are today—*in real time*.[1]

Fostering a live cam parenting mentality that honors a growth mindset means we perpetually ask questions such as:[2]

What do we see in our kids these days?

What do our kids need from us in our relationship with them right now?

Who do I need to be as a parent this week?

How are our kids' lives and relationships with God changing these days, and equally important, how are ours changing?

When we as parents start with these questions, we recognize that our parenting must be in motion. Growing With parenting assumes that our teenagers and emerging adults are . . . well . . . growing, and it doesn't take a PhD to know this is true. The evidence surfaces everywhere as our kids grow out of their clothes, empty out the refrigerator, and act a little less excited to see us at the end of the day. These obvious differences are symptomatic of deeper, more significant changes.

In order to embody our Growing With definition, we must respond to our kids' maturing process with a parenting posture that honors their current withing, faithing, and adulting progress and that positions our family for future growth. That posture is best accomplished through a new paradigm we introduce in this chapter. Your young people are *learners*, *explorers*, or *focusers* who consequently need *teacher*, *guide*, or *resourcer* parenting.

## Learners, Explorers, and Focusers: Tracking with Our Kids through Three Key Stages

Generally, young people ages 13–29 have been divided into two primary developmental categories: adolescents and emerging or young adults. While these are helpful pigeonholes, we believe today's young people actually warrant more specific and nuanced descriptions that best fall into three categories we call *learner*, *explorer*, and *focuser*.[3] The following figure depicts the relationship between the two traditional categories of adolescents and emerging adults and our preferred categories of learners, explorers, and focusers that better reflect today's young people.

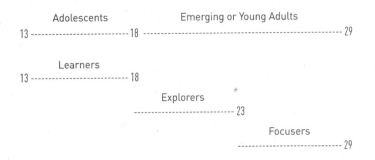

We have intentionally depicted these stages with fuzzy endpoints and with lines that overlap in order to acknowledge that because of our kids' various personalities, life situations, and cultural expectations, they progress through them in varied time lines. Some of us may determine that our kids are either ahead of or behind the curve. Others of us might find that our kids are learning in some areas (e.g., in their relationships) while they are exploring or focusing in other areas (e.g., in their vocations or spirituality). This is entirely possible. And normal. Our purpose in describing these three stages is to remind us all that our kids are changing and we need a live cam view of them that grows as they grow.

### Learners: Changing at Light Speed

When our kids are in late middle school through high school (typically ages 13–18), they are in the *learner* stage—a season of rapid physical, emotional, relational, intellectual, and spiritual growth and change. Parents who long to grow with their kids recognize that most 13- to 18-year-olds are:

*Learning how to use their increased intellectual capabilities.* Teenagers are learning to think abstractly and are able to form more robust arguments (as all six kids in our two families have demonstrated all too well). Abstract thinking gives them new capacities to envision an ideal situation or perfect world, thereby inspiring their imaginations, problem-solving abilities, and aspirational goals. Furthermore, they also more readily notice the imperfections in others, in our world, and even in themselves, which can be disorienting.[4]

*Learning how to live in their physically changing bodies.* They've entered puberty and notice change almost every time they look in a mirror. They have new energy and appetites, and how they care for themselves (through exercise and nutrition) starts having long-term effects.[5]

We are grateful to have been shaped by, and to have the honor of contributing to, the Phase resources created by Reggie Joiner, Kristen Ivy, and our other friends on the Orange team. To find out more about these resources, which also pay attention to your kid's ongoing maturity every year, visit justaphase.com.

*Learning how to manage their heightened emotional awareness.* Despite what we may sometimes feel, our high school students are not "crazy" or just "overemotional." Rather, their prefrontal cortex is developing and now integrating all they experience into an emotional milieu that is often intense and unpredictable.[6]

*Learning how to navigate a broadening circle of relationships embedded with expectations.* Their circle of peers increases in size and diversity. In-person and online relationships increase opportunities for connection and possibilities for risk.[7]

*Learning how to start living out their faith as their own.* They start recognizing that their relationship with God is bigger than Sunday and that not everyone sees God the way they do. They now grasp that belief isn't simple and that doubts are real.[8]

### Explorers: Sorting through Lots of Options

When our kids are roughly ages 18–23, they enter the *explorer* stage. As our kids leave adolescence and launch into emerging adulthood, they often venture for the first time away from home or home-oriented routines to pursue their goals, relationships, and beliefs. Legally they are expected to be more reasonable, and vocationally they are trying on different roles through service, training, education, and work. Explorers feel excited about the future yet still feel unsure about themselves.[9] Parents who grow with their kids recognize that most young people in this stage are:

*Exploring career paths through schooling, internships, travel, military service, new jobs, or gap year projects.* Most young people entering this stage say that they want to get more education and training. As we will further describe in chapter 8, this is the most educated generation, the generation with the most student loan debt, and the generation with a rising number of incomplete degrees.[10]

*Exploring their own interests, gifts, and talents.* They are often "trying on" many options that carry greater weight than the identity exploration of their younger learning selves. This often results in switching jobs and majors as they seek congruency between what they do and who they believe they are.[11]

*Exploring what they desire in deeper, more romantic relationships.* While this does not mean that their current relationships will lead to marriage (since many delay marriage until later), they are more emotionally invested and often more physically involved than in high school, which means more heartbreak when relationships do not work out.[12]

*Exploring new ways to relate to their parents.* Generally, this age group reports that their relationships with their parents are better than during their teenage years. They have richer conversations, are more open about their similarities and differences with their parents, and are more appreciative of their parents.[13]

*Exploring what they believe and how those beliefs inform their view of work, relationships, faith, and life.* Our kids at this age are introduced to a multiplicity of worldviews different from what they have known, which typically prompts them to reconsider their own assumptions. For some this is a liberating experience. For others it's disorienting. As we will explore further in chapters 5 and 6, some leave church, perhaps returning later or perhaps pioneering new spiritual paths.[14]

### Focusers: Landing on the Path(s) That Best Fits

When our kids approach the latter half of emerging adulthood (ages 23–29), they inhabit the *focuser* stage. They begin to gain a clearer sense of who they are and have likely made educational, vocational, and relational choices that set them on particular trajectories. These choices have opened up new opportunities and closed others. Parents eager to grow with their kids recognize that most in this stage are:

*Focusing on their careers.* They find themselves having to strive harder to find friendship, community, and love while working longer hours as they try to establish themselves vocationally and financially.[15] On average, they spend approximately 45 hours a week at work.[16]

*Focusing on their relationships.* Many no longer find themselves in the semi-structured environments of school, military, or gap-year organizations. The automatic peer connections they accessed in their early twenties diminish as they move to new cities and focus on their careers. They discover they must be more intentional with their friendships and sometimes endure seasons of loneliness. Their relationships are becoming more mature and emotionally closer as they learn to trust and support their significant friends and perhaps live with a romantic partner or get married.[17]

*Focusing on their beliefs.* While parents and churches hope that focusers will eventually "return to church," when and why some reengage with church is varied and complex. Thus, those who rely only on church attendance numbers to gauge young people's faithfulness will misunderstand focusers' faith journeys. Many emerging adults search for a spiritual identity but find it challenging to connect with churches that do not address their personal challenges and social concerns, or that fail to see them beyond their singleness.[18]

*Focusing on a reset.* Too many young people have bought the mantra that "30 is the new 20," and they are reaping the fruit of an unfocused decade. As a result, many are trying to get beyond cobbled part-time jobs to an established career. Some are recovering from drug and alcohol abuse. Others are smarting from the loss of failed relationships and are longing for a relationship that will last.[19]

## Growing Kids Need Growing With Parents

The following chart spotlights the unique journey of today's learners, explorers, and focusers.

| Learners | Explorers | Focusers |
| --- | --- | --- |
| In the midst of rapid physical, emotional, relational, intellectual, and spiritual growth and change, learners are increasingly aware of their abilities, flaws, and possibilities. | Often venturing for the first time away from home or home-oriented routines to pursue their goals, relationships, and beliefs, explorers feel excited about the future yet unsure about themselves. | Having developed a clearer sense of who they are and having likely made educational, vocational, and relational choices that set them on particular trajectories, most focusers feel on track with life. Yet others still feel behind. |

Based on the chart above and your own experience, it is pretty easy to surmise that the strategies you used to parent your kid last year (or even last week) do not always work today! As parents, we never have the luxury of saying we have cracked the parenting code. Success today with our kids does not guarantee success tomorrow. Kara and I confess that we often feel like we're just a few steps away from the next parenting challenge or surprise. While it takes effort and stamina to keep up with our growing kids, we believe we can anticipate their growth by holding on to this important piece of wisdom: young people need a different kind of parent in each of these three stages. Withing looks different with a 14-year-old than it does with a 24-year-old, as do faithing and adulting.[20]

Specifically, we propose that as kids enter each new developmental period, parents grow with their kids by starting out as *teachers*, then moving to *guides*, and finally becoming *resourcers*. The following figure extends our diagram of the three primary stages of young people by including these three parenting roles.

**Young Person**

```
            Learners
 13 --------------------------- 18
                              Explorers
                 ---------------------------- 23
                                            Focusers
                        ---------------------------- 29
```

**Parent**

```
            Teachers
 13 --------------------------- 18
                              Guides
                 ---------------------------- 23
                                            Resourcers
                        ---------------------------- 29
```

## Parents as Teachers

Growing With parenting of learner children (roughly ages 13–18) requires us to play the role of teacher. We recognize that the term *teacher* conjures up many different images. What we *don't* mean by teaching is merely telling our kids what to do, maintaining order, or expecting our developing teenagers to accept what we say at face value. Instead, our role as teachers requires us to do what educators describe as "learner-centered teaching." Learner-centered teaching asks something different of the teacher. It calls us teacher parents to integrate new ideas, skills, and competencies into the frameworks and paradigms our teenagers already possess.[21]

There is a vigilance inherent in learner-centered teaching since we are required to step closer to our teenagers' lives to see them, know them, and engage with them. In many ways, the characteristics of a learner-centered approach can be applied to Growing With teacher parents.[22]

*Teaching invites and endures practicing.* We assume that parenting our kids will be a messy process in which they will learn by trying, not just by listening. This means that teaching allows for the lawn not to be cut "just right," the dishes not to be put away perfectly, the makeup to be a little too much, and the hairstyle not to be our favorite. In this mess, teacher parents find opportunities for conversation and growth—both for their kids and themselves.

*Teaching trains specific skills.* We don't assume that our teenage kids know how to plan ahead, ask someone to the dance, introduce themselves to an adult, or track down missed homework assignments after they've been sick. In these moments, we have a chance to teach them to make a game plan and walk them through the skills they need to navigate the scenarios they will encounter.

*Teaching encourages reflection.* We recognize that a crucial part of our kids' learning is encouraging them to reflect on their experiences. So we cultivate space for our kids to process an event beyond what score they got on the test, whether or not they made the team, or if they "liked" youth group tonight. Our questions about their feelings, their methods, or their opinions teach them to reflect on their lives and grow in their critical thinking.

*Teaching introduces choice and agency.* Our learner kids are in a stage when we can encourage and motivate them by giving them new and expanded options. This may mean we hold more loosely to our opinions and our need for efficiency in order to encourage their agency and growing independence.

*Teaching fosters collaboration.* We value learning together and sharing what we're learning with each other. Instead of asking our kids, "Did you get your homework done?" we consider asking, "What is something interesting you've been learning lately?" In the spirit of withing, we invite them to share what they're discovering. We can also seek out others to help them grow in areas they are interested in or where they need help.

To envision a snapshot of a Growing With teacher, imagine how you would interact with your learner about how they might plan their weekend. A parenting reflex for pre-learner kids might be to dictate their weekend schedule or, in response to your kids' requests, offer yes or no responses based on the reasoning "because I said so." What if you instead played the teacher role and, prior to the weekend, began to dialogue with your kids about their school responsibilities, family obligations, home chores, and social plans? This approach likely would require more time and intentionality (not to mention occasional frustrations and adjustments!) but would allow opportunities for your learning teenager to manage time, think of others, and pursue their interests. To be a better teacher, in what areas might you need to loosen your grip and desire for control? What will you, as a teacher parent, learn about your child . . . and yourself?

We recognize that our young people today live in a variety of households. I (Steve) was adopted as a child and grew up with two adopted siblings, while Kara's parents were divorced when she was in elementary school and both remarried when she was in middle school. So our own experiences and the changing demographics of families today confirm that the adults who feel responsible to parent their young people may be married parents, single parents, stepparents, foster parents, adoptive parents, grandparents, or extended family members. Our proposal is that all of these caring adults must consider the type of parenting that best matches their young person's life stage.

## TOP QUESTIONS FOR TEACHER PARENTS

Beyond navigating weekend expectations, many parents misread a growing distance with their teenage kids and stop trying to connect with them.[23] But our learner kids need us to take new steps toward them and grow with them by asking ourselves these questions:

- Where is my child growing and how do I affirm their progress?

- Given my commitment to withing, what are new ways I might try to connect with my child in this learner stage?

- Where does my child need feedback to help them grow in their knowledge, habits, skills, or competencies?

- What is a goal that my child has, and what might it look like for me to support them while encouraging them to take responsibility?

- Instead of just telling my child what to do, how might I start asking their opinion on decisions in order to learn more about them and grow their confidence in using their voice?

- In what aspects of my teenager's life should I connect them with other adults who are better positioned to teach them than I am?

### Parents as Guides

Growing With parenting shifts a second time when our kids inhabit the explorer stage (roughly ages 18–23) and need us to embody the role of *guide*. As someone who loves hiking, I (Steve) often envision a guide as someone who leads other hikers through less-traveled trails so they can experience new sights and new challenges. I have also appreciated being guided through the biggest metropolitan centers by enthusiastic citizens who love their neighborhoods and want me to experience the subway, meet artists on the west side, or enjoy an incredible meal in an obscure restaurant.

Consider what guides on a hiking trip or city tour do and don't do. A guide is the experienced traveler who knows the terrain, uses their trained eye to gauge the weather, highlights the beautiful spots to stop, and anticipates what lies ahead that is either safe or dangerous. A guide doesn't carry your pack or do the exploring for you! They walk with you, attending to the novice traveler's untested instincts, wrong turns, missed opportunities, and awe-inspiring moments.

As parents who are guiding our explorers on easier or familiar terrain, we will encourage them to run ahead. On more dangerous or technical segments, we'll draw a little closer. With explorer kids, we shift our parenting focus away from setting goals for our kids and toward guiding them on the journey of setting their own goals. As guide parents we recognize certain elements of guiding.

*Guiding requires more empathy and perspective taking.* Our seasoned perspectives may be valuable to our explorers, but what is usually more important is that we do our best to understand their goals, their views, and their self-determined next steps. Parents as guides must expertly and artfully gauge how much help is most beneficial for their kids. This requires us to empathize with our kids in order to understand their hopes, fears, and aspirations. It means valuing the process of growing up as much as the result of reaching adulthood.

*Guiding discerns both novice and intermediate terrain.* As guides, we grow with our explorer kids by evaluating how closely they need us to journey with them. Good guide parents know when to encourage our kids by stepping away, encouraging them to take the lead, as well as when to step closer to support them through more taxing terrain. In this stage, we parent by expecting more of our kids while recognizing that they may still need initial assistance in learning how to live on their own, cook their own food, manage their time, pay their bills, plan their future goals, and advocate for themselves.

*Guiding values different forms of appreciation.* This stage signals a change in how our explorer kids view their relationship with us. While their increased physical distance and growing autonomy highlight the gap between us, explorer kids may discover a newfound appreciation for their parents' unique journeys. This new stage offers promise for a new adventure together, even if the previous teacher-learner relationship we had with our children was rocky.[24]

To envision a snapshot of a Growing With guide, imagine your explorer kid wants to switch jobs or their undergraduate major. The temptation might be to quickly solve their problem, offer them an ultimatum, or manipulate them into doing what you think is best. But this is your chance to empathize with them, seek to understand the crossroads they feel, and join them in the process, not just the solution. What might it look like for you to let your child take the lead? How can you phrase your questions with an aim of encouraging them to assess and think ahead for themselves? What will you, as a guide parent, try to learn in this process yourself?

## TOP QUESTIONS FOR GUIDE PARENTS

As guides, we grow with our explorer emerging adults by asking ourselves questions such as:

- What can I help them see or notice about the current situation they face?
- How might I encourage them to reflect on their past, present, or future?
- As they grow in adulting, what can I encourage them to try on their own?
- What is more technical terrain where they may need help navigating life's demands? How can I guide them toward tools that can provide that help?
- How are my child's encounters affecting me?

- How do I reconnect with my child after we've felt relationally distant for so long? What's a "path" that reflects our shared interests that might offer a starting point toward reconnection?

- When have I not been there for my child? What might I need to ask forgiveness for so that we can get our relationship back on a healthy path?

### Parents as Resourcers

As maturing emerging adults approach the focuser stage (roughly ages 23–29), they are now typically leaning in to their chosen career and relational trajectories. Our parenting journey shifts yet again. We do not lead them as teachers or walk beside them as guides, but instead we intersect with them as *resourcers* during crucial points in their lives.

They may now come to us for advice pertaining to new challenges and opportunities. They seek us out because we have lived through the life events they now anticipate, including career advancement, marriage, parenthood, renting or buying a home, and financial investments. As resourcer parents, we grow with our kids by recognizing particular aspects of resourcing.

*Resourcing exercises patience.* Being patient means resourcing our focusers when they ask for our input while resisting the temptations of being either too controlling or too aloof. We can be interested in their faith, relationships, jobs, families, or goals, but we must not demand full disclosure. Chances are that our forcuser kids will seek us out for some topics but not others. They may want to talk with us about careers but not faith. They may want to talk investments but not relationships.

In some cases, our focuser kids may not want to access our wisdom at all. This can be disheartening, but it is also an opportunity to grow in our patience, acknowledging that we cannot force our resourcing on them. Whether they reach out or not, we can always pray for them and consistently remain interested in them.

*Resourcing offers perspective.* As we both work with graduate students, we have found that many of them need help in asking the questions they don't know they're supposed to ask. The perspective of another person (including a parent) offers more questions, another angle, or a third-way option. When our forcuser kids seek us out, they are often looking not for the answer but for a bigger view of the situation. Some of us feel like we don't have much to offer, so we downplay the power and relevance of our advice.

But let's remember that we have lived longer, have succeeded and failed more, and have learned more life lessons. There's a difference between a peer saying to a focuser, "It's going to be all right," and an older person telling them, "It's going to be all right." The latter possesses the quality of a lived life that forcuser kids seek.

*Resourcing supports—no matter what.* During my pastoral work, I (Steve) have seen many families divided because some parents didn't approve of their forcuser kids' choices. While these situations are complex, resourcer parents remember their place in their focuser child's decisions. Once our kids choose, our role as a resourcer requires us to find ways to love and encourage them— whether or not we agree with their decisions. When we are hurt, offended, and distraught over their choices, it may be prudent for us to consider whether we overstepped our role and tried to take possession of a choice that was never ours.

To envision a snapshot of a Growing With resourcer, imagine your focuser kid is faced with two options. She's wrestling with whether she should move to another city to take a job promotion or stay in town with her boyfriend who she has been dating for a year. Perhaps you have even faced a similar choice in the past and you have a strong opinion about what she should do. She hasn't come to you for advice yet. How does that feel? If she does talk with you about her decision, how will you frame your questions and interactions with the aim of honoring her priorities rather than yours? What is your best posture as a resourcer parent who is encouraging but not enmeshed, and available but not anxious?

## TOP QUESTIONS FOR RESOURCER PARENTS

Resourcer parents are the trusted conversation partners who help forcuser kids see the bigger picture of the situations they face.[25] As resourcers, we grow with our focuser emerging adults by asking ourselves questions such as:

- How do I tend to be either too controlling or too aloof? What steps can I take to be a more available resource?

- What can I share from my life events?

- What questions can I ask to help them think about their situation from a broader perspective?

- What encouragement can I give them?

- How do I follow up without "checking up"?

- Who is another adult whose perspective would be beneficial to my young adult in this season?

- Why does their decision bother me? Even if I disagree with their choice, how can I still show support in order to maintain our relational connection?

In the following chart we build on the previous one by adding our corresponding role as teachers, guides, and resourcers.

| Learners | Explorers | Focusers |
| --- | --- | --- |
| In the midst of rapid physical, emotional, relational, intellectual, and spiritual growth and change, learners are increasingly aware of their abilities, flaws, and possibilities. | Often venturing for the first time away from home or home-oriented routines to pursue their goals, relationships, and beliefs, explorers feel excited about the future yet unsure about themselves. | Having developed a clearer sense of who they are and having likely made educational, vocational, and relational choices that set them on particular trajectories, most focusers feel on track with life. Yet others still feel behind. |

| Parents as Teachers | Parents as Guides | Parents as Resourcers |
|---|---|---|
| Lead their kids by teaching them how to integrate new ideas, skills, and competencies into the frameworks and paradigms their teenagers already possess. This role requires parents be patient, attentive, available, interested, and encouraging. | Accompany their kids as their kids articulate their own journey and goals. This role requires wisdom to know when to encourage independence and when to offer proactive support during trickier life scenarios. This role recognizes the changing yet potentially positive relationship that can develop with their kids. | Intersect with their kids' lives during crucial points by exercising patience, offering perspective, and preserving their relationship with their kids, even if their kids' beliefs, values, or goals diverge from their own. |

When we add our kids' maturing as learners, explorers, and focusers, as well as our subsequent role as teacher, guide, or resourcer, the Growing With path we introduced in chapter 1 becomes more complete.

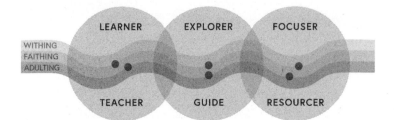

You can see immediately the overlap between the life stages (indicated by the darker sections of the intersecting circles). That's because the progress from learner to explorer and explorer to focuser is often gradual. In some areas of their lives, your 18-year-old will still act like a learner; in others they will already have transitioned to being an explorer.

While not to be taken literally, the dots on the withing, faithing, and adulting paths remind us to consider our kids' status and our relationships with them. Learners need teacher parents to take the lead and help them anticipate life's demands. Explorers need guide parents who walk alongside them, assisting them as they need support. Focusers need resourcer parents who watch their kids take the lead and are available as wise counsel when their kids ask for it.

### Three Mantras Growing With Parents Tell Themselves

As Growing With parents journey alongside their teenagers and emerging adults, they remind themselves of three key mantras.

#### Mantra #1: Today I Will Attempt to Be at the Right Place at the Right Time

Parents who understand that their maturing kids are working through learning, exploring, and focusing stages will make two commitments. First, they will discern which stage their kid inhabits. Second, they will then pinpoint the most appropriate parenting role, whether that's as a teacher, guide, or resourcer.[26]

When parents forget their most appropriate role for the current season and situation, confusion and tension ensue. Could it be that "helicopter parents" who are overly involved in their children's exploring and focusing stages are actually parents who haven't learned to be anything but teacher parents?[27] These overly attentive parents still assume that their role is to direct and protect their children rather than play a guiding or resourcing role.

Similarly, might it be that "distant parents" are merely acting as resourcers, making them seem hands-off and disconnected from their learner and explorer kids?

Sadly, the most heartfelt parenting calibrated for the wrong developmental stage keeps parents from parenting—and growing with—their kids. When we start to sense a disconnect in our relationship with our kids, this may be our signal that we are not being a bad parent but must become a *different kind of parent* to match our kid's new stage.

### Mantra #2: Today I Will Allow Grace to Give Me Courage to Take a Next Faithful Step

Sometimes it is hard to let go of the past, not because it is better but because it is familiar. Our past successes and failures have woven a narrative about our parenting that keeps us from seeing new ways we can grow and change ourselves. We get stuck, afraid, or cautious about taking parenting risks.

As followers of Jesus, we celebrate God's grace as a gift of God's faithfulness that saves us from our sinful motives or actions and strengthens us daily. This Christian reality of grace reminds us that every day is a new beginning filled with potential to learn and grow—no matter our past mistakes or successes. God gives us courage to embrace new ways of thinking, behaving, and believing as parents. It is a journey infused with this message of grace: Today you only need to take one faithful step toward who you want to become as a Growing With parent.

Perhaps Jesus said it best when he invited his disciples to "follow me." His invitation had long-term implications, but it also was a present, simple, grace-filled invitation to take a next faithful step. As Christians and parents, we believe that each day Jesus extends this same invitation to us.

### Mantra #3: Today I Have What It Takes to Be the Best Parent for My Kid

No matter how you may feel right now, remember that you are journeying with a generation of mothers, fathers, foster parents, and grandparents raising kids and grandkids who are experiencing new parenting opportunities and challenges. Lately I (Steve) have started parenting seminars with this phrase: "From one parent to another, remember that you are the right parent for your child and that no one loves your child the way you do." Often the crowd responds with a holy silence. And even with tears. There is a solidarity among parents and an unspoken understanding that we love our kids, we want what's best for them, and we want to be there for them. So let's just reaffirm that together now:

No one loves your child the way you do.
You are the right parent for your child.
You have what it takes to be the best parent for your kid.

To help you best love and parent your child, we've structured the rest of this book in order to increase withing in your family, faithing in your child's relationship with God, and adulting in their engagement with the world. In the following chart, we build on information presented earlier in the chapter and highlight our main concepts in order to offer a map for the remainder of the book.

| **Traditional labels for young people** | Adolescent (ages 13–18) | Emerging/Young Adult (ages 18–29) | |
| --- | --- | --- | --- |
| **Our suggested categories for today's young people** | Learner (ages 13–18) | Explorer (ages 18–23) | Focuser (ages 23–29) |
| **Growing With parenting role** | Teacher | Guide | Resourcer |
| **Thriving in family** | Withing chapters 3–4 | | |
| **Thriving in faith** | Faithing chapters 5–6 | | |
| **Thriving in future** | Adulting chapters 7–8 | | |

Chapters 3–8 are divided into three major sections, each of which propels your family forward in the quest toward withing, faithing, and adulting. Since each of our families is different, feel free to jump around through these chapters based on your most pressing questions. You are more than welcome to plunge into

faithing or adulting chapters before you dive into withing if those are your family's most urgent needs.

For those of you who gravitate toward data on parenting young people, focus on the *insights* section in each chapter that draws on our own experience as well as world-class research conducted on families and young people like yours.

Those of you searching for new and fresh parenting approaches for your growing kids might want to focus on each chapter's *ideas* section that puts the research into practice.

If you're especially eager to take a first or next step in your Growing With parenting, you'll be grateful that we conclude each chapter with *practical questions* to pinpoint the best few ideas for your family in this particular season.

Throughout all three sections, we provide sidebars that we hope are catalysts for your Growing With parenting. These "Growing With in Real Time" case studies (which may mirror your own parenting dilemmas), quotes from parent interviews, and additional insights from research are all geared to help you better respond to your maturing learner, explorer, or focuser.

Our hope is that these sidebars, insights, ideas, and practical questions help us all move away from distorted snapshots of the past and unrealistic images of the future. Instead, let's pay attention to the live cam of our family by moving forward and growing with our kids.

## Practical Questions to Grow With My Child

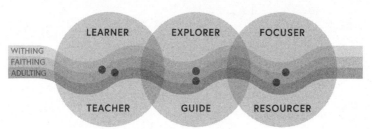

1. Most days I find myself parenting in the present rather than the past or future:

1 ........................................ 5 ........................................ 10
Never                    Sometimes                    Always

2. Take a minute to reflect on the kind of adolescent or emerging adult your child is and what kind of parenting role you play with them. In the first two columns below, write the name of your kid(s) and which life stage category best fits them. Then in the far right column, jot down your most appropriate parenting role.

| Name | Life stage (Learner, 13–18; Explorer, 18–23; or Focuser, 23–29) | Parenting role (Teacher, Guide, or Resourcer) |
|------|------|------|
| | | |
| | | |
| | | |
| | | |

3. After reading this chapter, what information, quote, or story inspired your thinking, or gave you a fresh perspective or something important to think about?

4. What is one way you are encouraged that you are becoming a Growing With parent?

5. What hurdle will you need to overcome in order to be more of a Growing With parent?

6. Think of others you know who embody many of the qualities of a Growing With parent. Jot down three questions you would like to ask them.

# PART 2

# THRIVING IN FAMILY: "WITHING"

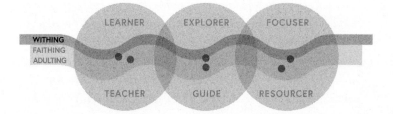

**Withing:** *a family's growth in supporting each other as children grow more independent.*

It's not that you don't want your kid to become independent. You just want to stay connected in the process.

One day she seems content to hang out with you. The next she is too busy. (And even if she weren't busy, you aren't sure she would want to.)

Some days you think you're tracking with him. Other days you wonder whose child he really is.

Enter *withing*.

At the heart of withing beats this truth: independence doesn't mean total separation. The goal of mature independence is really *interdependence*: learning that we were made for relationships—made to rely on others' presence and support in our lives, and to offer our presence and support in return. This healthy interdependence doesn't form overnight; it takes seasons of recognizing when we need each other more and when we need each other less, as our relationships change over time.

In chapters 3 and 4, we offer you practical steps to strengthen your withing bonds with your child on both an everyday basis and when those connections feel stretched. Our hope is that you'll gain all sorts of ideas that help you fight *for* your child, not *against* them.

*A prayer:*

*Jesus, we love our kids even more than we imagined we would. But sometimes we want to keep them overdependent on us and on the relationship we had when they were younger. We confess that it feels safer that way. As they gain wings, show us how our relationship can remain rooted without smothering. Prune away our selfishness, our insecurities, and our drive for control that fuel our fears rather than inspire our hope. May our love for our children mirror your unconditional love for us. And may this perfect love drive out all fear while drawing us and others to you.*

# 3. Getting Warmer

*Everyday Steps That Build Withing*

The Powell family abides by this general principle: if our kids are capable of doing something themselves, we want them to do it themselves. For us, parenting usually includes empowering our kids to take care of—and be responsible for—as many slices of their lives as is developmentally appropriate and possible.

Around age eight, each of our kids became capable of packing a simple school lunch, usually consisting of a bagel, cheese stick, fruit, and a granola bar. When their friends Charlie, Tyler, Abby, and Tori opened their lunchboxes at noon and were surprised at the contents inside, our kids realized that most second graders don't make their own lunches. But they also felt pride and accomplishment that they were cobbling together their own food.

Right around that same age, our kids also became adept at making their own breakfast. Toast with peanut butter and jelly. Cereal with nuts and fruit. These were not elaborate breakfasts, but our kids benefited from an early morning sense of achievement. Dave and I benefited from a few extra minutes in the morning to exercise or check email. These specific strategies for building competence won't work in every family, and you might focus your efforts on different areas of competence, but "make your own breakfast and lunch" became a pretty normal phrase for our clan.

Fast-forward eight years. Nathan, our oldest, was a sophomore in high school facing a rigorous week of midterm exams. Even busier than usual, Nathan was holed away in his room, and we saw him only a few minutes here and there for meals. Motivated by a desire to lessen my learner son's stress and increase his healthy caloric intake, I shook up our family routine and made breakfast for all three kids.

When they walked into the kitchen and saw pancakes and sliced apples, they looked at me—and then at each other—with puzzled faces.

"Mom, why are you making breakfast for us? Is something wrong?"

"Yeah, are we in trouble or something?"

"Don't you normally just make breakfast on the weekend?"

No, nothing was wrong. No, they weren't in trouble. And yes, it was still Monday.

The next morning, my French toast evoked the same bewildered looks and questions.

So did lemon muffins and eggs on the third day.

By the time Nathan had wrapped up his midterms week, the kids were no longer confused. And I had one of those Growing With flashes of parenting insight. Long touted as "the most important meal of the day," breakfast might also be one of my most important times with my son in this season of his life.

Driver's license fresh in hand, Nathan had begun driving himself to school in the morning. After school he headed to soccer or volleyball practice, and then often directly to youth group or worship practice. He was home for our family dinners less than half of the time. I loved having a son who could drive to his own activities (and also occasionally drive his sisters to theirs). But I missed our time together in the car and around the kitchen table. I didn't feel like I was with him enough for our relationship to keep growing.

So for the rest of that busy year, breakfast was the new dinner. Those daily 15 minutes over waffles and grapes were often my best conversations with my son. Sure, we chatted about logistics of the day, but we also talked about what was going on in his classes, in his friendships, and in his soul. Thankfully, he was a teenager who had the capacity to hold a conversation at 7:00 a.m. And I woke up to see a parenting pattern that no longer served its purpose in our family, sucked up my pride that my kids made their own breakfast, and changed.

Nathan was 16, and I needed new rhythms to grow with him.

## Withing: A New Goal for Your Family Relationships

From ages 13 to 29, one critical goal in our family relationships is to figure out the rhythms and rituals that propel our families toward *withing*. The goal of withing is *a family's growth in supporting each other as children grow more independent.*

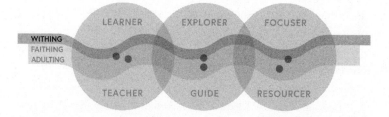

The withing journey is better when we pair two important parenting instincts: challenge and support. Developed in the early 1960s by Nevitt Sanford, the "challenge and support theory" posits that the typical person grows best when their environment holds the right balance of challenge and support. Too much support with not enough challenge results in status quo. Too much challenge with not enough support leads to surrender. Growing With parenting strides forward in both.

Withing beats at the heart of Growing With parenting. One of the most important phrases in our definition of Growing With is that it is a "mutual journey." It's impossible, not to mention unpleasant, to try to embark on a journey alongside someone else if you're not willing to walk *with* them.

The patterns of withing change as your child changes. Now that Nathan is 18 and transitioning to college, a 15-minute breakfast together is no longer possible. Withing during college is more about connecting over text and a screen than over toast and scrambled eggs.

Steve's twentysomething daughter moved home for a while after college. Even though her bedroom is ten feet away, her teenage life is *years* ago. Any inclination Steve or Jen feels to default to old parent-child roles doesn't work anymore. It *can't* work anymore. Forging an ever-evolving relationship of support and challenge means respecting her space and schedule, clarifying each other's expectations, sharing domestic responsibilities, and negotiating her financial commitments. All of which must be done mutually.

Some of you are in this same resourcer role with focuser young adults, but your kids are married and may have children of their own. You're expanding your withing circle to grow with your child's new family—in-laws and all.

In all three stages of teacher, guide, and resourcer parenting, as you think about the type of relationship you want with your maturing child, we hope you choose the on-ramp of withing. Even

As a reminder, the definition of Growing With parenting is a commitment to "a mutual journey of intentional growth for both ourselves and our children that trusts God to transform us all." If you need a refresher on the essence of the learner, explorer, and focuser stages, you can find those explanations in chapter 2 in the section "Learners, Explorers, and Focusers: Tracking with Our Kids through Three Key Stages."

though the traffic jams of your child's indecision or your own frustrations over the timing of their life and faith choices might slow you down, withing leads not only to the best destination but also to the most enjoyable road trip along the way.

## Withing Insights

True withing requires us to align with the particular pace and progress of our own family, but we can lean on research and the experiences of other families to inform our first and next steps.

### *Warm Is the New Cool . . . and a Primary Faith Conduit*

The fuel that powers your withing journey is your family's closeness. As we studied worship services and ministry programs at Growing Young churches, we quickly realized that today's teenagers and young adults aren't necessarily attracted to fog machines, laser lights, and loud music. In many of our nation's most effective congregations, it's not about hype or being hip. Given the relational hunger of today's young people, one senior pastor summarized in a simple phrase what we had seen in church after church: "Warm is the new cool."

As another pastor confessed, "We can hire and buy cool, but we can't hire—or fake—warmth."

While this data emerged during our study of churches, the best literature confirms that family warmth is just as important, just as impossible to fake, and just as vital in a young person's faith journey.

Warmth and withing go hand in hand. As your family gets warmer, you will get better at withing (and vice versa).

A recently completed 35-year longitudinal study of 3,500 family members from 358 three-generation families has convinced us that few attributes are more important in our own families than warmth.

The team conducting this massive research project, led by Vern L. Bengtson, described families as "warm" when the child perceives a close relationship with one or usually both parents.[1] In looking at the relationship between family warmth and young people's faith, Bengtson's team concludes, "When children perceive their relationship with parents as close, affirming, and accepting, they are more likely to identify with their parents' religious practices and beliefs, while relationships marked by coldness, ambivalence, or preoccupation are likely to result in religious differences."[2]

Across multiple measures of religiosity (including religious intensity and participation), and across multiple faith traditions ranging from Mormonism and Judaism to Christianity and atheism, there are greater parent-child faith similarities in families who maintain close relationships.[3] It seems that when a child feels close to a parent, they are more likely to follow in the faith footsteps of that parent. When a child feels distant from a parent, they tend to walk away not only from that parent but also from what is important to the parent, including faith.

Of course, there are never any guarantees. Lots of warm families have kids who are not currently following Jesus. Faith may come much later, and along the way you will still have a good relationship because of warmth. The arcs of both our relationships and our faith formation are long, and withing can continue to grow over time.

It turns out that rearranging my morning schedule to make breakfast and connect with my kids over French toast isn't just good for our relationship, it may be good for my kids' faith too.

### Adolescents and Young Adults Need Withing Dads

While both mothers and fathers are important in maintaining a balanced atmosphere of warmth and challenge, fathers or other male role models may be the more important barometer. In evangelical Protestant families, 46 percent of young adult children who feel "not close" to their fathers maintain the same faith as their parents. When young adult evangelicals feel "close" to their fathers, that rate jumps to 71 percent.[4] That 25 percent difference in faith adoption towers over the 1 percent gain in faith adoption between evangelical children who feel "close" (versus "not close") to their mothers.

Of course moms matter, and of course kids need more than just warmth from dads. But it's worth paying attention to this finding. Too often we lay the responsibility for the emotional climate of the home on moms; this research challenges us to reconsider our assumptions. The bottom line is this: dads and moms, your kids need the unique relational warmth you each bring to your family. In families where a dad is not present, it's all the more important to seek male role models who can build withing bonds with your learner, explorer, or focuser.

### It's Your Child's Perception of Warmth That Counts, Not Yours

As is the case in most research on family relationships, when it comes to detecting warmth and withing in our family, our child's radar is more definitive than our own. The same 35-year longitudinal study of families and faith highlighting warmth found that our child's perceptions of closeness matter more than our own perceptions. Interestingly, children tend to rank the quality of their emotional bonds lower than their parents do.[5] So not only do learners, explorers, and focusers tend to give their family warmth a lower grade, their grade also counts more than that of their parents.

What makes this extra challenging is that as our kids grow, their experiences—and perceptions—of our family warmth change. Our learner adolescents may have fond memories of feeling closer to us when they were in elementary school now that our conversations are punctuated with conflict over curfews and clothing choices.

Our explorer and focuser young adults who have moved away from home might remember feeling more family warmth when we were all living in one space for family meals, spontaneous burrito runs, or long conversations in the car. Our kids' experiences and perceptions are not static, which means we have to continually pay attention to—and ask our kids how they are feeling about—our family rhythms and relationships.

### Empathy Helps Us Journey With, Not Judge

Currently in academic, philanthropic, and for-profit fields, there is a fresh awakening to the power of empathy. By empathy, we mean "feeling with" young people. As defined by research professor Brené Brown, empathy is "simply listening, holding space, withholding judgment, emotionally connecting, and communicating that incredibly healing message of 'You're not alone.'"[6]

As we conducted interviews and visited worship services in Growing Young churches, we quickly noticed their commitment to empathize with learners, explorers, and focusers. In a world that patronizes young people, or greets them with judgmentalism cloaked in helpful suggestions (e.g., "Instead of being on social media all day, why don't you actually go and talk with real friends?"), Growing Young churches recognize that for today's young people, the starting line is earlier, the finish line is later, and the race in between is better when young people trek with supportive peers and adults.

When we as parents can take that same supportive posture, our teenagers and young adults benefit. Parental empathy has been found to be associated not only with more harmonious family

*"In our family, there is no conversation topic that is taboo. We talk about everything as a family. Topics that are gross or sometimes socially unacceptable—none of that is off the table." —Coby, an Indiana dad of an explorer and a focuser*

interactions, but also with a host of positive outcomes in our kids, including:[7]

- A greater ability to regulate their emotions
- Lower rates of depression
- Less aggression
- An increase in their own empathy

### Getting Warmer with Age . . . and Effort

Our success in finding the right withing synergy between support and challenge is especially complicated in adolescence when we are our child's teacher. During the high school season, we inherently take a more instructive posture that can feel like "nagging" to our learner kids. Our teaching-oriented responses to our teenagers' missing homework, dented cars, and broken curfews are needed but can eat away at the relational glue between us.

Good news: as our kids age, our relationships with them typically improve. Three-quarters of parents report that their relationship with their kids improved after age 15. And about that many agree that there is less parent-child conflict once their kids are no longer teenagers.[8]

Largely thanks to digital technology, over 50 percent of emerging adults connect with their parents on a daily basis.[9] Parents of young adults report that their kids seem to have greater appreciation for them than when they were teenagers, as well as a more nuanced view of them as complex people who face highs and lows just

> *"Well, I feel like we're most connected when we insist on family time or create opportunities for family time. We tell them that we expect that you'll be there and hope that you'll be there, and usually they do show up." —Keiko, a California mom of two explorers and one focuser*

like they do.[10] (Parents as people? How crazy is that!) As Jeffrey Arnett observed during over 300 in-depth interviews with 20- to 29-year-olds, "They begin to realize that their parents are neither the demigods they adored as children nor the clueless goofs they scorned as adolescents, but simply people who, like themselves, have a mix of qualities, merits as well as faults."[11]

Compared with high school, 18- to 23-year-olds report that they and their parents find it easier to talk, get stuck in fewer conflicts, and show each other greater mutual affection and understanding. Yet in the midst of these glowing relational report cards, some explorers resign themselves to mediocre or even failing family relationships. Often feeling emotionally or physically abandoned by one or more parents, many young adults are forced to confront the reality that the relationship is standing still or moving backward, and they have to salvage what they can from their parents while continuing to build life-giving relationships with those outside of their family.[12]

### Sibling Relationships Also Warm Up after High School

Typically some of the longest relationships they will ever have, our kids' relationships with their brothers and sisters change significantly as they move out of the family home or apartment. While in some families moving out exacerbates the distance, it's common for explorers' and focusers' relationships with their siblings and stepsiblings to grow warmer when relationships become more voluntary.[13]

Your emerging adult's growing relationship with their siblings is associated with higher levels of well-being, competence, life satisfaction, and self-esteem as well as lower rates of drug use, loneliness, and depression.[14] Without the seeds of dissent that come from sharing a bathroom, a chore list, and the family car, your explorers and focusers are likely to share more intimate information with their siblings, enabling their relationship to blossom into a true friendship laced with authentic support and advice.

## Grandparents on the Scene

Since your child was in elementary school, you've probably rubbed shoulders with grandparents volunteering in the art room and picking up kids after school. Across ethnicities, now that your child is a learner, explorer, or focuser, you're likely still seeing the tracks of grandparents crisscrossing this generation for a host of reasons.

First, grandparents are in overall better health than their predecessors.

Second, thanks to technology, grandparents have new and expanding ways to connect with their grandkids via text, video, and social media.

Third, grandparents are providing more financial assistance, not only through childhood gifts but also aiding with college tuition, wedding expenses, rent, or the purchase of a first home.

Fourth, with more dual-income parenting and an increase in single-parent households, grandparents are also providing more direct care. In some cases, adult children are unable to parent, making grandparents the primary caretakers for 2.5 million children.[15]

In the midst of the wide variety of grandparents' experiences and backgrounds, researchers suggest that your teenage and young adult children will have greater involvement with their grandparents (and sometimes even their great-grandparents) than any previous generation in the history of the US.[16]

This expanded support translates into expanded influence. Paralleling the research on parental empathy described earlier in this chapter, emotional closeness with grandparents is linked with a host of positive outcomes for emerging adults, including lower levels of social isolation, stress, depression, and loneliness. Many of the benefits of a warm grandparent relationship are more evident for explorers and focusers from divorced or single-parent families, suggesting that extended family relationships are especially advantageous for emerging adults whose parents don't live together.[17]

When it comes to faith impact, grandparents tend to follow one of four possible paths:[18]

1. They reinforce the parents' faith.
2. They substitute for the parents' faith.
3. They subvert the parents' faith.
4. They ignore faith altogether.

Whether our kids spend time with biological grandparents or adopted or "functional" grandparents (meaning they are not genetically related to our family but play the same role), senior adults often hold untapped potential to grow with our family. Many senior adults are discovering that beyond merely nurturing their own family tree, they are able to branch out and care for families like yours.

## Withing Ideas

As much as we love research, we love research even more when it can be translated into practical ideas and applied. We hope you pick one or two ideas from the following menu and adapt them as needed in order to maximize your family's withing.

### Time Talking: A Portal for Withing

One common withing habit in the moms and dads we interviewed was prioritizing time for conversations. In fact, time talking was ranked as the best way for parents to connect with their learners, explorers, and focusers.

Until each of my (Kara's) kids turned 16, one of my withing habits was to maximize my conversation time in the car with them, especially when I only had one kid along for the drive. The Powell family is not alone in cherishing conversation time on the road. Of all daily routines that our Growing With parents mentioned, the habit most frequently mentioned was taking advantage of car time.

When each of my kids received their driver's licenses, I had to find new ways to pursue conversation. In addition to the weekday breakfasts I described earlier, I came to prioritize weekend time with my kids. Usually on Thursday or Friday, I looked at our weekend schedule with an eye for possible one-on-one hangout and conversational time with my kids—whether it was having a leisurely Saturday lunch together, grabbing a coffee after church, or sitting on our couch and watching a game together on TV.

Instead of being discarded, some withing conversation habits have the potential to grow with your family as your learners, explorers, and focusers transition into new life stages. One Growing With family with daughters in high school valued Sunday night dinners at their favorite local Chinese restaurant. As each girl has moved out during college, the family still carves out time together every Sunday night, but now they connect over video instead of egg rolls.

One Texas dad who responded to our Growing With family interviews developed a creative strategy to prioritize conversation with his family members. He summarized, "As much as we would all love to sit down at dinner every night, my wife and three kids are too busy for that. So I have three dinners: one with my wife, one with my two elementary-aged kids, and one later when my teenager gets home. It's not about the eating. It's more about trying to find that time together when we are in the same space at the same time."

As we learned in our interviews with Growing With families, there is no one-size-fits-all list of withing conversation habits. Each family needs to find their own best warm routines, some of which might use technology instead of—or in addition to—face-to-face discussions. For many families, withing in particular seasons may be less about all being in the same place and more about giving our best time.

### *What to Do If You Don't Share Interests*

In the midst of seeking to increase your family's withing, many of you may wonder what to do if your learner, explorer, or focuser doesn't seem to want to spend time with you.

When parents ask me (Kara) what to do when their relationship with their teenager or young adult is rocky, my favorite answer is to share the story of Nora, a mom who has creatively built a withing bridge with her son.[19] The only time 17-year-old Sam leaves his room to interact with the family is when he's hungry (which, luckily for Nora, is often). But when she tries to start up a conversation while Sam's standing in front of the refrigerator or microwave, she's greeted with one-syllable answers: "Fine," "Nope," or "Uh-uh."

Longing for a deeper withing relationship, Nora has tried to connect with Sam. Every time she offers to take him out for a meal or to do something fun, he refuses. He would rather shut himself in his room and go online or play video games than be with her.

But Sam does love going to movies.

So Nora has become a student of film. She tracks movie release dates, visits movie websites, and has learned the fine nuances of various directors and actors.

The only time Sam says yes to Nora's invitations to do something with her is when she asks Sam to a movie. The round-trip conversation is Nora's best withing window into her son's life and heart.

Because of this, Nora wisely tries to pick theaters that are far away so they have more time in the car together.

Nora doesn't really like movies all that much, but she likes her son. As with many Growing With parents we interviewed, Nora is willing to leave the well-worn path of her own comfort and preferences to journey with her child.

Whether your child lives across the hall like Sam or lives a plane trip away, we recommend Nora's strategy in sparking a withing relationship: *start with your child's personality and preferences.* As one Connecticut mom of two explorers recommended, "Find out what really interests your kids and just do it, regardless of whether it interests you or not. If they want to play video games, go play video games with them. If they want to go for a bike ride, just do that, as opposed to thinking, 'That's not really what I want to do.'"

As is the case with one of Steve's daughters, is your child an active explorer who would rather go for a hike than sit and watch movies with you? Or, as with my 18-year-old son, is food helpful in unlocking the door to withing in your relationship? Pay attention to your child's predilections and intentionally create time for those shared activities. The older your child, the more you're going to need to offer those activities as suggestions for how your family can spend time together, and then be open and willing to accept your child's counterproposals.

### Be a Library

One of the wise Growing With moms we met during our interviews painted a compelling vision for how she tries to grow with her maturing kids. She summarized, "As my kids turn 18, I tell them, 'You are an adult, you can start making your own decisions. I am here as support. I am here for feedback. I am here for direction. I am here as your library. That is what I am here for, but I want you to start making the decisions on your own.'" As a result, her explorer and focuser children have sought her library-like advice in moments when they needed outside information and experience, like when they navigated a new tax situation or considered buying a home.

As you reflect on your teacher, guide, or resourcer role in your child's current life stage, what support can they "check out" from you that prepares them for their next stage? For example, even though you are a teacher for your high schooler, your goal is to help them prepare for greater independence and your corresponding

> *"I ask them all the time, 'How do I need to love you?' And there is absolutely no judgment on however they answer. Whatever it is, I will do my best to come through. If I want to be close to them, they need to know that I am there for them in the way that they need."*
> —Sharla, the single parent of a learner and an explorer

shift to a new role as their guide. The same holds true as you move from being a guide for your college-aged young adult to becoming a resourcer for your twentysomething.

When your growing kids ask you questions about life and faith that fall outside of your "card catalog," how can you best point them to other resources that can help them? Our time with remarkable Growing With parents has convinced us of the power of good questions in preparing learners, explorers, and focusers for what lies ahead. Instead of offering your best advice to your teenager about taking public transportation to their doctor's appointment or who to invite to prom, ask questions that enable them to figure it out themselves. Follow the example of Growing With parents who consistently replace "how to" and "I think" statements with "how would you" and "I wonder" questions. While it's tempting to give your 20-year-old your stellar guidance about how to find a church near their college or military base, instead ask them questions like, "How would you go about making a first step?" or "I wonder what you can do next to explore some possibilities?"

### When Withing Loses Momentum: Five Cooling Words to Avoid

If your child is like most, there is one five-word phrase they hate: "When I was your age . . ."

We parents use that expression to try to empathize with our kids, but given the cultural differences between today and when we were younger, those five words trigger warning signals in our kids. They think either we are trying too hard to relate (a cardinal sin few kids tolerate), or perhaps even worse, we are underestimating the differences between today and decades ago.

It's not that our learners, explorers, and focusers don't want us to talk about our past. Most young people want to hear their parents talk about the roller-coaster ride of their own adolescence and young adulthood. But we have to share those experiences in subtler ways, never prefacing them with "When I was your age . . ."

As our 19-year-old rents their first apartment, we look for indirect opportunities to volunteer mistakes we made with our own first landlord.

As our 21-year-old is preparing their résumé, we sneak into the conversation some glimmers of our own nervousness before past job interviews.

To help our single 29-year-old know we can relate to any angst they may feel about the likelihood of a future marriage, we circuitously share humorous (as well as not-so-humorous) memories about our own attempts to find—and impress—potential romantic interests.

Even though they don't always show it, most of our kids are open to hearing about our past. Our task is to find the less obvious back door (or maybe even trapdoor) that opens up the right conversation at the right time.

### Withing Gains Traction with These Three Warm Words

In my (Steve's) home, Jen and I have mounted a simple sign that reminds all five of us of one of our family mottos: "Tell me more." Jen and I chose this family mantra when our oldest was in high school and our youngest was in elementary school because in the midst of a society that is relentlessly self-focused, we want to fight for conversational momentum in our family.

Prior to adopting this motto, our typical conversation with our daughters often started with Jen or me asking, "How was your cross-country meet?"

"Good."

We would respond, "Cool."

That's as far as we got. So we added a new follow-up question: "Oh yeah? Tell me more!"

***Growing With in Real Time:***
**What do you do when you fear your explorer
or focuser is making poor choices?**

What do you do when you say, "Tell me more," but you're afraid that the next words out of your young adult's mouth will confirm your fears about their actions and attitudes? Or maybe you find something—like pornography or drug paraphernalia—that you never thought your kid would be stashing away in their room. What then?

Every kid and family is different, but following are a few helpful Growing With practices:

- *If they have confessed something to you, thank them for being honest.* The horrid truth is better than a blissful lie.
- *Reassure them you love them no matter what.* And make sure your actions the next few days continue to communicate that love.
- *Explore first-steps solutions that are needed to address the immediate need or crisis.* Discuss together various options that your child can take in the next 48 hours that would help. If they need to immediately stop a behavior or a relationship, think with them about what relationship or habit they can add to their life to fill that vacuum.
- *Plan to talk about longer-term lifestyle changes that replace bad choices with better choices.* Perhaps let your child know that you'll be back in touch in a day or two to talk more.
- *Consider whether you need to talk to a trained counselor, a pastor, or a friend who knows you and your child.* If you don't know what to do, get some advice from someone who will. Even if you have identified a plan for how to respond to your child, run that plan by someone you trust.

I remember walking past one of my daughters who was sitting on the couch and looking distraught. We caught each other's eyes and my daughter said, "I think I'm going to break up with my boyfriend." In that moment, my first instinct as a dad was to cheer. My second instinct was to worry and be inclined to ask her, "What's-wrong-what-did-he-do?" Instead, I managed to pause long enough for a "tell me more" moment and asked, "What's up?" She shared that her anxiety wasn't about her decision to break up but how to break up in a way that was kind, because she still valued his friendship. We talked about different approaches, and I had a chance to offer support in the way she really needed it. I still remember the hug she gave me that day and her whispered, "Thanks, Dad." But if I had followed my initial impulse, I could have blown the opportunity.

No matter how close you feel to your kids, you are likely getting an edited version of their lives. They often present a (very!) abridged version of their "fine" day at school, their killer Saturday night out with friends, or their rising credit card debt.[20] Remember that there's so much more to the story, but fear of your lectures or your increased anxiety may prevent them from sharing. Strategically asking your child to "tell me more" might open up some conversational doors that are otherwise locked tight.

### Warming Up Birthdays and Other Milestones[21]

Fuel the fires of warmth in your family by leveraging upcoming special birthdays and other developmental landmarks. Your child's 18th birthday may be one of their last at home. Take advantage of it. Capitalize on this birthday to look both backward and forward. Either with your own immediate family or with other adults who have significantly shaped your 18-year-old, share your favorite qualities about your child. Invite all family attending, as well as your child's close friends, to write down memories, wishes, or funny stories. Sign a soccer ball, a musical score, or a sweatshirt.

Three years later, use your explorer's 21st birthday as another catalyst to warm up your relationship. If your family drinks alcohol responsibly and occasionally, this may be a moment to take your child out and treat them to a first official drink together. At this cultural transitional moment, double down your withing commitment and say to them, "I see you growing up, and we can share this moment as peers."

If drinking alcohol is not appropriate or contrasts with your religious tradition, develop an alternative that holds special appeal with your emerging adult. Book a night in a downtown hotel. Surprise them with a movie marathon at home. Spend all or part of a day taking your 21-year-old to their favorite coffeehouses, restaurants, and hangouts. Invite your explorer to bring along a few friends for part of your celebration as a bonus chance that helps you get to know those closest to them.

Beyond birthdays, make a special effort to celebrate your child's graduation from school, military boot camp, or vocational training programs. One-on-one over coffee or perhaps during a dinner with family and close friends, ask questions like:

- What did you love most?
- What are you going to miss?
- How do you think you've changed?

Warm families pair honoring what their young people have *graduated from* with anticipation for what they are *graduating to*. Try weaving prayer and reflection together as you invite your child to answer questions such as:

- What are you most excited about in your future?
- What are you most nervous about?
- How can we best help you and pray for you as you look ahead?

Graduation and other inevitable transitions provide a plethora of Growing With opportunities to follow this pattern of remembering the past and celebrating the future. Moving into a first apartment. Getting a first job. Getting a first "real" job. Getting a first real job they love. Finding a new church on their own. Getting engaged. Getting married. Having a baby. If and when your child turns these corners, look for warm moments to remind your young person that you are there for them *no matter what*, and that you have growing confidence they can handle what comes their way.

### Withing on Their Terms: Asking Your Kids What Would Warm Up Your Relationship

To improve our family's withing, one of my (Kara's) favorite questions to ask each of my kids is, "If you could change anything about our relationship, what would it be?" It's scary and sometimes a bit nerve-wracking to wait those few moments for their responses, but I have been glad every time I've asked the question. Even if I can't—or won't—change what they wish I would, I'm glad I know what they find annoying or even hurtful.

Even these last six months, my teenagers' honest answers have prompted me to make some changes. "Mom, you give us too many chores to remember. When we forget to do something, you get frustrated with us and we don't think that's fair." As a result, I bought a whiteboard and now write a separate list of family chores for each day or week. Problem solved!

"Mom, your texts are too long. You text like an old person." Yes, I am someone who likes to express complete thoughts. And yes, no one ever accused me of being too concise. So that's something I'm still working on.

"Mom, you ask too many questions." This is a tough one for me to change. I'm inherently a curious person, and when it comes to my kids and their friends, my curiosity dial is turned to high.

> *"There is a fine line between wanting to be their friend and still having to be their parent. I struggle with where that line is sometimes."* —Romero, a Nebraska dad of an explorer and a focuser

But I'm trying to edit my questions and raise only the ones that are most important.

Why? Even though I don't believe longish texts or asking one too many questions is a big deal, my kids do. And while I think far more about our relationship than they do, their perception of our warmth matters far more than mine.

### iWithing: Using Technology to Increase Your Family's Warmth

One single mom we interviewed was pleasantly surprised by how frequently her college freshman daughter, Kanesha, called and texted her during the first few weeks of the fall semester. The fact that her daughter was initiating so much contact became a little less meaningful when Raquel realized that her daughter reached out to her whenever she was walking to class or the cafeteria. Kanesha didn't want to seem like a loner, so she tried to project the image of having a busy social life. And who could Kanesha count on to pick up the phone or reply immediately to her texts? No one was more responsive than Mom!

Regardless of the motivation, many parents find that technology uploads warmth into their relationships. The Growing With parents we interviewed used texting and phone calls with their learners, explorers, and focusers as their primary technological withing strategies. Slightly behind these two channels was parents' use of social media and video calls to foster warm relationships with their tech-savvy young people.

In restaurants or during long car drives, Growing With parents use word puzzles and game apps to strengthen family withing.

Parents and kids alike send pictures or funny short videos to each other that help the family build up their warmth muscles.

While the majority of my (Kara's) texts with my kids revolve around logistical needs or questions, I've found my kids more likely to affirm me via text than face-to-face. To be honest, sometimes the same is true when I text them. From simple "You're the best" phrases to emojis that capture inside jokes, many Growing With parents find technology adds kindling to the warm fires burning in their families.

### Clarifying Technology Expectations, Especially in the Learner Stage

Despite the fuel technology adds to the flames of family warmth, our interviews with exemplar parents confirm that families often grow closer when we limit our kids' use of technology, especially before and throughout high school.

Some families create rules for their learners' devices that prohibit all family members (including parents!) from using technology during dinner or in certain rooms of the house. With my (Kara's) teenage kids, it works well to give them a few minutes to text their friends once we get in the car together. But then I usually ask them to put away their devices so we can talk with each other. Some families even find it helpful to outline these practices in a "technology contract" they develop with their child to ensure that the family's devices strengthen withing instead of erode it.

### Withing's Perpetual Welcome Mat

Whether their home was a small urban apartment, a suburban two-story tract house, or a rural property with lots of acres to roam, the Growing With parents we interviewed wanted their kids and their kids' friends to feel welcome. In the midst of often-tight family budgets, parents created warm spaces and offered appetizing snacks to make their home one of their kids' main hangouts.

For more research-based insights and suggestions about navigating technology with your teenager, you might want to check out *Navigating Our Digital World* by Kara Powell, Art Bamford, and Brad M. Griffin (Fuller Youth Institute, 2018). See fuller youthinstitute.org/digitalworld.

I (Kara) have found that my face-to-face time with my kids' friends has evolved based on their life stage and my role in their life. When our kids have been teenagers, my husband and I have been quick to offer our home as a hangout hub. We keep brownie mix in the pantry and bought a firepit for our patio so the gang had a place to sit. Our kids and their friends like that we are usually inside the house and can't hear their outside conversations. We like that even though we can't hear them, thanks to our family room windows we can still see them.

Now that I (Steve) am more of a guide and resourcer to my college-aged and twentysomething daughters, I find that we spend more time hosting our daughters' friends when they come to visit or need a ride to the airport. In addition, while we don't have the consistent visits of the teenage years, we find that our girls' friends are hungry for a home-cooked meal and are eager to talk about what they've been doing or what they're planning to do next. Our role as guides is to take an interest in their life trajectories, listening to their hopes as well as disappointments, so we can learn about their journey and walk part of it with them. As an extra blessing, these discussions with friends often surface conversations with our daughters about their own hopes and disappointments. We are reminded that our kids aren't the only ones on a journey. Their friends are too, and so are we.

### Withing over Family Vacations

When my (Kara's) younger brother got married right after college, I handwrote a list of 40 of my favorite memories with him.

We had grown up together. Our bedrooms were next door to each other. Since we were only two grades apart, we had many of the same friends in our youth group. We had navigated our parents' divorce and later remarriages (to great stepparents we quickly came to both love and like). We shared a bathroom. To my brother's chagrin, we also shared his clothes.

To my surprise, despite our daily interactions, over half of my favorite memories were from the one or two weeks each year we were on family vacations. Whether our family was camping locally or had scraped together enough money to head out of state, the highlights of our relationship were playing cards late at night, making up songs during long car trips, and lots and lots of water fights (that still continue now that we have kids of our own).

My experience with my brother is not uncommon, and the family warmth stoked by vacations is not limited to siblings. In our interviews with parents who were growing with their children, one-fourth said they felt most connected to their learners, explorers, and focusers when they were on vacation.

So Dave and I try to look ahead and find the weekends and rare unoccupied week or two per year that enable the five of us to get away. As our kids have become teenagers and young adults, we have warmed up family vacations by letting them choose and plan more of what we do together. Usually that means fewer museums than Dave would wish and more movies than I would choose, but giving our kids greater ownership of our schedule increases their willingness to be gone from their friends and focus on our family.

As aging kids have less flexible jobs and school schedules that don't align with those of their siblings, it is harder to prioritize family vacations. So like a lot of other Growing With families, we focus less on weeklong adventures and more on extended days enjoying Los Angeles, as well as overnights or weekends away. Even a 45-minute drive to a campground at the beach gives us the chance for long dinners and even longer card games that we wouldn't have otherwise. Getting away and removing the distracting pull of local friends, work, and household tasks helps us do withing better.

### Withing Siblings: Encouraging Brothers and Sisters to Build Friendships

I'm not proud of it, but when my (Steve's) daughters were younger and embroiled in a massive sister fight, I stormed into their bedroom, sat them down, and told them, "Someday you'll be older. Your mom and I won't live forever, and all you'll have for family is each other. So you'd better learn to support each other now." While my statement was logically correct, evoking the image of their parents dying in order to get them to stop fighting was admittedly over the top. My girls still remember that moment and (thankfully) laugh about it.

As parents, we easily think about our own warm relationship with our kids while forgetting to help our kids develop warm relationships with each other and how those relationships change as our kids grow. When our kids were in elementary school, we acted as the relational catalysts for activities that included all siblings (e.g., dinner, ice cream, family outings, etc.). As our kids move into their more autonomous learner, explorer, and focuser stages, our role in fanning the flames for sibling relationships changes.

I (Kara) try to spark those blazes by removing obstacles that might keep our kids from spending time together. Like money. We live three blocks from a coffeehouse, and our kids know that if they ever want to walk there with one of their siblings, we will pay for them to get a small treat. So once or twice a month our kids take us up on this standing offer. But they know they have to focus on each other—not their phones—or we aren't buying.

In my (Steve's) own parenting evolution, as a teacher parent, I've encouraged my daughters to reach out to each other. As a guide parent, I've had to watch and learn from the ways they nurture their own relationships with each other. Some moments are more encouraging than others, but it's fun to see them grow their own connections. And they seem to know deep down that they need each other.

### Withing Grandparents

In my (Steve's) face-to-face interviews with college students, I was surprised by the number who spoke warmly of their grandparents and feared losing them when they would someday pass away.[22] There's often a special tenderness between senior adults and young people, but just as with all withing connections, the relationships between grandparents and grandchildren need to be developed intentionally.

That's why I'm so impressed with an idea from one of my mentors who has 13 grandchildren. He sends out a monthly email to his grandchildren called "Papa's Monthly Roundup." In the email, he asks his grandkids to share something they did, read, or experienced (their "doings") and something they're excited about, thinking about, or disappointed about (their "beings"). He reminds his grandkids that an answer like "Nothing much" is unacceptable, and that he's expecting not just a one-sentence reply but a paragraph.

Stuart then compiles the monthly "doings" and "beings" and sends out the summary to all the grandkids. None of the parents (i.e., his kids and their spouses) are involved, and all the parents want to see the list—but he won't give it to them, because it's *Papa's* Monthly Roundup! While Stuart says that some grandchildren are better at responding than others, all of them tell him, "Don't stop doing it, Papa!"

That's extraordinary warmth those teenagers and young adults will never forget . . . and may just repeat with their own grandkids. After all, every relationship can always get a little bit warmer.

*Growing With in Real Time:*
## More warm ideas for grandparents

Whether you are a grandparent or you simply want to help the generation above you connect with the generation below you, you may want to adapt some of these withing ideas in your own family.[1]

- Pray for your grandkids and tell them that you pray for them.
- Write a prayer of blessing for your grandchildren. Frame it for them.
- Share with each other what you're reading. Ask for book suggestions.
- Have breakfast together once a week or once a month—either in person or by video.
- Text them on an ordinary day and let them know you're thinking of them.
- Send packages! Your grandkids love getting small and inexpensive gifts by mail.
- Invite your grandchildren to stay overnight with you, or for a weekend or even a week.
- Ask your grandchild to teach you a new trick or skill on your phone or computer.
- Ask your grandchild to share their favorite music. You know, the "popular songs these days."
- When the mood is right, offer to tell stories about your life growing up.
- Serve together at a local ministry or philanthropy.

1. Adapted from Kara Powell, *The Sticky Faith Guide for Your Family* (Grand Rapids: Zondervan, 2014), 120–24.

## Practical Questions to Grow With My Child

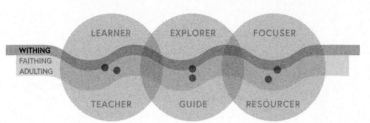

1. On a scale of 1 to 10 (with 1 being "we stink at this" and 10 being "we rock at this"), rate your family on the withing research insights presented in this chapter.

Our kids would describe our family's relationships as warm.

1................................5................................10

While we recognize that warm relationships with both parents are important, our kids have a close relationship with their dad (or stepdad or another adult male).

1................................5................................10

Our kids have warm relationships with each other (siblings and/or stepsiblings).

1................................5................................10

Our kids have a warm relationship with their grandparents or other senior adults.

1................................5................................10

2. What do you already do to build a warm withing relationship with your learner, explorer, or focuser?

3. Based on your rankings in question 1, as well as the ideas you've read in this chapter, what one or two changes might you want to make in your family?

4. What can you do in the next few weeks or months to move toward these changes?

5. Who might you share your insights with? Who might be a great listener or encourager to cheer for you as you pursue your goals?

# 4. Walls of Support

*Withing That Repairs and Reorients Your Relationship*

"But I don't want to ride with you. I want to keep riding with my cousins."

Having arrived at the beach for an extended family vacation with a case of bronchitis, it was day three and I (Kara) was finally feeling better. The first 48 hours of our vacation, Dave and I had asked our kids to ride with their aunts and uncles since I was still contagious. But now I was germ-free and wanted our three kids to hop in our rental car for an hour-long drive to a new beach. After two days of keeping a cool distance from my kids so they wouldn't catch my cough and sore throat, I wanted to warm up again. It was time for the vintage car games of "Twenty Questions" and "I Spy" along with a few favorite word game apps I keep handy on my phone.

Nathan and Jessica grabbed their towels, hats, and water bottles and buckled themselves into our back seat. Krista tossed her beach backpack over her shoulder but stood six feet away from our car.

With her arms crossed and her hazel eyes cool with determination, our 14-year-old bluntly told us that she liked riding with her cousins better.

My feelings would have been hurt even if we had been home. But losing valuable withing time during one of our few precious (and expensive!) vacation days was a slap in the face to my pride and my hopes for family warmth.

I had a 3-D picture in my mind of what our vacation was supposed to be like. Krista's assertion of her independence—a normal and appropriate tendency for an eighth grader—was ripping that image into shreds.

We let Krista ride with her cousins that day. In between the car games we played without her, I asked God to give me wisdom to know how best to respond to Krista when we arrived. As we were still en route, God brought to my mind an image that has been a favorite anchor of my Growing With parenting philosophy.

When you and I try to stoke the fires of warmth we discussed in the previous chapter, we will inevitably experience conflict with our self-reliant learners, explorers, and focusers. In those strained moments, we are wise to heed psychologist Lisa Damour's counsel for parents of girls—advice that Steve and I believe is relevant for parents and stepparents of sons and daughters alike:

> Your daughter needs a wall to swim to, and she needs you to be a wall that can withstand her comings and goings. Some parents feel too hurt by their swimmers, take too personally their daughter's rejections, and choose to make themselves unavailable to avoid going through it again. . . . But being unavailable comes at a cost. . . . Their daughters are left without a wall to swim to and must navigate choppy—and sometimes dangerous—waters all on their own.[1]

Like all relationships, those with our maturing kids ebb and flow emotionally. As I found at the beach with Krista, sometimes when our independence-seeking child moves away from us, they don't just let go and drift; they kick off the wall. And they kick hard. So hard that it hurts, leaving us feeling cracked, dented, and leaky. We love our teenagers and young adults more than we ever dreamed possible, so when they turn their backs on us—whether for an hour-long car drive on vacation, a week of ignoring our texts, or a month of rejecting all offers to get together—the pain is more than we can bear.

Motivated by either our anger or self-protection, it's tempting to turn our backs on our kids when they turn their backs on us. Instead of being a wall for our kids to return to, we put up walls that keep them away. In the midst of our trip to a coastal paradise, everything in me wanted to punish Krista.

To shame her into getting in the back seat.

Or take away her phone as a consequence for her attitude.

Or verbally lash out at her so she understood how she had hurt me.

Or ignore her and shower my attention on her brother, sister, and cousins. (That would really show her!)

Or all of the above.

I'm sure that in my disappointment, traces of all those so-called parenting strategies seeped into my interactions with Krista. But in the midst of my frustration, and even a few parental threats, I mentally repeated this mantra that I felt the Lord brought to mind: *Be a wall. Be a wall she can come back to. Be a wall. Be a wall she can come back to.*

Krista remained aloof for the next 24 hours. She rode in the car with my brother and his wife, not us. She offered to help with family meals only if I was not already in the kitchen. When I walked toward her, she picked up her phone and started texting a friend.

It took everything in me not to aggressively confront her or passively distance myself from her. Especially when I did the math on the daily cost of our vacation.

*Be a wall. Be a wall she can come back to.*

With two days left on the trip, Krista did come back. I can't point to why it happened. There was no breakthrough conversation. No heartfelt apology. No fantastic sunset walk along the beach that changed everything.

Krista simply started to act like herself. Whatever thoughts and feelings had deepened the rift between us seemed to disappear. She started riding in our car more. She joked with us, making fun of my subpar basketball skills (at six feet, I'm all height and no skill) and Dave's tendency to get lost on small, winding coastal roads. She looked at her phone a whole lot less and directly at us a whole lot more.

I'm so glad that during the two days Krista was distant from us, I didn't say or do something that would create a permanent barrier between me and my teenager. That would dent my ability to be *with* her.

While Jesus is the ultimate "wall" we want our kids to cling to, during the ups and downs of our vacation all I could do was cling to this phrase: *Be a wall. Be a wall she can come back to.* But that phrase gave me enough courage to continue to be available for Krista—asking her periodic questions, affirming her contributions to our extended family's fun and conversations, and smiling in her direction—all of which were cues I hoped would prompt Krista to reach for me when she was ready.

My vacation experience with Krista highlights the crucial role we parents play in withing. As we described in chapter 1, while withing is about our relationship with our child, we generally take the lead in laying the relational bridges that keep us connected. Our goal is to keep building new bridges that enable us to love and care for our teenagers and young adults as they (and we) grow older.

## Withing Insights

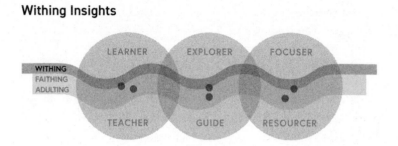

Whether we are vacationing or staying at home, our goal in withing—namely, a family's growth in supporting each other as children grow more independent—is repeatedly stymied. Based on our interviews with parents as well as multiple studies of families nationwide, we've found that even when we want to be a wall that our kids can come back to, a host of questions plaguing either us or our children erode our relationships and threaten our family's withing. Paying attention to these questions, and responding to them with the right warm strategies, is foundational to our ability to be the wall of support our (sometimes drifting) teenagers and young adults need.

### How Is Pushing Away a Normal Step on the Path toward Interdependence?

The starting point for our relationship with our kids when they are infants is dependence. If we mentally rewind time, we recall how much our babies needed us—for food, for security, for a place to sleep, and for diaper changes.

If we fast-forward and imagine our kids as adults, our desired end point is interdependence, which in many respects is a synonym for the "mutual journey" that beats at the heart of our definition of Growing With parenting. We remain the parent and our child remains our child, but as our child ages, the hierarchy between us decreases and reciprocity increases.

But typically in between dependence and interdependence is the stage of independence.[2]

## DEPENDENCE > INDEPENDENCE > INTERDEPENDENCE

Independence is the apex of our children pushing away from our withing wall of support. But it's an (almost) essential liminal state that propels our kids toward the self-confidence and autonomy that enable them to transition to the next stage of interdependence.

Krista's move away from me during our vacation likely had less to do with negative feelings toward me and Dave and more to do with her stepping into her independence stage. While that's easy to tell myself in hindsight, the pain of her rejection in those moments short-circuited my rational (or even semi-rational) assessment of her actions.

Experienced Growing With parents are able to remove the blinders of their own anger or fear and view their kids as walking down a developmentally normal path from dependence to (the oh-so-painful) independence to (the oh-so-delightful) interdependence.

The journey from dependence to independence to interdependence can vary based on our family system or ethnic identity. For example, white teenagers (or learners) are often socialized to be independent from family obligations, which may make them more susceptible to risk behaviors and social isolation. While often manifested in different ways, learners from African American, Latino, and Asian American families often receive generous support and spiritual mentoring from extended family, which can result in inner conflicts as they negotiate family expectations along with Western assumptions about autonomy.[1]

1. Richard W. Flory, Korie L. Edwards, and Brad Christerson, *Growing Up in America: The Power of Race in the Lives of Teens* (Redwood City, CA: Stanford University Press, 2010), 40; Ken Johnson-Mondragon, *Pathways of Hope and Faith Among Hispanic Teens: Pastoral Reflections and Strategies Inspired by the National Study of Youth and Religion* (Stockton, CA: Instituto Fe y Vida, 2007), 141.

## *How Busy and Stressed Is My Teenager or Young Adult Right Now?*

Those of us parenting learners are likely not surprised to hear that our kids are stressed, but we may be surprised by just how stressed they are.

- Teenage stress levels during the school year are higher than adult stress levels (on a 10-point scale, teenagers average 5.8 while adults average 5.1).[3]

- Even during the summer, teenagers report stress levels that are higher than what is believed to be healthy.[4]

- Almost one-third (31 percent) of teens say that their stress levels have increased in the past year, and 34 percent believe their stress levels will increase in the coming year.[5]

- While school is the most commonly mentioned source of stress for teens (labeled a "somewhat" or "significant" source of stress for 83 percent), more than half (59 percent) of teens report that managing their time to balance all activities is also a somewhat or very significant stressor.[6]

- Nearly a third of children ages 8–17 surveyed report that in the past month they have experienced physical health symptoms often associated with stress, such as sleep problems, headaches, and an upset stomach.[7]

Given the roller-coaster ride of adolescence, many parents are surprised to find that life after high school is typically even more

> *"When our kids were teenagers, they had a lot of homework. Looking back, I think we should have carved out some time when we said, 'Nope, no homework.' Almost like a Sabbath—just a time when we are going to have fun without any homework." —Adrian, a California dad of one learner and one focuser*

emotionally jarring. Chief among explorers' and focusers' stressors are those related to "daily life management," most notably new pressures related to time and money that accompany post–high school freedom and responsibilities.[8]

### Growing With in Real Time:
### For busy teens and young adults, are church activities a burden or a blessing?

Churchgoing young people and families are not inoculated from this busyness and stress. In fact, congregations contribute a few degrees to the feverish pitch of young people's schedules. When asked whether their church adds to or lessens their busyness, the learners, explorers, and focusers in our Growing Young study reported that their church involvement increases their busyness. Attending or leading church events erases any spare blocks of time that your teenager or young adult might have otherwise walled off for themselves.

Whether we as adults think learners, explorers, and focusers have enough discretionary time is immaterial. Most young people perceive that they have little extra time or resources. As a result, their choice to attend church-related activities feels like a big sacrifice for them. It's worthwhile to pause and acknowledge this sacrifice that young people are making.[1]

But unlike other sources of busyness, that which is caused by the faith community isn't necessarily harmful. Approximately 50 percent of the learners, explorers, and focusers who believe that their church involvement increases their busyness mentioned that these activities are life-giving and noticeably different than what they do the rest of the week. As one young person gushed, "Serving in the church has been a joy to me, so I do not consider it something that just takes up my time."

1. Tim Clydesdale, The First Year Out (Chicago: University of Chicago Press, 2007), 66–67.

### How Stressed and Busy Am I?

As our young people wade through their "quarterlife" crisis, many of us are hip deep in our own "midlife" crisis. New pressures stemming from declining health, fractures in our family relationships, financial burdens, challenging jobs, and shifting relationships poke holes in our ability to be a stable wall of support for our family.

Sometimes these gaps are widened because of our frustration with our teenagers and young adults. When it comes to our withing goals, the good news is that parents of young adults categorize their relationship with their child as one of their top three joys. The not-so-good news is that these same parents also name it as one of their top three stressors.[9]

Whatever the cause, multiple studies confirm that parental stress trickles, or in some cases surges, through our families. Following are some interesting (and may we say personally convicting) findings about the effects of our own stress on our children.

#### FOR THOSE OF US WITH TEENAGERS[10]

- One-third of children surveyed ages 8–17 believe their parent has been "always" or "often" worried or stressed-out about things during the past month.

- Four in ten kids report feeling sad when their parent is stressed or worried.

- One-third of kids (34 percent) say they can tell their parents are worried or stressed when they yell. Other signs of parental stress perceived by kids are arguing with other people in the house, complaining or telling family members about their problems, and being too busy or not having enough time to spend with them.

Not only do our kids know when we're stressed, they don't like it. One study asked over 1,000 kids ages 8–18 with one or both

## Additional Stressors Affecting Parents' Withing

Many parents face additional stressors that affect their family, such as:

- *Aging parents*, especially given that 15 percent of middle-aged adults in the US are part of the "sandwich genera-tion" that is providing financial support and/or care to both their children and their parents.[1]
- *Children with learning disabilities*, which are experienced by 8 percent of US children ages 3–17.[2] While 34 percent of parents whose children have learning disabilities are optimistic about their ability to cope, slightly more (35 percent) have serious concerns about their ability to cope with their children's learning issues. These parents feel isolated, guilty, stressed, and worried about their children's future.[3]
- *Children with autism*, which is estimated to be experi-enced by just over 2 percent of US children.[4]
- *Financial stress*, given that 31 percent of American adults, or 76 million people, say they are struggling to get by or just barely making it.[5]
- *Unemployment*, which is experienced by 3 percent of fa-thers and 4.2 percent of mothers with children ages 6–17.[6]

1. Alana M. Boyczuk and Paula C. Fletcher, "The Ebbs and Flows: Stresses of Sandwich Generation Caregivers," *Journal of Adult Development* 23, no. 1 (2016): 51–61.

2. National Survey of Children's Health (2012), http://childhealthdata.org/browse/survey/results?q=2540&r=1.

3. Amanda Morin, "Learning Disabilities Facts, Trends and Stats," Understood.org, accessed January 5, 2018, https://www.understood.org/en/learning-attention-issues/getting-started/what-you-need-to-know/learning-disabilities-facts-trends-and-stats.

4. Ariana Eunjung Cha, "Autism Cases in U.S. Jump to 1 in 45: Who Gets the Diagnosis, in 8 Simple Charts," *Washington Post*, November 13, 2015, https://www.washingtonpost.com/news/to-your-health/wp/2015/11/13/autism-cases-in-u-s-rise-to-1-in-45-a-look-at-who-gets-the-diagnosis-in-8-simple-charts/?utm_term=.456852c976cf.

5. Tami Luhby, "76 Million Americans Are Struggling Financially or Just Getting By," CNN Money, June 10, 2016, http://money.cnn.com/2016/06/10/news/economy/americans-struggling-financially/index.html.

6. A. Kalil and P. Wightman, "Parental Job Loss and Children's Educational Attainment in Black and White Middle-Class Families," *Social Science Quarterly* 92, no. 1 (2011): 57–78.

parents working outside of the home what they would change about how their parents' work affects their lives. The parents of these kids expected their top wish would be for more time together as a family.

The parents were wrong. The kids' number one wish was that their parents would be less stressed and less tired. Only 2 percent of parents surveyed expected that would be their kids' top wish.[11]

### FOR THOSE OF US WITH EMERGING ADULTS[12]

- While high proportions of emerging adults feel that their current stage of life is stressful, so do their parents. Parents are nearly as likely as emerging adults to report that they often feel anxious or depressed.

- Forty percent of parents report greater anxiety about their emerging adult's finances when their child is living with them. Having an emerging adult living at home gives a front-row seat to their ups and downs, ranging from arguments with romantic partners to disappointments at work, all of which magnify parental concerns.

- One study found parents of young adults in lower socio-economic groups gloomier than other parents. The lower the education level, the more likely parents are to agree that "I often feel depressed" (32 percent for parents who have a high school education or less; 18 percent for those who have a college degree or more) and that "I often feel anxious" (46 percent for parents who have a high school education or less; 33 percent for those who have a college degree or more).

### How Much of My Kids' Life and Choices Am I Trying (or Hoping) to Control?

Dave and I (Kara) once watched a TV drama about jury selection. During the juror selection process, one question the fictional defense attorney used to screen and understand potential jurors' proclivities was, "How do you catch a cold?"

My immediate response was that I catch a cold when I haven't been diligent in washing my hands, especially before I eat.

Dave's answer was that he catches a cold when he's been around someone who's ill.

Note the difference in our responses and what that difference reveals about our sense of control. If I catch a cold, I assume it's my fault. I didn't control my surroundings well enough. In Dave's mind, catching a cold isn't a result of his own actions; it's the often inevitable by-product of sitting near a sick child, friend, or colleague.

This will come as no surprise to anyone who has met Dave: I have a stronger sense of control—or really, a stronger drive to control—than he does.

The pattern in our marriage is not unusual. About 17 percent of mothers of emerging adults are highly controlling, compared with 7 percent of fathers. Unfortunately for me (and for our kids!), more controlling parents tend to have emerging adult children with lower levels of self-worth and higher levels of depression and anxiety.[13]

Much of what motivates my own attempts to influence (okay, yes, my attempts to *control*) my kids' circumstances and choices is my desire to protect them from pain. Ironically, what I most deeply desire and dream for my kids often comes from the very experiences I am trying to safeguard against. As our good friend and colleague Scott Cormode, himself the parent of two young adult daughters, has confessed to Steve and me multiple times, "As a parent, I want to protect my kids from pain. And yet I want my kids to display the maturity and character that usually comes only from experiencing pain."[14]

Two months into high school, our son Nathan was selected by his ninth-grade class to be part of the homecoming court. It was no big deal to him. In fact, he knew for three days before he even mentioned it to us. Nathan only let us know because we had to sign a permission slip for some extra court-related homecoming activities.

Fast-forward three months to the next high school dance—the winter formal in which the girls invite the guys. I was sure he'd be invited. I made sure his one and only dress shirt made it to the dry cleaner's and back. Unbeknownst to him, I even scheduled a haircut for him a week before the dance so that on the big night, his hair would look good but not too freshly cut. (Don't judge! I know some of you reading have done the same thing.)

Three weeks before the dance, a few girls started inviting boys. But no one invited Nathan.

Two weeks before the dance, more invitations were offered. But not to Nathan.

A week before the dance, Nathan got his scheduled haircut. But he still had not been invited.

During the 48 hours prior to the dance, the final flurry of invitations was extended. But not to Nathan.

This is embarrassing to admit, but if I could have found a way to bribe a girl in his grade to invite him, I would have. I didn't want him to feel the rejection of not being invited—partly for his sake, but also for mine. If I'm honest, a tiny speck of rejection in my kid's life becomes a black pit of shame in my own.

The night of the dance, Nathan hung out with a few of his friends who also hadn't received invitations. He wasn't that disappointed to skip the dance. He hates wearing a suit and tie (and don't get him started about wearing freshly starched dress shirts), so a night of pizza and Netflix with a few buddies was just fine for him.

And I came one step closer to coming to terms with this truth: Nathan's going to be rejected. It's part of life. Even if I could Bubble Wrap him such that he'd never feel any pain, that's ultimately not what's best for him. What's best for Nathan—and for me—is to experience the full roller coaster of life, knowing that growth comes from both the lows and the highs (and often *more* from the lows than the highs).

My (Steve's) own struggle with my lack of control was crystallized when we dropped off our middle daughter at college. A few minutes after we walked away from saying our last good-byes to our daughter Elise, Jen said to me, "We've done all we can and now it's time for Elise to live her own imperfect life." Her comment jarred me at first (I was still wallowing in sentimentality), but I soon realized the profundity of Jen's statement. She was naming that we aren't perfect and neither is our daughter. I can't control Elise's life or decisions. My goal is to be a wall she can return to before, during, and after she makes those decisions.

## What Conflicts Are Driving Us Apart?

Is conflict over money cooling your relationship with your young adult? If so, you're not alone. In fact, one study of parents of 18- to 29-year-olds found money to be the top source of stress in their relationship with their child, experienced by 48 percent of those surveyed.[15]

Frequently our young adults' college debt is like kindling that fuels the fires of conflict over finances. For the undergraduate class of 2015, the average amount owed for education debt was over $35,000.[16] In one survey, 30 percent of young adults admitted that they would sell an organ to rid themselves of student loans.[17]

Older family members living in a dominant culture different from their own may feel tensions with younger family members. For example, parents or grandparents may want to preserve traditional cultural values (including family roles and obligations) while young people often prefer to give more attention toward fitting in and being accepted by their peers. These divergent perceptions may negatively affect the quality of the parent-child relationship.[1]

1. Khanh Dinh and Huong Nguyen, "The Effects of Acculturative Variables on Asian American Parent-Child Relationships," *Journal of Social and Personal Relationships* 23, no. 3 (2006): 12.

Other sources of stress for families with young adults include the following: [18]

| Focus of conflict | Experienced by what percent of families | Commonly expressed by parents as |
|---|---|---|
| Money | 48 percent | "I'm still waiting for them to become financially self-sufficient." |
| Occupational progress | 39 percent | "Will they ever get off the couch and find a job?" |
| Substance use or abuse | 36 percent | "I wish they partied less." |
| Educational progress | 27 percent | "I fear that they won't finish their degree or training." |
| Romantic life | 19 percent | "I think they could find someone better." |
| Sex life | 9 percent | "I'm worried about them being sexually active. I'm even more terrified about them getting pregnant." |

Perhaps the order of these stressors is different in your home. Regardless of what bubbles—or boils—to the top, it's helpful to name and discuss your family's hot spots before the next conflict emerges.

## How Does Divorce Affect a Family's Withing?

You may have heard the statistic that 50 percent of all marriages in the US end in divorce. It's time—actually, past time—to correct that myth. According to the Census Bureau, 72 percent of those who have ever been married are still married to their first spouse. Included in the remaining 28 percent who are not married to their first spouse are those whose spouse has passed away. Given this data, one reliable estimate concludes that 20–25 percent of first marriages end in divorce.[19]

Statistics aside, we recognize that stigmas attributed to divorced parents can be painful and discouraging. If you're reading this book as a divorced parent, we know there's more to your story and parenting than your marital status. These findings on divorce are not meant to pile on more blame but to remind us all that fragmentation in our family systems creates unique challenges for us, and especially our kids, to navigate. We are wise to watch for these symptoms with the aim of growing with our kids, not blaming ourselves and other parents.

While that lower divorce rate is something to cheer, we would hold our applause if we understood how divorce can scar a child's sense of attachment and a family's sense of warmth. Divorce leaves children feeling permanently conflicted, bouncing back and forth between two parents and often two homes. For young people from intact families, special events such as birthdays, holidays, and graduations enhance their sense of family withing. For teenagers and emerging adults from divorced families, these same events reinforce their sense that they stand with one foot in each parent's world. When divorced parents start dating and perhaps remarry, teenage and young adult children often experience the conflicting emotions of joy over a parent's new partner along with uncertainty about how to relate to their new stepparent and sadness that their original parents' marriage is decidedly over.[20]

In the midst of these obstacles to family warmth, children of divorce are three times as likely to feel alone, twice as likely to feel unsafe, and almost four times as likely to disrespect their parents.[21] As they age, young adults from divorced families tend to have higher rates of alcohol and drug use, less academic success, and are more likely to be depressed and withdrawn.[22]

Given both sets of our parents are divorced, the most heartbreaking statistic to Steve and me is how poorly the faith community supports young people affected by a family breakup. Of young adults who regularly attend a church or synagogue at the time of their parents' divorce, two-thirds report that no one from their faith community reached out to them during that painful season.[23] As a young person's fabric of family is ripped apart, we who are in their faith community have the opportunity to weave ourselves into their relational network if we pay attention and proactively reach out to families in transition.

## How Can Our "Welcome Home" Help or Hurt Our Withing?

In the US today, the typical age for leaving home is between 18 and 19, the lowest age on record. Yet in the midst of this early mass exodus from home, nearly half of today's emerging adults move back in with family, the largest percentage in the last century.[24]

In addition to those who "boomerang" home, 30 percent of young adults don't move away from home until their middle or late twenties. These young adults often grew up in Latino, Black, and Asian American families who prioritize family closeness and interdependence. In other cases, young twentysomethings stay at home because they are simply not ready or financially able to live on their own.[25]

Whether your child never left home or left home and returned, having your young adult living down the hall or basement steps can challenge your family's withing. You and your child have both grown used to your independence. In the name of family warmth, you now have to readjust privacy patterns and personal space arrangements. Your child may resist any limits you try to set on their behavior and schedule, or your expectations that they pay rent or help with chores and meal preparation.

Yet many families find that the withing benefits of having a twentysomething at home outweigh these potential hazards. You and your explorer or focuser can pool finances to support the family's housing. You can be a source of comfort and motivation as your young adult is finding their vocational and relational way.

Living under the same roof gives you a real opportunity to establish a warm adult relationship with your son or daughter.

Furthermore, as boomeranging or staying at home through the early to middle twenties has become more common, there is less stigma and embarrassment—for you and your kids. In fact, 70 percent of 18- to 34-year-olds who are living at home with their parents report being satisfied with their family life and relationships.[26] Admittedly, the parents of those young adults were not asked the same question, but this remains good news for parents who want to grow with their young people not despite but because of their shared living space.

## Withing Ideas

### Helping Learners, Explorers, and Focusers Slow Down and Set Limits

One primary way that Growing With parents tangibly support their children is by helping them slow down and set limits for their schedules and commitments. By middle school, many of our kids have outgrown the parental rule of thumb common during elementary school that says "only one extracurricular activity at a time." And by high school, they may need to begin earning income to help with family expenses or looking ahead to pay for college. As we move into our roles as teachers, guides, and resourcers, we need better rules of thumb for making decisions that grow with our maturing kids.

While both Steve and I have had our kids tell us "I don't like choosing," helping our kids make the hard—but necessary—choices is not only better for them overall, but also makes it more possible for our families to be greenhouses of warmth.

One of the challenges of learning, exploring, and focusing is that young people are beginning to bump up against their limitations. They can't do everything. They can't be everything. They can't go everywhere. They're also learning more about the limitations of their social location, family financial realities, and their own abilities.

One Growing With parent we interviewed had a high school sophomore son who was stretched in multiple directions. She recalled, "Finally, he basically said, 'I'm doing too much.' He didn't feel like he was enjoying anything he was doing. He felt like he was just padding his high school résumé, not because he was called to those activities. So he prayed about what God was calling him to pursue, and he dropped out of sports."

In all three stages, we can help our kids understand that saying yes to one commitment generally means saying no to something else (either at that moment or later on). At first this seems like a life-limiting reality, but we have both tried to reframe the nos through dialoguing with our kids about specific questions that match their life stage.

So we'll ask our learners: "Are you getting enough rest? If you had to eliminate one activity or commitment, what would it be?"

With our explorers, we'll invite them to consider: "Who do you want to become as you're headed into young adulthood? If you say yes to this and no to that, what new opportunities might come your way? What opportunities might you miss out on?"

And as our focusers are hip deep in adult-like schedules and tensions, we'll nudge them about their schedule by wondering: "What do you sense God is calling you to work on? What's most important to you, and how can your schedule reflect those priorities? What are the practical realities that you'll have to hold alongside your priorities and longings?"

> "The number one difficulty in our family is allowing the children to develop without letting them get too busy. Events and commitments just start to collide. We do not enjoy that, and our kids don't either."
> —Beth, a Wisconsin mother of a learner and an explorer

Adding to the schedule dynamics for those kids living at home is that families may also have expectations such as sharing in chores or joining the family for certain evening activities. While those who have left home have more schedule freedom, we can play a crucial guide or resourcer role by asking them questions like:

How do you plan to invest your summer?

What are your plans for spring break?

How are you feeling about your balance between work and play?

Where do you feel the most stressed and why do you think that is?

When can we plan a time for you to visit (or for me to visit you)?

Here are our hopes about the holidays. How does that plan sound to you?

When asking these questions, both Steve and I have found that as our kids age, we need to shift from being a teacher to a guide or resourcer. The type of schedule direction we give a 16-year-old is inappropriate, if not insulting, to a 26-year-old. Growing with our kids' schedules means offering fewer suggestions and more questions.

### If It's Not a Definite Yes, It's a No

I have yet to meet a parent of a learner, explorer, or focuser who doesn't feel busy. If I (Kara) could change one aspect about my life, I would replace 10 to 15 percent of my calendar commitments with relaxed downtime with my family.

While I struggle to find the skill and self-discipline to make that goal a consistent reality, my calendar has become more manageable thanks to this simple principle I adapted from *Essentialism* by Greg McKeown: "If it's not a definite yes, it's a no."[27]

In my family, as well as with our team at the Fuller Youth Institute, I conducted a six-month experiment of using "definite yes" as a litmus test for whether to pursue a certain activity. Using that criteria was a game changer for my family's warmth (as well as our team's focus).

Should Dave and I accept an invitation from our son's school to coordinate his grade's camping trip? We already lead an annual camping trip with a bunch of families at our church (my husband is an Eagle Scout, so when we got married he introduced me to backpacking and I introduced him to a good hotel concierge). That makes hosting the school trip a maybe at best, so we said no.

Serving on a local nonprofit board we care about but that would involve monthly meetings at night? That's more than a maybe but still not a definite yes, so I said no.

Driving my high school son to a week-long summer school intensive, giving us five hours in the car together? Heavens yes. Definitely yes. Can't-wait-to-go yes.

We all live with commitments beyond our control that temper our ability to choose yes or no for ourselves. An inflexible work schedule, a chronically ill family member, or extended family obligations can put some of us in places where saying no feels like an incredible privilege. But many of us do have more choice than we act on.

I probably still set too low of a bar for my definite yes cutoff. But using that phrase as the criteria for making decisions about my schedule has given me more energy and time to be with my family.

### During Family Conflict, Focus on Your Main Growing With Goal

In his advice to parents of young people, noted scholar and author Eugene Peterson encourages moms and dads to view conflict as an opportunity to exchange faith, hope, and love.[28] I'm better able to do that when I keep in mind our main Growing With goal: to foster a mutual journey of intentional growth for both ourselves and our children that trusts God to transform us all.

When it comes to nurturing a "mutual journey of intentional growth," our wise friends and fellow ministry leaders, Reggie Joiner and Carey Nieuwhof, astutely describe the difference between

> Dave and I (Kara) have found this phrase helpful in maintaining a warm posture in the midst of conflict with our kids: "If I were in your position, I'd feel the same way. The answer is still no, but you are doing a great job expressing yourself."[1]
>
> 1. Adapted from Jim Burns, "Lead with Love, Purpose, and Authority," *HomeWord* (blog), November 13, 2017, https://homeword.com/jims-blog/lead-with-love-purpose-and-authority/.

fighting *with* our kids and fighting *for* our kids: "When you fight *with* someone, you want to win. When you fight *for* someone, you want that person to win. When you fight *with* people, walls are built up. When you fight *for* people, walls come down."[29] In the midst of your family conflicts, you're not trying to show your teenager or emerging adult you're right. You're trying to help them make right decisions while keeping a right relationship with them.

In the midst of trying to fight for and not against your young person, if your child is doing something risky—to themselves or others—don't go radio silent. Speak up, and speak up promptly.

But before speaking up, ponder whether your child's choices are truly dangerous or merely different than you wish they would make. As Jeffrey Arnett and Elisabeth Fishel wisely recommend, "If your son hasn't shaved in a few days and looks rather scruffy and a family reunion is scheduled, well, that might not be pretty, but it's not life threatening. But if your daughter shows signs that she's smoking pot every day instead of looking for a job, that habit can be harmful." At that point, "Parents need to step up, speak up, and be ready with resources for outside, professional help."[30]

### What Do You Disagree With? What Do You Agree With?

Many parents who seek to build withing find that family relationships struggle when our maturing kids develop new convictions about morality, politics, or religion that differ from (and, more often than not, lean more progressive than) our own. If you've had your twentysomething come home for Thanksgiving and hint over turkey and mashed potatoes that they think you're narrow-minded, out of touch, or even worse, a [insert political party name here], then you know what we're talking about.

While Growing With families are bound together more by our relationships than our beliefs, we still need to have honest discussions about our diverging convictions and opinions. Normally I (Kara) am a big proponent that when it comes to evaluating an idea or debriefing an event with others, it's best to start with the positive. Voicing together what we liked or what we appreciated about a shared experience creates an encouraging tone that makes us more open to constructive feedback.

But with my own kids, I've found it works better when I reverse the order. When I'm making an observation about our family or offering my opinion about politics, religion, or any other hot button topic, I can quickly tell when they aren't jumping on my bandwagon (my kids' body language is not very subtle). At that point I often ask them, "What do you disagree with, or what do you think is wrong, in what I'm saying?" I listen as they offer their (often very perceptive) criticisms of my perspective. I try not to respond with any counter-perspectives. I do my best to keep my ears open and my mouth shut. Whether or not they convince me that I'm wrong and they are right, I celebrate that they are finding and using their voices, and I thank them for opening my eyes to a different path forward.

Then I ask them, "What do you think is right, or what do you agree with, in what I'm saying?" I've found that once my kids have had a chance to critique me, they are far more open to verbalizing what they agree with, even if it's just a few sentences here and there.

Growing With parents move past conflict and kindle the fires of warmth by asking their own kids for input on tough decisions. As one mom of teenagers we interviewed remembered, "My oldest son was floored when I asked for his opinion. He was like, 'You want to talk to me?' I said, 'Yes, I want your opinion about this.' He couldn't believe it."

### Seeing Your Child through the Lens of Genesis 1, Not Genesis 3

One warm parent we interviewed offered his goal of viewing his children through the lens of Genesis 1, not Genesis 3. Genesis 1 describes the creation of the earth and humankind prior to the entrance of human sin. Sin enters our world in Genesis 3 when Adam and Eve eat fruit from the tree of the knowledge of good and evil, disobeying God's gracious boundaries that allowed them to eat from any tree but that one.

This dad continued, "I want to affirm that my two college-aged daughters are good, created in God's image. Of course they sin, but I don't want sin to define them. I want them to first of all know that God created them and loves them." Not only does this vision help parents connect with their children when their relationships are sweetness and light, it also helps parents who have experienced more distance to gain a new start. Since our kids are created in God's image, all is never lost.

The choices and journeys of far too many young people (as well as parents, including the two writing this book) are blown off course from the truth of Genesis 1 by shame. According to the understandably popular writings of social work researcher Brené Brown, shame is feeling bad about ourselves for who we are. In contrast, guilt is feeling bad about ourselves for what we do.[31]

Your theology of sin might lead you to a different conclusion, but we believe that Growing With parenting emphasizes our kids' sinful choices (i.e., "You made a bad choice") more than their core sinfulness (i.e., "You are a bad person"). The first gives your young person hope that through the cleansing power and grace of Jesus, they can make better choices in the future. The latter often paralyzes your young person, robbing them of hope that they can ever change. While there are (lots of) moments when you need to share your concerns about your child's choices with them, they will be far more likely to hear about your uneasiness—and make different decisions—if they know at their core that they are loved and valuable to God and to you.

As a result of our research, Dave and I (Kara) have framed our kids' poor behaviors through the language of their bad decisions rather than a core bad quality that defines them. Often we tell our kids we're surprised that they made a poor choice since we know they have a good heart.

But one vivid Saturday when one of our learner children (who shall remain nameless) was treating their sister poorly, I lost my temper. I broke my normal parenting rule of calling their behaviors bad and instead spoke in frustration, "You are selfish. You are treating your sister poorly because you are selfish."

Immediately, the look on my child's face told me that my harsh words had penetrated—and poisoned—their sense of themselves. My child started crying—not tears that streamed down their cheeks but tears that were so virulent they appeared to launch horizontally out of their eyes.

Choking back tears, this child asked, "I'm selfish? So you think I'm selfish?"

Instantly, I apologized. I confessed that I had misspoken. It wasn't that they were a selfish person but that they were making selfish decisions.

That child graciously accepted my apology. But during three different conflicts over the next nine months, that child reminded me that I had called them selfish. They haven't talked about that regretful day for the past few years, and I hope and pray that God will prevent my condemning words from robbing my child's core awareness that not only does God love them, God likes them. They bear God's image. The same God who knit them together in the womb is especially fond of them today. And so am I.

## Two Words to Draw Them Back

"I don't think you should be interviewing me for this study."

"Why?" I asked Julio, a dad who had been nominated as an amazing parent of teenagers and college students.

"Because in the last 72 hours, I've had to ask each of my sons for forgiveness for how I've blown it as a parent."

My response: "That's exactly why we want to talk with you."

This dad from a medium-sized Midwest city then explained how he recently had lost his temper with each of his boys. Each accepted his apology, and the fact that Julio repented stoked the fires of warmth in their family.

I (Kara) apologize at least once a week to one—or all—of my kids. Most of the time it's because of my tone of voice. If you were to read a transcript of what I say to my kids, it wouldn't seem too problematic. But if you were to hear the anger, frustration, and bitterness that taints my voice, you would understand—and affirm—my need to apologize.

If you're like me, when you apologize, you're often tempted to still criticize your child: "I'm sorry I yelled, but if you would have been less selfish, I wouldn't have raised my voice."

Or you give an excuse: "I shouldn't have misjudged you, but I was really tired from a tough conversation with my boss."

While many cultures frown on apologizing, based on our research, we recommend you instead say this: "I'm sorry. I was wrong. Will you forgive me?" No other additions are needed.

None of us are perfect—at parenting or anything else for that matter. If perfect parenting existed, we wouldn't need Jesus. But it doesn't and so we definitely do.

### Seven Questions When Your Child Boomerangs Home

In order to increase the odds that your young adult's return home is a blessing and not a burden, young adult scholars Arnett and Fishel offer the following questions to ask *before* the boomeranging begins:[32]

1. Do your kids have a plan while living at home—more education, networking and job applications, part-time or volunteer work?

2. Is there an end date (e.g., a few months or no more than a year), or is the arrangement open ended?

3. Will they pay rent, contribute to household expenses, or provide other kinds of regular help (e.g., errands, grocery shopping, cleaning the bathroom)?

4. Will they help with caring for younger siblings or grandparents, or prepare meals, or do laundry either regularly or once in a while?

5. Will they be allowed to borrow the car or be expected to use public transportation?

6. Do they need to call or text if they'll be out for dinner or past a certain hour?

> Since we described earlier in this chapter that conflict over money is one of the greatest tensions between parents and their young adults, you may be interested to learn that about half of young adults who boomerang home pay rent, and about 90 percent help with household expenses.[1]
>
> 1. Jeffrey Arnett and Elizabeth Fishel, *When Will My Grown-Up Kid Grow Up?* (New York: Workman, 2013), 117.

7. What are the boundaries around romantic partners, smoking, and drinking alcohol at home?

## In Their Pain, Acknowledge Your Own

Core to Growing With is the conviction that parenting is one of God's greatest life curricula for us. Since the birth of our oldest, I (Kara) have learned more through parenting about myself, my sin, and God's ongoing work in me than through any other facet of my life.

For those of us who are inclined to be the best goalie we can, deterring as much pain as possible from the lives of our teenagers and young adults, it's time to ask ourselves these questions:

- What about my tendency to protect my child is furthering their growth?

- What, if anything, about this tendency may be hampering my child's growth?

- What fear is motivating me to protect my child?

- As I think about my child's potential future suffering, how much of my anxiety stems from my concern about what *they* will feel?

- How much of my anxiety flows from my fear of what their struggles will cause *me* to feel about myself and my own parenting?

Admittedly, these questions are heavy. But they invite us to a depth commensurate with the depth of Growing With parenting—namely, as our kids grow, *we are growing also*. There is no such thing as healthy status quo parenting, just as there is no such thing as healthy status quo living. We are ever evolving and ever developing.

On those days when we find it easy to be a wall for our kids to come back to, and on those days when we feel kicked and bruised and ready to crumble, Steve and I take comfort knowing that just as God is continuing to transform our children, he's transforming us too. Just as we seek to be with our kids, Jesus is *Immanuel*, the God who is with us in our family highs and lows—and everything in between.

## Practical Questions to Grow With My Child

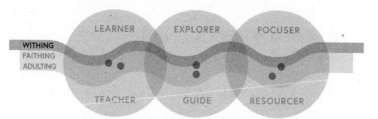

1. On a scale of 1 to 10 (with 1 being "we stink at this" and 10 being "we rock at this"), rate your family on the withing research insights presented in this chapter.

   I know how to handle my child's progression from dependence to independence to interdependence with the grace and patience that prevents that journey from fracturing our relationship.

   1⋯⋯⋯⋯⋯⋯⋯⋯⋯⋯⋯⋯⋯5⋯⋯⋯⋯⋯⋯⋯⋯⋯⋯⋯10

   We are not overwhelmed by the busyness and stress that often erode parents' resolve and ability to be a wall of support for their kids.

   1⋯⋯⋯⋯⋯⋯⋯⋯⋯⋯⋯⋯⋯5⋯⋯⋯⋯⋯⋯⋯⋯⋯⋯⋯10

   We navigate conflict—both large blowups as well as little annoyances—that can eat away at our family's commitment to journey with each other.

   1⋯⋯⋯⋯⋯⋯⋯⋯⋯⋯⋯⋯⋯5⋯⋯⋯⋯⋯⋯⋯⋯⋯⋯⋯10

2. In your opinion, which of the questions discussed in this chapter is the biggest culprit in cooling your family's warmth? Which question do you think your child would choose? If

they would choose a different question than you did, why do you think that is?

3. In what seasons have you felt like you were a warm wall of support for your learner, explorer, or focuser? What does that tell you about yourself, your parenting, and your family?

4. Who do you know who embodies the warm wall of support you would like to be for your teenager or young adult? What about their withing do you respect and wish to incorporate into your own parenting?

# PART 3

# THRIVING IN FAITH: "FAITHING"

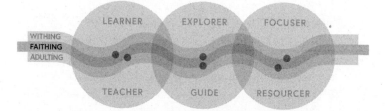

**Faithing:** *a child's growth in owning and embodying their own journey with God as they encounter new experiences and information.*

As parents and adults who care about adolescents and emerging adults, we have accrued enough parenting experience to feel like we can handle certain topics with our kids, or at least find the resources to support them.

Faith often feels more elusive.

Their questions about life, Jesus, good, and evil become more pressing and complex.

You may feel like no one trained you to be a theologian.

You and parents like you barely remember your high school or college philosophy lessons. There's much you fear you don't understand about God and the Bible.

And their questions, if we are honest, sometimes still haunt us.

Faithing provides grace, explanations, and conversational spaces to explore the deeper questions our growing kids are asking.

Faithing invites us to reengage our own faith journeys too.

In chapters 5 and 6, we propose that through the concept of faithing, we can encourage meaningful conversations about faith and explore renewed ways for our kids (and us) to connect with Jesus along with faith communities. Our hope is that we all continue to develop a faith that grows with us.

*A prayer:*

*Jesus, our kids' faith is changing and so is ours. We feel the weight of their search to make sense of our world, themselves, and God. This process also makes us more aware of our own questions and emotions, which can feel both exciting and terrifying. Grant us wisdom to listen well, patience to hold ambiguity, grace to receive their doubts, and courage to further our own faithing. Please also grant us a community who can hold all of this with us, journeying together toward you.*

# 5. Personal Faithing

*A Quest for a Faith That Grows With*

My (Steve's) firstborn was less than 48 hours old. As Jen held our precious newborn daughter, the hospital nurses wheeled her from her room to our car. All of a sudden it hit me: we were about to be all alone.

No more pit crew of nurses checking on us, attending to Jen's needs, offering ongoing encouragement to us as new parents while constantly telling us that our baby was the best. Surrounded by a support team of caring medical professionals, parenting seemed easy—albeit sleepless—those first 48 hours.

But now those same nurses were rolling Jen out the door, helping her into our sedan, watching while I buckled our baby into her car seat for the first time, and saying with a smile, "Have a great life!" At that moment, parenting got real. Our confidence evaporated. "Have a great life"? Seriously? That's all the help we get as we're launched into uncharted parenting territory?

These "I'm in over my head" moments surface for us as parents more often than we would like. We think we are getting the hang of one parenting stage. Then our kid or circumstances change and we're faced with another new frontier. The predictability we have grown to appreciate that stems from routines, resources, and relationships is often upended that first time we drop our kid off at school, let them stay at a friend's house, empower them to join the sports team, witness them get their driver's license, help them figure out prom, watch them pick a career, and greet a special friend they bring home to meet us. These crucial moments challenge us to pause and recognize that the ways our parenting worked in the past may not work today or tomorrow.

Kara and I have found this especially true for growing with our teenagers and young adults in their faith journeys. The family routines of prayer, reading the Bible, and going to church that worked through elementary school often unravel when we need to incorporate our growing kids' new schedules, new pressures, new questions, and even new resistance.

As our kids navigate new faith questions and experiences during their learner, explorer, and focuser stages, we have new opportunities as teachers, guides, and resourcers to encourage their growth. In this chapter, we explore practical research and tools to help us support our teenagers and young adults as they trek through new territories of faith—and doubt. In the spirit of Growing With, we'll also probe the new twists and turns emerging in our own faith paths as parents. Then in chapter 6 we'll explore the relationship learners, explorers, and focusers have with faith communities.

## Faithing: The Fuel for Our Spiritual Journeys

Prior to the teenage and young adult years, one of our primary faith-oriented goals was to pass on the faith tradition to our kids. This meant talking to them about Jesus, modeling faith in our actions, taking them to church, enrolling them in Sunday school, or ensuring that they made it to summer camp. Kara and I have each tried to keep up these practices in our respective families with our own kids, motivated in large part by research confirming that family instruction, traditions, and rhythms are correlated with deeper faith in young people—both now and in the future.[1]

While this faith foundation is important, it cannot—and will not—be the fuel that carries our kids forward for the rest of their spiritual journeys. We cannot "fill up" our kids in their early years and then hope there is "enough in the tank" to make it the rest of their lives. A relationship with Jesus does not work that way.

Which means we parents need new perspectives and goals regarding faith—both our own and that of our kids. These renewed views and aims are rooted in a concept called *faithing*. By *faithing*, we mean *a child's growth in owning and embodying their own journey with God as they encounter new experiences and information.*

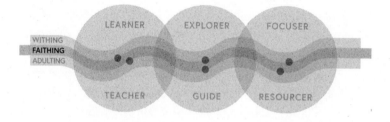

Inherent in this definition is a view that faith isn't just a noun, it's a verb. When we treat faith only as a noun, it often gets reduced to a possession.

You may have heard someone say that they "have faith" or "found faith." As parents, we worry that our growing kids will "lose their faith."

Stop and think about how faith is being used in these phrases. Relationship with God is treated as a thing to find, an object to own, or an item that can be lost.[2] It's treated like a commodity.

If relationship with Jesus is perceived only as a noun, we feel that our job is to load up more faith-like items into our kids' lives to offset any current or potential doubts or struggles. Like a cosmic faith balance sheet, we strive to bank enough pro-faith experiences for our kids to offset the anti-faith elements they will encounter. So we add more church, more youth group, more Bible verses, and more religious education. We believe the myth that if the balance sheet stays positive, the faith of our learner, explorer, or focuser will stick until they grow old enough to worry about their own kids.

Thus, while Christian traditions, practices, and faith-oriented language provide frameworks for younger children to interpret, live, and talk about their spiritual lives, we must build on these crucial foundations with strategies that support their walk with God as they age. Their faith becomes qualitatively different; therefore, so must our approach to navigating faith with them. So a Growing With commitment to faithing relies on three new premises:

*Faithing is about making sense of our spiritual journey, not merely learning more information.*[3] Faithing is about the *quality* not the *quantity* of our believing. It is about developing an agility that allows us to negotiate our personal, relational, and vocational trajectories. Faithing encourages us to keep developing our connection with God.

*Faithing seeks to integrate, not separate, spirituality and life experiences.*[4] Sooner or later our learners, explorers, and focusers will need to integrate their spiritual and religious beliefs with political platforms, social issues, economic challenges, global relationships, and scientific discoveries. If our young people keep their convictions about Jesus separate from their lived experiences, they run the risk of embracing a faith that is unable to keep pace with their lives. Faithing inspires us to live holistically.

*Faithing is more than intellectual; it also has relational and emotional qualities.*[5] When young people are working through belief crises, many adults assume that the problems and solutions are informational. They believe that if the young person just reads the right book or memorizes more of the Bible, then the process of following Jesus will work itself out. Far more than mere intellectual assent, faithing also

Some researchers suggest that the religious beliefs and commitments of young people can vary by ethnicity. While broad generalizations, some of these patterns can be helpful to understand as we consider the young people in our families and communities. African American teenagers often exhibit "personalistic absolutism," meaning a greater tendency to see God (who is often viewed as pretty demanding) as someone who has to be obeyed and who also wants to have a personal relationship with them that influences every aspect of their lives.

Latino teenagers often demonstrate "religious familism" by speaking of their religious beliefs as tied to family relationships more than institutional commitments. From the perspective of religious familism, the church exists to support family connections, and a personal encounter with God is often viewed as a catalyst toward positive outcomes for the entire family.

Family connections are often the catalysts for Asian American teenagers' entrance into both church and faith. As a result, while many young Asian Americans make autonomous faith discoveries through church relationships and serving, others continue to describe their religious involvement through the lens of their parents' expectations.

White teens often hold to a view of moralistic therapeutic deism that is expressed as "therapeutic individualism," meaning God helps them through personal struggles, and religious groups provide help in times of need.[1]

For more resources exploring the realities of multicultural families and communities, see fulleryouthinstitute.org/multicultural.

---

1. Richard W. Flory, Korie L. Edwards, and Brad Christerson, *Growing Up in America: The Power of Race in the Lives of Teens* (Redwood City, CA: Stanford University Press, 2010), 141; Jerry Z. Park and Elaine Howard Ecklund, "Negotiating Continuity: Family and Religious Socialization for Second-Generation Asian Americans," *The Sociological Quarterly* 48, no. 1 (2007): 93–118.

encompasses what we feel and how we relate to others. Faithing legitimizes our quest to make sense of our beliefs, permits us to be emotionally honest, and encourages us to reach out to others for support.

The bottom line is this: We do more than "have faith." We "faith." This is faithing.

Kara and I both value conversations with young people because we find their perspectives enlightening. I once asked an 18-year-old about his experience transitioning out of high school and how that affected his own spiritual journey. A phrase he offered stuck with me and has shaped the way I have parented my own kids. He explained, "The adults in my life didn't tell me *what* to believe but *how* to believe."

As he explained what he meant, I realized that what was most helpful for his journey with Christ was the way his parents, youth group leaders, and mentors gave him room to grow in his faith beyond saying the right answer or agreeing with everyone else. His faithing grew as adults in his life taught him *how* to believe. I got the sense that his parents grew with him in their own faithing too.[6]

## Faithing Insights

### When Faithing Moves Us from an Abstract God to a Reliable Jesus

When we train ministry leaders to help their churches grow young, we often ask the adults in the room to share their responses to the following questions:

What words come to mind when you hear the term *Christianity*?

What are some words that describe God?

What are some words that describe Jesus?

Often those in our seminars notice that their descriptive answers to the first two questions favor abstraction. They label Christianity as "a religion" or "the church." They offer abstract Christian words that characterize God as "almighty," "holy," and "triune."

But when they describe Jesus, they use more intimate words such as "friend," "healer," "loving," "present," or "forgiving." During our Growing Young research, we discovered that young people wanted to talk less about abstract Christian beliefs and more about Jesus.[7]

The gospel means "good news," and good news for young people is rarely an abstract theological concept. It's concrete, and it's lived out in concrete terms.

It's offering forgiveness to a family member who has wronged you.

It's finding one's place in a competitive world.

It's listening to the marginalized and feeding the poor.

It's confessing our sin of racism.

It's welcoming the stranger and loving the people right in front of us.

Jesus had dirty feet, was a partygoer, stood up to oppressive power, cared for the mistreated underdog, and ultimately gave up his life for those he loved.[8]

Just as Jesus embodied flesh-and-blood good news, young people long for a tangible gospel that matters to their everyday lives. Faith must match their ground-level, gritty, real-time minutes and hours. Young people want to know if the religious concepts they've been handed up until now are relevant enough to handle their current relationships, decisions, and actions. Their religious beliefs shift from theoretical ideas to everyday realities when the bills arrive; when diversity becomes their roommate; when violence is no longer a news story but their friend who has experienced sexual assault; when choice means pursuing one option at the expense of another; or when their politics are activated by stepping into the voting booth.[9] The faith traditions they have inherited from their families and churches must now be pursued on their own volition, in their own lives.[10] They need a faith that grows with them.

## Faithing as Searching

Let's be honest: the statistics regarding young people and their faith do not appear promising. As referenced earlier, the National Study of Youth and Religion (NSYR), a comprehensive study of the faith of over two thousand 13- to 17-year-olds, tracked teenagers into their early emerging adult years (ages 18–23) and found that the influence of religion in their lives diminished.[11]

Furthermore, the number of Americans described by the Pew Research Center as "Nones"—meaning those who claim to have no religious affiliation—has risen nationally from 16 percent in 2007 to 23 percent in 2014. More alarming is that 35 percent of those in the Millennial generation (of whom the majority are in their twenties) claim to be Nones, outpacing religiously unaffiliated members of Generation X (23 percent), the Baby Boomer generation (17 percent), and the Silent generation (11 percent).[12]

Parents who read these statistics and watch their own kids' behaviors often assume that young people are walking away from faith. While that may be happening, there is often more bubbling under the surface than we realize. Having conducted a vast review of the major studies on 18- to 23-year-olds, researcher and professor Tom Bergler describes a clear pattern in their religiosity: "Public religious practice declines a lot, private religious practices and felt importance of faith decline somewhat, and basic theistic beliefs decline only a little."[13] In other words, while faith-related *behaviors* may plunge dramatically, our kids' *beliefs* might actually only dip slightly.

Perhaps our concept of faithing allows us to reinterpret our kids' behaviors and questions and forge new ways to support them. To start with, let's assume that their faith journeys are more about *searching for* God than *walking away from* God.

While our young people's religious behaviors may be dropping, the encouraging news is that their hostility toward faith is not rising.[14] Even in the midst of describing college-aged young adults' move away from public, corporate faith practices (such as attending church or a campus Bible study), the NSYR reports that 80 percent have positive feelings about the religious traditions in which they were raised.[15] Relatedly, most Nones say they consider themselves spiritual and believe in God.[16]

### Doubt: Faithing's Friend

Faithing acknowledges that the quest to integrate their faith with new life experiences brings new struggles and doubts for our learners, explorers, and focusers. So we might hear them say:

"I don't believe in God anymore."
"If that's what Christians are like, I don't want to be one."
"I've outgrown my faith."
"I'm not sure I believe what our (or sometimes even more painfully, *your*) church teaches."

Disappointed by a faith that feels too small, our kids often seek new ways to hold their beliefs while simultaneously feeling disoriented and vulnerable. In one study, 78 percent of college students expressed a fluctuating sense of feeling connected with God and felt "considerable" or "moderate" distress over their religious dilemmas.[17]

Tom, a college student we met during our research, realized how a shift in his spiritual outlook could impact other parts of his life: "You start thinking, if I was wrong about this, or I have a different perspective on this, what else am I wrong about? You change your opinion on one thing and it affects everything else."[18]

At this point, it's normal for parents who have tried to raise their kids in a faith tradition to become anxious.[19] But let's suspend our anxieties for just a moment and view these doubts through the lens of faithing. Let's acknowledge the qualitative shifts our kids are trying to make and recognize that faith is more of a verb than a noun. It is much more a *process* than a *possession*.

The good news when our growing kids ask new questions is this: *Faithing invites doubt rather than avoids it.*[20] In many family and church contexts, doubts about God are often viewed as embarrassing or maybe even unfaithful. Few want to express their spiritual struggles for fear of being seen as less of a Christian or maybe not a Christian at all.

Growing With parents fight to reverse this trend. They realize that doubt is part of the faithing process and a necessary portal toward mature faithing. Often, young people's questions about God and current topics are their attempts to keep their spirituality relevant, not rebel against it. In one of our interviews, a mother with three post–high school kids reflected on the changes she's witnessed: "I think if I were to go back and re-parent, I actually would allow my kids more freedom in their high school years to explore and express their questions about faith."

Her instincts align with what teenagers need. Over 70 percent of churchgoing high schoolers report having serious doubts about faith. That statistic emerged from a three-year longitudinal study of 500 youth group graduates launched by the Fuller Youth Institute to help parents and churches build faith that lasts, or what we call Sticky Faith. Sadly, less than half of those young people shared their doubts and struggles with an adult or friend. Yet these students' opportunities to express and explore their doubts were actually correlated with greater faith maturity. In other words, *it's not doubt that's toxic to faith; it's silence.*[21]

> To find out more about our Sticky Faith research and resources, please visit fulleryouthinstitute.org/stickyfaith.

In our nationwide interviews for this Growing With project, mothers and fathers noticed both how their kids experienced doubt and how their kids tried to harmonize their beliefs with their new life experiences. Such efforts raised new faithing questions for their kids and called on new parenting skills that encouraged their kids to work through doubt rather than ignore or avoid it.

An East Coast couple shared the changes they were seeing in their high school daughter. The dad described their observations this way: "Her faith seems to be becoming more personal, which has driven more questions for her. There is lots of, 'Why would God not like this?' or 'Why would God support something like that?'" Mom chimed in: "She's no longer willing to just regurgitate something she has been told. She's trying to understand and figure it out herself."

One Indiana mother reflected on the parenting shifts she needed to make as her son went to college: "Finally God was saying to me, 'It is still your faith you are trying to give to your son, but you need to allow him to make his faith his own.' I realized I could pray for him and encourage him, but for his faith to stick, he had to own his faith journey."

Another mom we interviewed realized that she had to monitor and contain her own emotional and physiological responses to her explorer daughter's new questions: "During her sophomore year in college, my daughter came home and told me that one of her senior friends who she really looks up to said she wasn't sure if there was a God or not because there's so much destruction in the world right now. My daughter said she agreed with her. As I listened to her, my stomach was in knots as I resisted overreacting."

## Faithing Grows Best with a Solid Starting Point

In the midst of seasons when a child's faith stalls or diverges from our own, the spiritual influence of parents is still paramount. When our kids strive to make their faith their own, they need a solid launching point and, at times, even something to come back to. In their 35-year longitudinal study spanning four generations, sociologist

Vern Bengtson and a team of researchers found that religious transmission, meaning faith habits and perspectives held by parents and passed on to children, remained almost unchanged with their adult

### Growing With in Real Time:
### Faithing's three dimensions

Faithing has intellectual, emotional, and relational dimensions that affect the way young people make spiritual sense of their world.[1] All of these elements impact and are impacted by the way we embody our faithing in our everyday tasks, relationships, service, and worship. The following table depicts these three dimensions associated with faithing.

| | What faithing asks | What doubt looks like | What young people need as they navigate faithing and doubting |
|---|---|---|---|
| **Intellectual** | What do I believe? | Beliefs and experiences do not add up, leading to confusion and questioning. | Space and opportunity to question, challenge, disagree, and wonder. |
| **Emotional** | How do I feel? | The onset of doubt brings anxiety, frustration, or feelings of being overwhelmed. Working through doubt leads to feeling hopeful and energized. | Time and empathy to grieve and be authentic. |
| **Relational** | With whom do I believe? | Diverging from one's family or faith community's beliefs can lead to experiences of abandonment, loneliness, rejection, loss, and distance. | People who are relationally committed to them, even if they believe differently. |

children. For example, parents who reported being "more religious" also had adult children who similarly identified themselves as "more religious." Beyond self-reported religiousness, parents and children

*The intellectual dimension of faithing.* Young people are often the most articulate about their spiritual struggle in this intellectual dimension of faithing. After all, they want to understand why something about God is true or how to synthesize previously held beliefs with conflicting data or experiences.[2] Parents must resist the temptation to short-circuit adolescents' and emerging adults' intellectual quests by only reinforcing prior beliefs or by downplaying their questions. Instead, we can nurture the intellectual dimension of relationship with God by encouraging honest conversations, creating room where everyone is free to ask any question, and being willing to learn together.

*The emotional dimension of faithing.* When children experience doubts, they may feel anxious, confused, angry, sad, or hurt because life does not add up. Or they may feel let down by their faith, their church, or even God. As they work through these challenges, they may eventually begin to see a way forward and then experience relief, joy, renewed energy, or inspiration.[3] Parents can help their kids by recognizing that faithing includes an emotional element that usually seeks an empathetic ear before a logical argument.

*The relational dimension of faithing.* We have discovered that some students who experience spiritual struggle worry most about the effect doubts and questions will have on their relationships with parents, clergy, and peers. They anticipate that their intellectual doubts may result in relational consequences. Parents can help their kids' faithing by reminding them that, even in disagreement, we are committed to the relationship—no matter what.[4]

1. Sharon Daloz Parks, *Big Questions, Worthy Dreams: Mentoring Young Adults in Their Search for Meaning, Purpose, and Faith,* 2nd ed. (San Francisco: Jossey-Bass, 2011), 53–103.

2. Steven C. Argue, "Undergraduate Spiritual Struggle and the Quest to Remain Faithful," *Journal of Youth Ministry* 16, no. 1 (Fall 2017): 19–20.

3. Argue, 18–19.

4. Argue, 17–18.

consistently reported similar responses regarding church participation, view of Scripture, and attitudes toward teaching religious values. Their conclusion: "In religion, parents really matter."[22]

## Faithing's Contagiousness

Supporting our children's faithing requires paying attention to our own faithing. Some researchers have noted that spirituality has a "contagiousness" to it; the faithing and doubting of those close to us impacts our own faithing and doubting.[23] Relationally, we might sense that our kids are pulling away from us. Emotionally, we might wrestle with our own spiritual uncertainties and wonder if that's okay. Intellectually, we could have questions just like our kids do. If we are honest, we may have uttered phrases like:

"I get worried that I can relate to my stepson's feeling that church sometimes doesn't make sense."

"I feel anxious when my daughter asks a question about Jesus and I don't know the answer."

"I feel scared when my teenager raises a legitimate point that contradicts our church's stance, because I think I agree with her."

In the midst of this inner whirlwind, we're tempted to focus on our kids while missing how God may be transforming our own lives.

I (Steve) remember having a "conversation-turned-lecture" experience with my high school daughter, Lauren, as she was packing for a month-long service trip. Both of us were a bit more sensitive as we were tired from tackling her long to-do list, excited about her adventure, and anxious about all the unknowns. Our conversation took a negative turn when I realized that I was barking at her more than talking with her. I could see that she was shutting down, and we finished packing in silence.

Later that night, I returned to her and confessed, "Hey, I'm sorry that I started lecturing you. You weren't doing anything wrong. I just realized that I was scared about you heading out on this trip by yourself. Will you forgive me?"

Honestly, I get discouraged when she sees the anxious parts of me. When she forgave me that night, I realized that perhaps these are the moments our own kids help us as much as we support them.

### Growing With in Real Time:
## What if my spouse and I do not see eye to eye on faith-related issues?

While there is evidence that same-faith marriages can perpetuate religious continuity over generations, parents often disagree on religious topics, or parents are growing in their faith at different rates.[1] The same dynamics can emerge in a single-parent family supported by grandparents or a multigenerational family sharing the same living space. When our kids start raising questions and sharing their own opinions about God, spouses and other family members often are invited—or forced—to consider trying the following:

- *Check each other's assumptions.* Do not assume that you and your spouse hold the same position on a particular faith-related topic.
- *Make time for honest conversation.* You do not need to agree with your spouse, but you need to understand where each of you is coming from.
- *Model dialogue.* Show respect for each other, especially as you interact with your kids about religious topics. Acknowledge that, at times, there can be multiple faithful solutions.
- *Think win-win.* Our goal for our kids is for them to grow into holding their own faithing perspective, not to choose between disagreeing parents.
- *Keep talking.* Recognize that our kids' faithing journeys unfold over time. As parents, check in with each other on the conversations you both are having and work to keep the dialogue generative and encouraging.

1. Vern L. Bengtson, Norella M. Putney, and Susan C. Harris, *Families and Faith: How Religion Is Passed Down across Generations* (New York: Oxford University Press, 2013), 127.

My daughter's journey impacted my own faithing. I realized that I was trying to control the situation so that I wouldn't feel anxious. My impatience and stress were about *my* faithing, not hers.

Sometimes the words we say, the emotions we feel, or the relational tensions we experience are not about our kids' spiritual journeys. Instead, they are symptoms of our own faithing and doubting. When we get scared, anxious, and overwhelmed, Growing With parents stop and admit it—to themselves and to their children.

### Faithing's Linguistic Connection

The glue of faithing in our family is communication. In other words, Growing With parents actually *talk* about our faithing.

The vast NSYR highlighted that young people have become inarticulate about their faith, often lacking the language to express their beliefs and convictions.

Further exploration revealed another telling part of this story: so have their parents.

Somehow, young people and their parents have lost the ability to speak of faith in real life.[24] Like learning Mandarin as a young person then forgetting it as an adult, Christian adolescents and emerging adults often become less fluent in faith over time. Faithing needs to be talked about and processed, and if these conversations diminish as our kids get older, we miss opportunities to help them remain fluent in faithing. Faithing depends on practice and use for it to become deeply part of us.[25] It is through faithing that language, behaviors, beliefs, and values are internalized.[26]

The good news for parents is we don't need to be theologians or super-Christians to talk with our kids about our faith or theirs. We only need to be willing to go there.

Take a risk by offering to pray for them. Share what you're trusting God for. Discuss the sermon together. Or read the Scriptures together during the holidays when everyone's home. Our good friend and fellow practical theologian from Princeton Theological

Seminary, Kenda Creasy Dean, says it best: "Do something radical and give Jesus the credit."[27] When our faithing process becomes part of our conversations, faith itself becomes easier and more natural to talk about.

## Faithing Ideas

### Help Your Kids Figure Out Their Unique Faithing

I (Kara) tend to feel closest to God when I'm reading my Bible or writing in my prayer journal. Or both. But the older I get, the more I am coming to terms with the reality that not everyone is the same as me.

So every once in a while, I ask my kids this question: "When do you feel closest to God?"

Nathan's answer: "During worship." He has felt close to God through worship music since fourth grade. He now plays guitar and regularly leads worship at our high school ministry. Thursday night worship practices are a priority in his schedule.

Krista tells me she feels closest to God when she's at church. With her friends. She's always been social, and she comes alive when she's with people who get her.

For Jessica, our most introverted child, it's in our backyard. By herself. She loves nature and experiencing God's creation. As much as she loves her friends, she cherishes time on her own outside to read, swing on a swing, ride her scooter, or just lie in the grass and look at the sky.

God has wired each of my kids differently. As much as my default is to assume my kids are like me (or at least *should* be like me), I'm coming to appreciate their unique ways of faithing. I want to model faithing to them, but I cannot expect them to copy my faithing. If you want to try to do the same with your learners, explorers, and focusers:

- *Ask your kids when they feel closest to God.* If I really thought about it, I could probably guess my kids' answers based on what I observe about them. But even having the conversation provides one more way to faith as a family.

- *Carve out time in your family schedule so your kid gets that type of time.* I have a confession to make. Sometimes I don't want Nathan to go to Thursday night worship practice because I treasure time with him at home. I am learning that encouraging his faithing requires sacrificing my preferences for what he values.

- *Expose your kids to other ways to connect with God.* While Scripture reading and prayer are foundational to faithing, I want my kids to know that they can be creative in their faithing. Like any relationship, we grow when we try new things together, and we can offer this vision to our kids. A talkative kid might find a contemplative prayer group transformative. A talented performer might discover a new kind of engagement with God through manual labor. We may need to be the catalysts who invite them to try something new.

## Bring Faithing into Their Challenging Dilemmas

Now that we understand faithing, let's return to the challenging statements we raised earlier in this chapter. What if we tried to approach our kids' challenging dilemmas in light of what we now know of faithing?

*I don't believe in God anymore.* What if you responded, "Please tell me about the God you don't believe in anymore"? Encourage your teenager or young adult to articulate their doubts so that they, and you, can better understand what they might be working through. Acknowledge that their confession is courageous. Honor the moment by asking them how they're feeling rather than debating them. Remind them that you are present with them, love them, and are for them. You might even find you can say, "I don't believe in that kind of God either." And eventually share what you believe about God instead.

*If that's what Christians are like, I don't want to be one.* What if you were to acknowledge that you also have observed mixed messages sent by both churches and individual Christians? Compliment them for noticing the contradictions. Ask them how they would live differently. Talk about how your family can live more consistently, extend grace to each other, and forgive each other.

*I've outgrown my faith.* What if you respond with a calmness that comes from remembering that faithing grows and that this moment is not the end of their faith journey but the beginning of a new chapter? Might it be possible to acknowledge your teenager or young adult's growth, empathize with their emotions, or encourage them to find new inspiration for their faith journey? Suggest reading a biography of someone who may have charted a similar journey, such as a scientist who believes in God or an artist who expresses faith through unique mediums. Or read of a woman who overcame her experience with discrimination. Or maybe study a person of color who found God through experiences within his cultural background. Remind your child that when they outgrow something, they are likely growing into something else.

*I'm not sure I believe what our church teaches.* Comments like these can move a family from conversation to debate in no time! Be slow to assume that a statement like this is only an intellectual one. Recognize that intellectual dissent or questions often are evoked because of new and broadening relationships and experiences. Simplistic faith responses to issues of equality, science, and politics that previously may have been acceptable to your kids now feel unsatisfying. Acknowledge new complexities and make room to dialogue about topics that are important to them. Invite other adults to join your family conversation who will listen, honor, and respond well to your kids' questions. Avoid offering either-or solutions that constrain them to only two options when there may be more. Work toward considering new, creative ways that honor their experiences and faith journeys.

### Speak Fluently of Faithing

As we interact with parents nationwide, they confess that when it comes to discussing spirituality, they're worried about saying the wrong thing and either messing up or revealing their ignorance. Let's acknowledge right now that we all will say the wrong thing sometimes! The good news is that faithing needs fluency not correctness.

Faith in families has become a lost language, a segmented category, the fancy room in the house that we visit but don't live in. Parents can bring faithing language back into everyday life by finding small ways to speak it again. Like any language, it will seem awkward at first, but consistency will bring fluency.

Before my (Steve's) kids could drive, I would take them to school in the morning. I realized that this task was also a ritual when I had my kids all to myself at the beginning of the day. So somewhere along the way, I made it a point to turn down the music and pray a simple prayer over them. I would typically end by praying, "May we follow you to live in ways that make the world a better place today."

One morning on our drive, I was moody and quiet, making our typical fun morning drive not very fun. My daughter sensed it. She grabbed my hand, started to pray for me, and ended the prayer, "And may we follow you to live in ways that make the world a better place today." I squeezed her hand, wiped my tears, and said, "Amen."

If car-time prayer doesn't work or is too awkward, pray for them as you occasionally make their lunch or dinner. Tell them you're praying for them. Ask them what you can pray for.

When my kids have been at college or lived on their own, I have tried to text them regularly. I try not to be overbearing. In fact, we have an agreement that if I text, they don't need to text back! These texts aren't "Don't forget to turn in that paper" texts or "We miss you—please come home this weekend!" texts. Instead,

I tell them what I love about them, that I'm praying for them, or I send them a quote that resonates with their interests.

My family has tried regularly to take time over dinner (usually on Sunday before the week begins) for each one of us to share what we're anticipating for the week. Usually we ask two questions: (1) What are you excited about? and (2) What would you like us to pray about? Then we each pick someone to pray for. This small ritual seems to keep us connected with each other throughout the week. For those who have kids away from home, you can still find ways to connect and ask these very same questions by text, email, or video.

Having said all that, I can also list the numerous times when I forgot to ask the questions over Sunday dinners, failed to pray for my daughters, or just plain blew it. So we know that even our best intentions will at times fall flat or simply lose steam. Our goal is not to be perfect but rather to ask ourselves, What are the simple ways we're making our faithing conversations fluid and natural? Like any language, the more we practice, the easier it comes.

### Create Spaces for Faithing to Happen

When my (Steve's) daughters were in their late teens and early twenties, I made a point to use coffee outings to talk about meaningful topics. I'll be honest, it was hard at first. As a parent, you want your kids to come to you and ask you about the meaning of life, but that rarely happens! What I found is that they often expected *me* to bring up important topics. So I learned to take some risks with them by asking them about friends, politics, current events, and God.

One question that I regularly brought up with them is this: "What is something you don't believe that you think I still believe?" I've also turned the question around: "What is something you believe that you don't think I believe?" Sometimes the answer would be, "I can't think of anything." Sometimes they had a list.

Each time I held my breath, wondering what they might say! But what gave me courage was knowing that faithing is a process—a process that is best fueled by honest, regular conversation.

## Tell Your Own Faithing Story (It's Part of Their Story Too)

Somewhere along my parenting journey, I realized that even though I was in ministry and our family shared many faith rituals, I had not really told my girls the story of my spiritual journey. So with each of them, I have tried to find moments to ask, "You know, we do all these religious things and talk a lot about Jesus, but have you ever wondered why or how I found a connection with Jesus and his story?" Each said that they didn't know; when I asked them if I could share my story, each one graciously responded, "Yes."

Tell your story. It doesn't have to be told perfectly. But share about times when God's grace has sustained you. Offer pieces of it as you can. And if you told them once long ago, don't assume they remember. Tell it again or share how you are experiencing God in your daily living. Let's give our kids context and a starting point for their spiritual journeys by telling them our own stories.

## Support Learner, Explorer, and Focuser Faithing

Once we accept that doubt is part of faithing, that it's not *if* doubts will come but *when*, and that faithing topics will arise the more our faithing communication becomes common, we become aware that faithing changes over the years. To best grow with our families, we need to develop unique postures that match the key struggles and questions of the learner, explorer, and focuser stages.

### WHAT LEARNERS NEED FOR THEIR FAITHING

As high school students, learners make sense of their faith through the groups they belong to and the modeling of others. They can envision a perfect world, a perfect church, a perfect parent, and a perfect self while realizing that none of these truly exist. They need help grieving the reality that they do not live in a perfect world, making sense of the new questions they're discovering, and learning to live congruently with their beliefs. Parents as teachers can help their kids' faithing by:

- Recognizing that learners highly value what adults and peers think. For them, being faithful often means fitting in. Doubting can challenge their sense of belonging in their church, leaving them asking, "What's wrong with me?" Assure them that they belong and that their questions can help their faithing and faith community, not hurt them.

- Accepting their questions about God and teaching them how to seek helpful answers that encourage their maturity. Encourage them to talk with an expert, read an article, or listen to a podcast. Follow up with them and ask them to teach you what they've discovered and what new questions have now surfaced for them.

- Gently pointing out moments when what they say they believe appears incongruent with how they're living. Patiently explore solutions with them to align their beliefs and actions more closely together. Remember that this is a gradual process that requires us to show them grace, and encourage them to keep working at it.

## WHAT EXPLORERS NEED FOR THEIR FAITHING

Since explorers are journeying through the first half of emerging adulthood, they make sense of their relationship with God by asking more critical questions, often comparing and contrasting what they have been taught by their families and faith communities with their new encounters with diverse people, experiences, and worldviews.[28] This is often a time of doubting more, challenging more, and stating what they don't believe more than what they do believe. They wonder if it is safe to question and critique, and worry that they will be rejected. Without encouragement from parents and other adults, they'll default to talking about their doubts with their peers or trying to work through them on their own. Parents as guides can help their explorer kids' faithing by:

- Creating room for explorers to question and critique their families and faith. They need adults who will be patient with their underdeveloped and sometimes harsh judgments and who can resist becoming defensive.

- Gently encouraging them not only to voice the problems in their families or home churches, but also to reflect on what they may have appreciated.

- Receiving their spiritual quests as part of their journey, encouraging them to move beyond doubting, and coaching them to search for new answers to their new questions. There have been times when my daughters have asked my opinion on social issues they were working through. In my best moments, I've resisted giving them my opinion and suggested that they find a resource on the subject. I want them to learn how to search for solutions themselves. In solidarity, I offer to read or listen to the resource too and then promise to talk about it.

## WHAT FOCUSERS NEED FOR THEIR FAITHING

As focusers move from emerging adulthood toward adulthood, they are likely gaining clarity in their careers, relationships, and beliefs. They do not need to associate only with those like them (like learners) nor reject those who disagree with them (like explorers). Rather, they are becoming more comfortable with their own relationship with God and are searching to find common ground—even with those who hold differing perspectives. Parents as resourcers can help their focuser kids' faithing by:

- Recognizing that focusers are starting to consider the fingerprint they want to leave on our world. They want to invest in causes that matter. Their doubting surfaces their longing to make a difference and their fear about whether they will live up to their aspirations. They ask, "What's wrong with the world and what can I do about it?"

- Creating space to talk with them about their relationships, vocations, and spirituality. They need a mutual conversation, not a teaching session.

- Connecting them with other adults who may have similar vocations, passions, or aspirations.

### Their Faithing Needs Our Faithing (and Vice Versa)

Our kids' faithing affects our parenting as well as our own faithing and doubting. What our kids need most is not for us to protect them or solve their problems, but rather to faith with them. This is a great moment for you to pause and reflect on your own journey with God. Consider asking yourself the following questions:

- On a scale of 1 to 10 (with 1 being low and 10 being high), how would you rate your own faithing process, meaning the way you personally are trusting God, working through doubts, or taking risks to align your life with your faith? This is not to shame you, only to encourage you to be honest with where you are right now.

- If your kids could describe Christianity based on how they see you live, what would Christianity look like to them? (If you're like us, likely there are some bright spots and some dimmer ones.)

- What doubts or struggles have you had or do you have now? How have those questions impacted your faith?

- What are some areas in your life where you would like to grow in your own faithing?

## Remember That God Seeks Out All of Us

We offer this important truth at the end of this chapter to prevent parents from defaulting to two unhelpful responses toward the faith of their growing kids. The first makes spirituality too magical, as though God will somehow work in our kids' lives and there's nothing we need to do. The second assumes that our kids' faith journeys and decisions are so influenced by our attitudes and actions that we have to do it all. The reality is somewhere in the middle. Our actions and attitudes matter, but there is no formula—or magical tip or trick that we can say or do—that can perfectly predict our kids' relationship with Jesus. In this middle space lie the peace and strength that come from knowing that God loves each of us, is pursuing us, and desires to give us a full life.[29] We can rest in knowing that, while we want our kids to believe in God, God always believes in them. And in us.

## Practical Questions to Grow With My Child

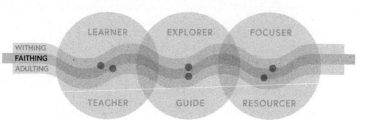

1. In our family, faith is part of our everyday conversations, decisions, and routines:

1................................5................................10
Never              Sometimes              Always

2. What information, quote, or story in this chapter inspired your thinking or gave you a fresh perspective on faith and faithing?

3. Describe a scenario when your child's faithing and/or doubting has challenged your own faithing and doubting.

4. We grow with our kids as we acknowledge their (and our) unique faithing challenges and breakthroughs. How might your learner, explorer, or focuser need your support in their faithing right now?

5. If you could describe your faithing journey over the last year to your adolescent or emerging adult, what would you share?

6. What parent, friend, or religious leader might help you grow in your own faithing as you interact with your kids in their faith journeys?

# 6. Faithing Together

## *Searching for Communities That Support Our Faith Journeys*

If you grew up in a churchgoing family—and if you're honest—you might remember those times when you faked sleeping in on Sunday mornings. I (Steve) will admit it. On those sleepy Sunday mornings, I would strategize that if I just stayed in bed long enough, my parents would overlook that I wasn't up or would sleep in themselves and give me a pass on church. Our own kids have tried the same tactics, but we were on to them!

But let me continue to be honest. As parents, we face that go-to-church/not-go-to-church dilemma every weekend. In the past few months . . .

There have been mornings when our kids didn't want to go to church and we really wanted them to go.

There have been times when they wanted to go to church and I wanted to take the day off.

There have been surprises, like when our high school daughter visited her older sister at college and, instead of sleeping in after attending a concert the night before, they went to church on Sunday.

There have been moments when they wanted to go to church and I really wanted them to stay home, rest, and recover from their dizzying schedules.

And continuing in this theme of being honest about weekend worship services, church creates all sorts of tension within us as parents, as well as in our relationships with our kids.

Relationally, this is often where fights break out between parents and children. Parents think their kids need to go to church, and kids are resistant.

Practically, we often get frustrated when all that our kids experience at church is a program—no relationships or integration beyond the peer-specific group.

Emotionally, we get nervous when our kids attend less frequently or stop attending church altogether, because we worry they'll lose their faith.

Adding to our anxiety are the less-than-promising reports on the decline of young people's religious lives that hit the headlines and crowd our social media feeds:[1]

Millennials Are Leaving the Church in Droves

Young People Are Biblically Illiterate

Religious "Nones" Are Atheists and Agnostics

What Will We Do About America's Empty Churches?

These headlines about young people are generally a bit exaggerated. Writers, bloggers, and marketers are trying to attract your attention and your dollars. Alarmist headlines often do the trick.

While we need to take such headlines with a grain of salt, we also need to recognize the truth that beats behind them. Many young people, including perhaps your own teenagers and young adults, are distancing themselves from the church today. While 18- to 29-year-olds comprise 17 percent of the US population, they represent only 10 percent of US churchgoers.[2] As people who love teenagers and young adults, Kara and I are deeply concerned by how young people are missing from churches. We hope you are too.

But in the midst of our worries, what fills us with optimism and inspired our Growing Young research project is all the amazing

Given the drift from churches we are seeing in our nation and in our homes, we might be inclined to demand that churches adjust to reach our kids. We agree with you that part of the solution is for churches to take a renewed look at the way they engage young people. We believe that our research in *Growing Young* maps out core commitments that can help churches serve young people. We encourage you to read this resource and to pass it along to your ministry leaders!

faith communities loving and attracting young people today. In the midst of the discouraging bare spots in churches, there are some hope-inspiring bright spots.

Further, let's remember that the faith journeys of young people are more complex than their church attendance. Dr. Nancy Tatom Ammerman, sociologist at Boston University's School of Theology, gives insightful perspective that if "we do not find as much of [religion today] in those predictable places as we did before, we cannot assume that it is disappearing."[3]

As a parent, you may wish the church was different and feel frustrated that you don't have much influence over your own church. That's why we focus this chapter on what *you* can do to encourage your kids' faithing in community. If we stick with our terminology that describes faithing as an ongoing journey, we suggest that when people are faithing together, they're *churching*. Church, then, is less of a place young people seek to attend and more of a community with which young people participate.

We might be tempted to direct our cheering or blaming over the current state of our kids' belief in God onto ourselves. All of us—including Kara and me—have made mistakes in how we've helped teenagers and young adults come to love the church. But the good news is that it is never too early and never too late to take positive steps toward encouraging the faithing journeys of your adolescents and emerging adults.[4] Our hope is that your church can be a supportive community both to you and to your growing kids.

## Faithing Insights

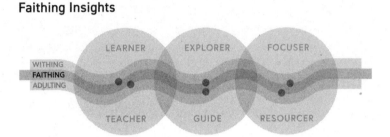

### *Looking Out for Young People*

During our Growing Young research, we discovered that churches doing great work with young people tend to "prioritize young people everywhere." Making young people a priority means that churches do more than empathize, relate, or say they care about them. Instead, these vibrant faith communities move beyond rhetoric to reality by making strategic choices in their buildings, schedules, budgets, and programs to position themselves to advocate for young people. Adults in Growing Young churches turn their focus *outward*, putting the needs of young people ahead of their own.

Prioritizing young people doesn't mean that older generations don't matter. In fact, our Growing Young research revealed that when young people are prioritized in the church, *everyone* benefits. Members of all generations learn from each other, help each other look beyond church culture, and develop new relationship muscles they have not exercised before.[5]

### *If—Not When—They Return*

We explained in chapter 1 that young people are taking longer to develop their careers, get married, and have children. Many eventually achieve these personal goals, but we must not extrapolate that this is the same for church. We cannot assume young people will just come to their senses and return to church at age 30. This false hope is rooted in studies of previous generations who returned in part to church once they got married or had children.

But this generation is different and less likely to return when they become parents. Their educational and vocational pursuits require emerging adults to be more mobile, extending the time it takes for them (should they choose) to settle into a community, get married, and start a family. Thus, if the stabilizing factors that may encourage them to reengage church are occurring later, their church non-attendance may lengthen. If this is true, churches must consider that young people who return to church may be coming back not from a short hiatus but after a decade-long absence.[6] Let's not assume that reentry is easy for them.

In addition, while overall church participation numbers have only declined slightly, when we look at the data by generations, those in their twenties are more likely to identify as *not* religiously affiliated. Pew research findings reveal that by generation, 35 percent of Millennials identify as religiously unaffiliated, compared to 25 percent of Generation Xers and 17 percent of Boomers.[7]

This rise in religiously unaffiliated Millennials seems common across race, ethnicity, socioeconomic status, and gender. It does not mean that today's young people are anti-God, however. Of the unaffiliated, two-thirds report that they believe in God, and a majority believe that religious institutions can be a force for good. Yet, 88 percent of these unaffiliated say they are not seeking to be connected with churches.[8]

## Learners and Their Relationship with Church

It is common to think that the only real connection teenagers have with church is through youth groups. We remain convinced that youth ministries play an important role in the life of Christian teenagers and their families. However, we also believe the *whole* church plays a crucial role in supporting and impacting adolescents' faithing. In fact, research supports that faith transmission from parents to children increases when family connections with churches are tighter. When families engage with faith communities, there are more opportunities for intergenerational support, spiritual modeling, and the development of religious practices.[9] Churches remain faithing greenhouses for teenagers where intergenerational relationships are cultivated, conversations about God are sparked, and faith development is extended into their real lives.

"Religious capital" refers to the religious or spiritual knowledge, beliefs, behaviors, and social structures that can be leveraged for an individual or collective good. Given how different ethnicities prioritize the individual over the collective, or vice versa, diverse teenagers often have different faith leanings.

- White teens have a propensity to value their individual journey and emotional well-being while seeing God as loving and supportive of their desires and autonomy.
- African American teenagers are inclined to find support through religious institutions. Churches are seen as authoritative, promoting a life ethic that includes commitment to family and community.
- Latino teens are likely to see church as an authoritative institution they trust to contribute to the well-being of their families. Belief is often understood as part of upholding family unity.
- Asian American teenagers tend to view faith from a pragmatic approach where their beliefs help them accomplish their life goals, and they often experience church as a safe haven to express their identity.[1]

1. Richard W. Flory, Korie L. Edwards, and Brad Christerson, *Growing Up in America: The Power of Race in the Lives of Teens* (Redwood City, CA: Stanford University Press, 2010), 157–61; Sharon Kim, *A Faith of Our Own: Second-Generation Spirituality in Korean American Churches* (New Brunswick, NJ: Rutgers University Press, 2010), 50–82.

## INTERGENERATIONAL SUPPORT

The promising insight for our learner kids is that churches can offer significant support to our adolescents, support that is appreciated by their parents. In our nationwide sample of family interviews, parents of teenagers consistently reported that their churches helped them parent their kids. In particular, they were grateful for the support of other adults from their churches who invested in their children's lives or served as mentors to them.

One father of two boys from the West Coast explained it this way: "I feel like over the years, each of our kids has had significant individuals in our church who have invested and connected with them deeply, whether that be a Sunday school teacher, youth group leader, or a small group leader somewhere along the way. That was huge in their spiritual development."

Thanks to the wisdom of our friend Chap Clark, we suggested in our Sticky Faith research that teenagers benefit from a five-to-one ratio where they can name five adults in their lives who support them with no strings attached.[10] This does not mean that there are five adults following one kid around everywhere they go! It means that a young person can name five adults supporting them—an aunt/uncle, grandparent, church leader, teacher, coach, or family friend. Our parent interviews confirmed that the most significant way parents felt their churches helped them parent their growing teenagers and emerging adults was by providing adults who invested in their kids.

## CHURCH IS WHERE THE CONVERSATION STARTS (NOT ENDS)

During our nationwide interviews, many parents reported that church events such as confirmation, catechism, or worship services provided them with opportunities to talk about God with their kids. One mother of four teenagers from California reflected: "When we drove home together from church, we would quite often have great conversations. I'd ask, 'What did you think?' I enjoyed letting them form their thoughts and responses."

From our interviews as well as research on religious transmission, we see that church programs are not merely an end in themselves but can be sparks that ignite more faithing conversations between parents and their teenagers.

## FAITHING THROUGH (AND BEYOND) YOUTH GROUP

Perhaps some of our young people struggle with attending church because they do not feel that church addresses the topics that really matter to them. Half of 13- to 17-year-olds desire to pursue science-related careers, yet only 1 percent of youth pastors report addressing any science-related subject in the last year.[11] While some youth leaders may attempt to address "faith versus science" debate topics, young people are often more interested in harmonizing their faith and science convictions. Many who aspire to work in the STEM fields (science, technology, engineering, and math) seek to have generative conversations about global warming, genetic engineering, the sanctity of life, fighting diseases, and alleviating poverty.[12]

As leaders deeply connected with the trends in US youth ministry, we remain concerned that church leaders at times fail to help young people make faithing connections between their beliefs and their life experiences. Our work at the Fuller Youth Institute provides portraits of youth group graduates who now seem unable to translate their youth ministry experiences into college, the military, or the workforce.[13] Youth group often prepares its graduates for more youth group, not life after youth group.[14] For many young people, they need help moving faith from an abstract religious term to everyday good news. Perhaps it is time for parents to have new conversations with our ministry leaders about our children's search for identity, belonging, and purpose and the support churches can provide for them.

### Explorers and Their Relationship with Church

Traditionally, the explorer period immediately after high school is when churchgoing drops most dramatically. Christian Smith and

Patricia Snell's study of the religious lives of 18- to 23-year-olds revealed that their regular religious attendance decreased by 25 percent, and those young people who reported that they "never attend" church increased by 25 percent.[15] In our national interviews, parents of explorers noticed shifts in their kids' spiritual lives and church engagement, and expressed their own conflicting emotions as they watched their kids make their own choices. For example, we heard statements like:

"And then I don't think he really went to church in college, despite me really harping him about it."

"I am praying that my kids would trust God. I am praying that they would trust that God loves them and is good, and the same for myself."

"But I think as a parent, you sit back and you are awed by how the Holy Spirit can just work in them. And there are a lot of parents who have done exactly what I have done and prayed with them every night and prayed for them and coached them and worked with them, and still things happen and your kid can walk away from church."

"I think it is always a challenge when your kids are living away from home to know how much do you push and say, 'Are you going to church? Do you have a church?' Do I care if they just go to church? I do not care as much if they go to church as that they are plugged in to a Christian community. What does that look like? Maybe that is harder to do than to just go to church on Sunday and check that box."

## DECLINING CHURCH ATTENDANCE (BUT STILL FAITHING)

Explorer young people are starting to learn to take responsibility for their decisions, including how they will engage church on their own. Some religious leaders misinterpret college students' decline in church attendance as evidence of the anti-faith agendas of university campuses and professors.[16] This perspective isn't supported by the newest data. Recently surveyed college students were 2.7 times more likely to report that their religious beliefs were strengthened during their college experience rather than weakened.[17] Further, there is evidence that those who do *not* attend college are more likely to experience declines in religious service attendance and affiliation.[18] Another study reinterprets statistics of declining church attendance of first-year college students as a by-product of learning to manage one's daily life more than rejecting God or religion.[19] More studies need to be conducted about the effects of college on a young person's faith, but while it's understandable that parents bemoan their undergraduate's drift from church or small group, it doesn't necessarily mean their beliefs, or their affection for those beliefs, have waned.

## FAITHING FACES DISRUPTIONS, DISTRACTIONS, AND DIFFERENTIATION

Adults may push back on the findings above and suggest that young people have a responsibility to develop their own walk with God. While we aspire for young people to own their faith journeys, churches must recognize that young people still need support. Smith and Snell observe that explorers participate less in church because of "disruptions," "distractions," and "differentiation."[20]

*Disruptions* are the social, institutional, and geographical transitions that upend the familiar religious practices of their once settled lives.[21] Hence the transitional states of most college-aged young people require a tremendous amount of effort to reengage in a new community, making it logistically more difficult for them to find a new church. It's quite likely that for our explorer children, religious practices diminish due to life changes as much as, if not more than, changes in religious beliefs.

*Distractions* reflect the increased activities and involvements that pull explorers in more directions. College-aged young people are busy—and feel busy—which often means attending church gets sidelined.[22] As with disruptions, it again appears that lower church attendance may not be because of young people's unbelief but rather because they feel overwhelmed by life's demands.

*Differentiation* is a central life task of explorers as they gain a sense of identity based not just on their family, faith, and cultural

---

### Growing With in Real Time:
### Can parachurch ministries on college campuses help?

Yes and no. In research I (Steve) conducted prior to coming to Fuller Seminary, college undergraduates revealed that parents consistently offered two main points of advice when they moved away for college. The first was to be careful because college can be hostile to their faith. The second was to join a parachurch ministry (meaning an on-campus religious group) as quickly as possible.[1]

On the positive side, campus religious groups offer alternatives to parties and other toxic social environments. Many Christian students discover campus religious groups to be safe social spaces where they can make friends. For a freshman especially, these groups often provide the support they need as they begin their new college careers.[2]

However, some university students struggled with parachurch ministries when leaders were perceived to be unwilling to dialogue about their life questions, resisted science and intellectualism, were insensitive to their academic commitments and goals, or were committed to certain theologies that limited women in leadership. So while both Kara and I celebrate how God works through parachurch ministries (and Kara herself was deeply impacted by one during college), we advise both explorers and their parents to research campus religious groups and interview their leaders before choosing one.

---

1. Steven C. Argue, "Undergraduate Spiritual Struggle and the Quest to Remain Faithful," *Journal of Youth Ministry* 16, no. 1 (Fall 2017): 8–29.
2. Peter Mark Magolda and Kelsey Ebben Gross, *It's All About Jesus! Faith as an Oppositional Collegiate Subculture* (Sterling, VA: Stylus, 2009), 89–91.

background, but also from the way they lean in to or push away from that background.[23] For example, a college-aged young adult who has been told all their life to go to church may decide *not* to go to church on the first Sunday after they move away from home. In situations like these, our children's actions may reflect how they are expressing their autonomy, not their disbelief.

The compounded power of disruptions, distractions, and differentiation is evident in one nationwide study of college students' drop in religious participation. While one-third of young people with a faith background in high school reported religious skepticism as a reason for being nonreligious in college, 50 percent reported other vague reasons such as losing interest, just stopping participation, or not knowing why.[24]

Let's be clear, however, that while there may be many reasons for our explorers' declining church attendance, stepping away from faith communities can be harmful for their faith journeys. In our Sticky Faith research, we learned that college students who found connection with off-campus churches or on-campus Christian fellowships demonstrated greater faith maturity, attempted to live out their Christian faith narrative, and sought God for support during their freshman year.[25] Additional studies report that those who both value religious participation and prioritize religious practices have a great sense of meaning, purpose, and flourishing.[26]

### FAITHING'S FIRST TWO WEEKS

In our interviews of over 500 college students for our Sticky Faith research, we were struck by how students repeatedly pointed to the importance of their first two weeks in college. During these first 14 days, students make key decisions about sex, drinking, and other high-risk behaviors along with their potential allegiance (or lack thereof) to a local church or on-campus ministry. An explorer's decisions during this short introductory period can set them on a trajectory that lasts for the rest of their college experience.[27] Given this trend, conversations about college decision-making must begin long before the first day of orientation.

### Focusers and Their Relationship with Church

As focuser kids approach adulthood (generally ages 23–29), they likely feel confident in some of their acquired competencies while still remaining uncertain about others. They need adults' support in more customized ways pertaining to their vocational choices, long-term relationship decisions, financial advice, and even input for their own parenting. In our national interviews, one mother from the Northwest highlighted common worries and desires she had for her child who was becoming a focuser: "I wondered, are they going to get a job? Are they going to get married? You know, no one can do it for them. We still want to be there for them in some way. And I think this is the biggest tension we feel—that communication gap between us believing that our kids can do it for themselves and us accepting that sometimes our kids want us to know that they cannot."

As we observe our focusers moving toward adulthood, perhaps churches can offer another layer of needed support, but that will require reorienting the ways churches see and relate to them.

#### THE DTR

At one time or another, you've probably had to define the relationship (or DTR) with someone. It's that moment in a significant relationship when you ask, "Who are we, together?" "What can I expect of you, and you of me?" and "Where is this thing going?" Relationships that don't have one (or more) DTRs live in ambiguity and eventually dissolve because neither party is clear on how to relate. Relational ambiguity can lead to a breakup.[28]

We use this DTR metaphor with ministry leaders to help them consider their churches' relationships with focusers. Those working through the second half of emerging adulthood may find their relationships with churches less defined and more ambiguous. As learners or even as explorers, their experiences generally match those of their peers, making it easier for the typical church to provide a cohesive and meaningful social environment. But the variability in late twentysomethings' lives and experiences creates ill-defined and awkward connections with churches.

For example, some focusers may not be married, but they do not want to be relegated to a "singles ministry." In fact, one of my (Steve's) graduate students told me, "Singleness is not an issue in my classes or my work. It's only at church that I feel labeled this way."

### Growing With in Real Time:
### Do focusers need a specialized "young adult" ministry at church?

The variability and ambiguity in focusers' relationship with the church begs a bigger question: At what point does a person really need a specialized age-based ministry anymore? When I (Steve) stepped into a new pastoral role at a church, I was charged with developing a ministry for emerging adults. I proceeded to interview those in college, those out of college, and those working. The twentysomethings told me they wanted a chance to gather with peers, have low-key music for singing together, and hear reflective teaching that prompted great discussion. As I compiled my notes, I realized what they wanted: youth group!

I did not fault them for what they said they wanted. For them, this was the familiar (and perhaps the only) way they knew how to relate to their church. But I recognized that I had a choice: I could give them a twentysomething youth group experience, or I could work at redefining their relationship with our community. This also meant that I wouldn't create a young adult ministry, which upset some people (especially some parents). But I knew that a youth group–style ministry would communicate to these emerging adults that all our church wanted from them was to

Or some may be married but have friends who are not, and they don't want church programs to divide them by marital status.

It's not easy for churches to work with focusers to negotiate a new, defined relationship that gives both emerging adults and church communities clarity and the relational support they need. But we think faith communities need to have a DTR with their focuser young people before more blame is launched or another "young adult program" is created. I often tell ministry leaders that they do not have to guess about what their focusers need. They only have to do one thing: ask them. Invite them to coffee

relate to them like high schoolers all over again. This is formation *backward*, not *forward*.

In order to remain committed to formation-forward ideas, our ministry team challenged ourselves to think of creative solutions to help our focusers find relevant ways to engage with our congregation. We rented out a local theater for monthly film and discussion gatherings that explored current events and faith. We held concerts where bands would play and talk about their creative process. We reoriented our training to encourage our volunteers' (the majority of whom were focusers) formational growth through mentors, training events, and regular conversations about their own journeys with God. We funded people's ideas directed at solving problems in our community. So instead of creating more age-based programming, we developed interest-based spaces where focusers in our congregation could express their faithing through their gifts, concerns, and aspirations while we did our best to support them.

In addition, we experimented with ways to anticipate focusers' challenges by starting to address "young adult topics" during their junior and senior years of high school. While what we created for our focusers (and soon-to-be focusers) was different from what they initially wanted, we all agreed that our efforts addressed a deeper need and set up our focusers for a more meaningful connection with our community.

or dinner and start to get to know them. This is where the DTR begins (and grows).

## QUALITY MENTORS

"The closest thing I have to a mentor is my boss." Over coffee, a 27-year-old summarized his connection to older adults with this phrase. His statement got me (Steve) thinking about the role and availability of older people in focusers' lives. From what I gathered from subsequent conversations with this young man, while he was grateful for what he learned from his boss, he wanted—and needed—something more significant.

Researcher and former Harvard professor Sharon Daloz Parks underscores that it's crucial for young people who are asking big questions and searching for worthy dreams to find good mentors and faithful mentoring communities. Parks believes that when it comes to twentysomethings, the most effective mentors possess the following qualities:[29]

*Mentors recognize young people.* As people in general, we have a need to be seen and known. Mentors see focusers for more than what they do but also who they are in their entirety.

*Mentors support young people.* Jen and I have been hosting monthly chili nights for emerging adults. It is a low-key night where we gather at our home, talk, and take the last portion for a "question of the night" discussion. I asked them recently, "What is your gift to the world, and how are you trying to develop that gift?" For the next few moments, you could have heard a pin drop. No one wanted to share their gift because, as they explained, "We're not that confident in our gifts yet." Their hesitation and inability to name their own gifts confirmed that focusers need mentors who support them and call out the gifts we know (and we want them to know) are there.

*Mentors challenge young people.* A mentoring relationship is most alive when both mentor and protégé are working on the edge of new knowing and possibility. Mentors bring a vigilance that challenges young people to grow and not just play it safe vocationally, relationally, or spiritually.

*Mentors inspire young people.* A good mentor is an antidote to mere cynicism. I remind my graduate students, many of whom are focusers, that every paper they write and every class they attend has the potential to change the world. Mentors inspire young people by reminding them of the bigger picture.

*Mentors hang in there with young people.* Mentors ask questions to nurture an open-ended dialogue rather than give quick answers that shut down their process.

## MENTORING COMMUNITIES

Parks's emphasis on effective mentoring is situated in an equally important opportunity for focusers and the church: mentoring communities. Emerging adults often need more than great mentors, they need mentoring environments.

In a world where focusers feel like their every move has little margin for error, mentoring communities become safe laboratories where they can try, grow, receive feedback, and know grace.[30]

To glean more specific ideas for how your church can better love and serve young people, check out our Growing Young resources available at fulleryouthinstitute .org/growingyoung.

For a focuser starting her first job after graduate school, working 80 hours a week . . .

For the focuser who is a new father, anxious about every parenting situation . . .

For the single focuser who just got dumped by "the one" . . .

For the focuser newlyweds navigating accrued debt on a shoestring budget . . .

For the focuser who just transferred to this new community . . .

Mentoring communities embody good news.

Kara and I often muse with our students, "Where might we find mentoring communities who care for families, advocate for young people, or make transplants feel at home?" Together we reflect on the incredible potential that churches have to be the very communities that young people long for and need. We believe churches can embody very good news for young people who crave support and mentorship.

### Learners, Explorers, and Focusers Faithing Online

Technological advances have made online interaction between users much more "human." While we have witnessed the advantages of technology connecting us with the world, we also have suffered from what Dr. Sherry Turkle, professor of social studies and technology at MIT, describes as existing "alone together."[31]

Does "going to church" online count? Tim Hutchings, a sociologist of religion, media, and culture who has tracked the development of online ministries, observes that most online engagement stems from existing churches taking their worship services online. Thus, churches in geophysical locations are simply using the internet to extend their ministries in various online forms.[32] Young people still have opportunities to connect with local communities either at the main church or, as I (Steve) saw in our previous church, through small groups that gathered around the world and listened to our church's podcast. Though these groups were nowhere near our local church, they felt connected and saw our church as their own church. Dave Adamson, the social media pastor at North Point Ministries, emphasizes that his main pastoral goal is to ensure that he is building community around the content their church develops. He also suggests that because of the online options now available, "Church attendance is not declining, it's decentralizing."[33]

Online spaces are more than gimmicky tricks to make religion cool again. For digital natives like the teenagers and young adults we're raising, "online" is a valid space for connection and community. Twentieth-century church leader and pastor Dietrich Bonhoeffer asserts in his book *Life Together* that "the physical presence of other Christians is a source of incompatible joy and strength to a believer."[34] But our learners, explorers, and focusers experience "presence" in more diverse ways than previous generations. While embodied relationships are essential, might even our current local church congregations lack consistent connection when parishioners only gather for Sunday services or once-a-week programs? Is not presence also found in the daily online interactions people have within their communities? Nancy Duff, associate professor of Christian ethics at Princeton Theological Seminary, suggests that online faith communities have the potential to "promote human understanding, combat loneliness, and share the Gospel."[35]

Furthermore, Duff observes that some people attend online services not because they are unwilling to attend physical churches but because they are unable. Author and editor Emma Green writes that for some Millennials, church attendance decline may be because fewer young people own cars.[36] Perhaps young people attending online church isn't about laziness but rather reflects faithfulness. Maybe they attend online church because of their desire for consistent community rather than their avoidance of it.

While we grew up in an age without digital connection to the world through the internet, social media, and smartphones, it's the only world our kids have ever known. What we learned to navigate as adult "digital immigrants" they've been breathing as natives since birth. That means we tend to see and experience technology differently, which makes this yet another area in which we can grow with our kids as they grow into adulthood.

Certainly there are limitations to online churches, and we both encourage our own kids to experience face-to-face faith community. But physical Sunday morning church services in their current forms may have seasons when congregations are just as "alone together."[37]

## Faithing Ideas

### *The Best Church for Young People*

Our Growing Young research made it resoundingly clear that the churches young people appreciate are not uniquely new or old, large or small, urban or suburban, rich or poor, cool or not. Instead, they are diverse churches who share common values that position them to be committed to young people. The good news is that when we are asked what type of church is the best for young people, we usually quote the answer given by our FYI colleague and *Growing Young* coauthor, Brad Griffin: "Your church."

As parents, spend less time trying to find the "perfect" church and more time leveraging the strengths and beauty of your own church. Chances are you have a compassionate minister, a professional who is willing to talk with your child about their desired vocation, or a senior citizen who cares about young people. Our default is often to think about what "programs" churches offer our kids. As our learners, explorers, and focusers mature, the people who will grow with them matter more than the programs they'll grow out of.

So start taking advantage of the unique beauty of your church by reflecting on these questions:

- Who are the people in your church that you'd like your son or daughter to meet?

- What are the initiatives, activities, or needs in your church that connect with your child's interests? (e.g., feeding those who are poor, working for justice, tutoring young people, cultivating the arts, developing technology, or sports ministry)

- What worship services or opportunities are the best fit for your child in this season?

- What types of community would be most healing (and maybe most stretching) for your learner, explorer, or focuser?

Young people from different racial or ethnic backgrounds often navigate cultural conflicts between their family and their peers. Some navigate social situations and obligations on behalf of their parents, in particular when language is a barrier to understanding. Institutions like the church offer a great opportunity to bridge this gap between the culture of home and that of the dominant society, reducing the risk that young people will feel alienated.

It's often helpful when church leaders and members pay attention to the symbolic and cultural expressions of young people who are from non-English-speaking cultures. For instance, some may feel a special closeness to God, or connection through prayer to God, when a church offers prayers in other languages or attends to the discipleship needs of bilingual teenagers and young adults.[1]

1. Beverly Daniel Tatum, *"Why Are All the Black Kids Sitting Together in the Cafeteria?" and Other Conversations About Race* (New York: Basic Books, 2003), 245; Ken Johnson-Mondragon, *Pathways of Hope and Faith Among Hispanic Teens: Pastoral Reflections and Strategies Inspired by the National Study of Youth and Religion* (Stockton, CA: Instituto Fe y Vida, 2007), 124.

## Attendance, Participation, and Exchange Zones

Kara and I admit it—we feel better when our teenage and young adult kids go to church! However, let's not assume that their attendance means they are participating.

Think of *attendance* as opportunities for young people to simply connect with other believers. *Participation*, on the other hand, means more than showing up; it means our young people are relationally investing in others and becoming part of the work of the church (in worship and in ministry to the community and world). To help your kid get the most out of attending—and hopefully eventually move into true participation—try asking the following questions:

- Who did you meet or see today?
- Who was the most interesting person you talked with?

- For those attending online church services: What podcasts are you listening to?

- How would you describe the message you heard this week in your small group or the Sunday sermon? What resonated with you, or what didn't?

Further, don't assume that your kid's lack of attendance means that they have turned off their spiritual dial. Regardless of your child's church involvement, tune in to their spiritual quest by asking the following questions:

- What are you praying about, reading, or reflecting on these days?

- What's a social cause you can see yourself supporting?

- How do you think you could use your education, degree, talents, and skills to help people in our faith community?

- Where might you want to serve in our town, and what might you need from our church to support you?

Let's take this concept of participation further. Using the metaphor of a triathlon, what if we envisioned church more as an "exchange zone"? The exchange zone is where triathletes transition from one discipline to another—from swimming to biking, or later from biking to running. In the exchange zone, the goal is to gear up efficiently for the next leg of the race. Exchange zones can make or break the race for athletes, but exchange zones are *not* the whole race!

If we envision churches as triathlon exchange zones, then the difference between attendance and participation becomes clearer. If all we encourage is attendance, our young people may show up for brief exchange zones (e.g., worship gatherings and church activities) but have little vision for the race they are part of all week long.

But if we encourage participation, then our goal is to support, equip, heal, and send our young people on to the next leg of the race. They are most faithful to the course set out for them not by loitering in the exchange zones but by pouring themselves into the goals to which they have been called. Coming to the exchange zone (church) now has purpose beyond attendance. Its purpose is participation. Church isn't the destination. It's the exchange zone—for ourselves and everyone around us. We each have something to offer one another. This is churching.

## Teacher Parents Who Support Their Learners' Churching

Last year, my (Steve's) high school senior was "so done" with high school. Regularly she came home reminding us that she was ready to move on to college (which at the time she had "narrowed" to ten options). We knew that she did not hate school, but she was growing out of the form of the high school environment and setting her sights on what was coming next.

Jen, a counselor, reminded me that part of the leaving process is to critique what we leave as a way to cope with transition. Thus, telling ourselves (and our parents and everyone else within hearing distance) that we are leaving a "boring, immature, annoying" high school is much easier than leaving a happy, perfect one. Likely, there are similar moves our learner kids make when they get closer to graduation that help them emotionally prepare for life after high school youth group. They may say it's boring, immature, or less interesting. Instead of assuming that our kids are "falling away," let's celebrate that they are growing up and engaging with our churches in new ways that match their growing maturity. Teacher parents can work with their kids by:

- Normalizing their experiences and empathizing with them as they grieve the absence of older friends who have graduated and moved away.

- Encouraging your teenager to play a different role in their youth group. Instead of just showing up, can they lead a project or mentor a freshman?

- Looking beyond youth group. Connect your kids with other adults in your church who have the ability to nurture their interest in teaching, technology, carpentry, travel, or finance.

### Guide Parents Who Support Their Explorers' Churching

Through our youth ministry work, we have recognized that many parents (and youth leaders!) assume that graduating high schoolers know where and how to connect with churches. For those who move for school, job, or the military, finding a new church is not always easy. For those who remain in town after graduation, their post–high school connection with church can also feel disruptive, especially if many of their church friends leave town or if their church (like most) doesn't have a vibrant college ministry. Parents can help their explorer kids find church connection during this phase in their lives by trying the following.

*Role-play.* Invite your explorer child to walk through how they plan to find a church connection. For some of our kids, this is the first time they have ever had to find a new church or have felt the freedom to do so. Give them space to find a congregation and diffuse the anxiety they may feel to get connected in a few weeks (likely it will take at least a whole semester). Discuss some potential answers to the following questions, and maybe even come up with a short written plan they keep on their phone:

- Where and how will you search for a church and/or campus group?

- Who could you ask for recommendations?

- How do you read a church's statement of faith and discern what a church believes, and then determine how those beliefs align with your theological values?

- How could you determine what the leaders are like?
- If you met the minister, what could you ask her or him?
- What are the theological views of the religious groups (on campus, on base, or in town) about issues you care about, such as evangelism, service in the community, racial reconciliation, and women in leadership?
- Do they respect your commitment to academic studies or your vocation? How would your academic and vocational pursuits be strengthened in this church?

*Be patient.* While your explorer kid may take time to find a church, do not wait to ask them about their process. Shift from asking them, "Did you go to church?" to "How has your search for a church been going?" Help them process their experiences and remember that their search can itself be formational. In their quest for a church, your child inevitably will bump against questions about their own identity, faith, and sense of belonging that are worthy of exploration and conversation.

*Send cookies.* Keep in mind that their transition away from your home church does not mean that your church doesn't matter to your kids anymore. As parents, work with your ministry leaders to reach out to young graduating high schoolers. Based on what we've learned in our Sticky Faith research, we believe that recent high school grads need tangible expressions of support from adults those first two weeks in their new setting. Send a note, prepare a care package, or make a phone call. Every text and box of chocolate chip cookies reminds explorers that though they're moving on, your church and your family haven't forgotten them. And we think they want to be reminded.

One Sunday, a father from my (Steve's) church rushed up to our youth pastor. Our youth pastor thought he was in trouble, but the father, choking up, shared: "I visited my son this weekend. In his dorm room I saw an opened UPS box on his desk shelf and asked him why he didn't throw it away. My son smiled and said, '*That's the box they sent me. It was filled with cookies and personal notes. My youth group remembered me.*'"

### Resourcer Parents Who Support Their Focusers' Churching

We assume that our focuser kids are on their way toward establishing their own relationships, careers, and habits. While that is at least somewhat true, focusers are in a unique stage of learning how to connect with church. During the monthly dinners when my wife and I (Steve) open up our home to emerging adults, the majority of those who show up at our doorstep are in the focuser stage.

Recently, in the midst of our chili and cornbread, the topic of "home" came up. Most all of them, both married and single, shared how their lives were in so much transition that the concept of home felt elusive. Some were trying to establish their own traditions but felt the tension to please their parents. Others admitted that they didn't see their current context as long-term, so they were prone to remain detached from people here and instead dream of a future home. I found their confessions powerful as I began to understand the extra stress they felt about family relationships, holiday expectations, and their decisions to go home or to create home right where they live. Perhaps resourcer parents can help their focuser kids by nudging them to discover home again, especially when it comes to their church connections.

Accept that the faith community they join may be different from yours and that they may attend it for different reasons than you attend yours. While we always encourage good and even robust discussions about God with your growing kids, ensure that your conversations do not turn into divisive debates. Start with where you agree, and learn to appreciate the way they are finding relational and spiritual connections.

Recognize that for many of our single young people, church is not always a welcoming place. Avoid "feeling sorry" for your unmarried child or trying to match them with a "nice Christian" boy or girl. (And try to convince their grandparents to avoid the same pitfalls!) Encourage them to connect with a church that values them for their gifts and talents, not their marital status.

Invite your focuser to use their gifts, skills, or profession to express their faithing within or alongside churches. In my former church, we had a grassroots program that enabled young people to apply for small grants to implement their great ideas. Some projects worked better than others, but our entrepreneurial invitation freed young people to let our church support their best ideas. In our church's case, some of these grassroots ideas turned into full-fledged established ministries that made clean water available in African countries and opened a homeless youth drop-in center that filled a gap in social services within our community. Young people don't need a church simply to attend as much as they need faithful people who are willing to support their great ideas, which leaves all generations inspired.

## When Church Gets Tense

### DO I MAKE MY HIGH SCHOOL LEARNER GO TO CHURCH?

Remember that learners need teacher parents, but our invitation to grow with our kids means we do more than either make them go to church or throw in the towel. Further, let's remember that at its core (and in the original Greek term for "church" used in the New Testament, *ekklesia*) church is about a people we gather with, not a place we attend. So part of our job as teacher parents is to help our learner kids reimagine their connection with church through the following ideas:[38]

*Ask why.* Help them articulate their reasons, and work with them to understand the validity of their feelings and opinions. Perhaps there will be times when you agree they can stay home and other weeks when you will point out that their attendance is not only good for them but also encouraging for those who care about them. Periodically (and not just 30 minutes before your weekend worship service begins) ask them why they go to church and why they think *you* go to church.

*Seek advice.* If your learner kid doesn't want to attend youth group, seek out other people (a youth pastor or small group leader) who can shed light on your child's past experiences. It may be that they had a bad experience at youth group or they are struggling to connect with friends. A clearer picture of what might be driving their behavior will impact how you handle your learner's resistance to church.

*Plan ahead.* It is easy to assume that our kids will know how to connect with others, but that may not be the case. Talk about what they will do when they go to youth group. Anticipate scenarios and pre-plan some questions they could ask their peers. Help them think about how to find and develop new friends. When our kids are entering new social situations, Dave and I (Kara) encourage them to look for other kids who seem to be standing on their own, who may feel just as awkward and eager to meet new friends as they are. In preparation for Sunday morning, discuss appropriate etiquette for interacting with and showing respect to older generations.

*Find their best points for connection.* If they think the church service is boring, are there ways they can serve in the church (kids' ministry, tech support)? If youth group isn't their scene, are there groups in your church that share similar interests (art, music, homeless ministry, sports team)?

*Brainstorm other options.* For some of our kids, our churches may not be a good fit in their current season of life. If that's the case, brainstorm with your learner kid about trying a different church or youth group. Perhaps they will want to attend with a friend. Or, if they are curious about other churches, offer to visit with them.

### HOW DO I NAVIGATE MY EXPLORER OR FOCUSER'S WANING INVOLVEMENT WITH CHURCH?

As our explorer and focuser kids navigate their life and faithing, some may choose not to go to church. As parents, what do we do when our kids say, "I don't like our church" or "I'm not going anymore"? At our growing kids' ages, they're too old for us to just pick them up and make them go. And given our own ages as parents, we often are too tired to keep fighting. So what do we do? While the uniqueness of each child and family (not to mention church) makes it impossible to give a universal one-size-fits-all answer, we hope you keep the following principles in mind:

*Don't make church attendance a battleground.* Fighting over going to church probably won't make your relationship with your kids better, since someone always loses. Take time to talk with them about their choice not to go. Seek to understand their perspective. Expect them to give valid reasons and help them process what's going on in their spiritual lives. Don't turn church into the goal itself. Don't make church into a magical panacea, somehow thinking that if they come to church their angst will disappear. After all, church attendance is not the ultimate spiritual litmus test.

*Give them space to try another church.* At some point, they will likely choose their own church when they move away, live on their own, or want to attend church with a different group of friends. Again, talk about this with them. Use this as a chance to talk about their, and your, spiritual journeys. Celebrate any inclination they have toward being involved in the faith community, even if it's not your own church or your own denomination.

*Give them room to take a break from regular church attendance.* Remember that it is natural for young people to suspend going to church as they learn to live on their own. It is possible that they will access church online. It is also normal for some to leave the church where they grew up and take time (often more time than you would wish) to find a faith community that resonates with them.

*Encourage them to stay in the conversation.* If their reasons for avoiding church seem to center on differences in belief, positions on social or political issues, or critique of church practices, you might offer the perspective that *the church needs them.* Their ideas, questions, and even new experiments just might be the breath of fresh air the church has been needing. If they pull out of the community altogether, the church misses the gifts and perspectives they can bring. Leaning in to the church presents the possibility that everyone might experience a faithing opportunity.[39]

*Invite them.* It's okay to invite them occasionally to your church. Think about how it can be a true invitation and not one laced with guilt or shame.

### FAMILY CHURCHING: BEYOND SLEEPING IN

Your kids (and maybe you!) will continue to feel the urge—even the need—to sleep in instead of attending worship. As parents, let's keep this tension in perspective, recognizing that our kids' connection with church is essential for their spiritual lives but does not represent the entirety of their spiritual journeys. We need the church and the church needs us to grow with our adolescents and emerging adults. Together we can be the churching exchange zones that encourage and support their lifelong faithing.

### Growing With Parents' Faithing and Churching

Embedded in our Growing With parenting philosophy is an emphasis on not just our kids' faith journeys but also our own faith journeys. Laced throughout the research insights and practical ideas presented in this chapter is a shift away from asking the church to provide programming for our young people and toward supporting our young people in making their own authentic connections with faith communities. As parents who are part of these churches, each of us also has something to give to and receive from young people (both inside and outside our family) as we make the following commitments.

*Stay connected.* As much as we believe in print and online tools for parents, often our most helpful sources of support are each other. Too often parents can feel isolated and overwhelmed. We can change that by making time to cultivate friendships that mutually care for each other and our families. Meeting with other parents of learner, explorer, and focuser kids provides implicit empathy, needed support, and safe places to process as we all attempt to parent well.

You don't have to make this a big production. Find another parent or two and meet for coffee. Connect periodically with another couple over dinner. Celebrate parenting wins as much as challenges. Every good parenting moment is worth celebrating, and every parenting struggle needs an ear, a hug, and a prayer.

*Be a bridge.* Family friends of the Argues have a daughter who graduated one year ahead of our youngest daughter. Their church encouraged graduating seniors to ask one adult outside of their families to pray for them in their next chapter of life. Allie asked my wife, Jen, to be that person. Jen loves it, and Allie gets periodic notes and texts from Jen. Allie came home for her fall break and met with Jen for lunch. What we love about this experience is that Allie's church set us up to *be* the church rather than developing a program for Allie and Jen to attend together. Their church is setting up their graduating young people well by asking other adults to be important bridges of support beyond high school. You can bet we've done the same for our daughters.

*Value belonging before belief.* Relational connection, more than religious instruction, keeps kids connected to faith. Young people need to know the unconditional connection they have with their parents. Treat differing beliefs as opportunities to get to know your kid, help them grow in their own convictions, and fine-tune your own faith. Work to sustain a close relational connection with your kids throughout their teens and twenties.

## Practical Questions to Grow With My Child

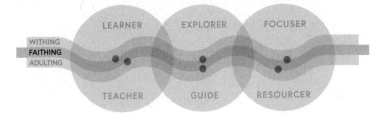

1. Respond to the following questions by rating yourself and your church:

Church is a vital part of my daily life and relationships.

1..........................................5..........................................10

Never                    Sometimes                    Always

My church is attuned to and helpful for teenagers in their faith journeys and quests for community.

1..........................................5..........................................10

Never                    Sometimes                    Always

My church is attuned to and helpful for early twentysomethings in their faith journeys and quests for community.

1..........................................5..........................................10

Never                    Sometimes                    Always

My church is attuned to and helpful for mid to late twentysomethings in their faith journeys and quests for community.

1..........................................5..........................................10

Never                    Sometimes                    Always

My kid is involved with a local church or faith community.

1 ································· 5 ································· 10
Never                    Sometimes                    Always

Reflecting on your answers above, describe where you are most encouraged, where you hope for something better, and where you feel you could use some help.

2. After reading this chapter, what information, quote, or story inspired your thinking or gave you a fresh perspective on faith and faithing?

3. How does your learner, explorer, or focuser view their relationship with church? How do you know? (Perhaps this is a future conversation topic with them.)

4. We grow with our kids by seeking out and creating community that encourages faithing. What might be a next step for you in your faithing together?

5. How has your relationship with your church shifted or changed as your kids have grown older? In what ways have you been encouraged, challenged, or disappointed?

6. Based on what you have learned in this chapter, what ways might you (and other parents) help your church community support learners, explorers, and/or focusers?

7. What parent, friend, or religious leader might you seek out to process your role in your kid's connection with a faith community?

# PART 4

# THRIVING IN FUTURE: "ADULTING"

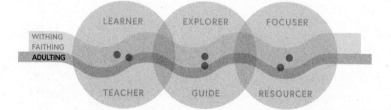

**Adulting:** *a child's growth in agency as they embrace opportunities to shape the world around them.*

As parents and caring adults, we see our growing kids inhabiting more adult spaces with us. They look more like us. We stand eye to eye while increasingly not always seeing eye to eye. We find ourselves negotiating their schedules (that conflict with ours), debating politics (that conflict with ours), or questioning their aspirations (that conflict with our hopes for them).

Perhaps it is fair to say that we simultaneously desire and dread their adulting. Relationally, they are learning to grow and deepen their friendships and romantic interests. Vocationally, they are discovering their true passions and real limitations as they consider their contribution to this world.

How do we offer input without being too controlling?

How do we stay connected as they become more independent?

How do we encourage them to figure things out on their own while reminding them that we're here for them?

How honest will we be with ourselves when their relational or vocational decisions challenge our values or family image?

In chapters 7 and 8, we propose that through the concept of adulting, we can encourage our kids to be agents in their relationships and vocations. Their journey of adulting will challenge and bless our parenting. We must be prepared for both as we remain committed to growing with them.

*A prayer:*

*Jesus, our kids' adulting will lead them toward new opportunities and challenges with their relationships and vocations. They will feel the weight of their decisions, and so will we. Grant us the ability to encourage their agency, strength to endure life's joys and pains, and commitment to stick with them even when their trajectories diverge from ours. Grant them vision to see and utilize their unique gifts, while protecting them from a self-centeredness that misses the ways those gifts are given for the sake of the world and the life of the church. We trust your calling on their lives, just as you have called us. May their adulting journeys bless our families and our world.*

# 7. Relational Adulting

*Friends, Love, and the Search for Connection*

"Okay, bye."

That's all she said as she sprinted toward our front door, one hand texting and the other grabbing her purse.

There was no doorbell ring. Not even a honk from the driveway. Only a stealthy signal by her friend who was parked in her car at the curb outside of our house. Jen and I (Steve) looked at each other. Like two referees throwing a flag for an infraction in the game, we both said, "Whoa, wait!" For us, the moment felt off. Too fast, too disconnected.

It wasn't that our daughter was doing anything wrong. But we felt that we were cut off from an important relational dimension in her life—meeting her friends. Our mantra has been that we seek to get to know the great friends our kids choose. When they come to pick up our kids, we work to invite them in, say hello, learn more about them, and allow them to get to know us. All of a sudden, one text message was short-circuiting this ritual!

Beyond the dynamics that technology brings, we believe there is something more foundational we experience every time our maturing kids walk in and out that front door. When they were young, we walked out that same door with them, setting up their playdates and shuttling them to the activities we thought were best for them. But with our learners, explorers, and focusers, it's rare that we take them with us anymore. Now it's time to grow with them as they grow into the friendships and relationships that may stick with them for the rest of their lives.

## Adulting: Owning Their Future Trajectories

While often used in humorous ways on social media (just search #adulting if you don't know what we're talking about), Kara and I think there is a primal longing in young (and all) people to grow up, to be relationally connected, and to find their place in this world. We define adulting as *a child's growth in agency as they embrace opportunities to shape the world around them.*

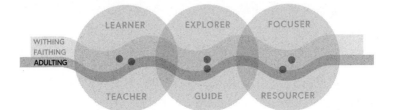

Key to this definition of adulting is the concept of agency. By "agency," we mean our maturing kids' growth in owning and clarifying their own interests, goals, and values.[1] Since the process and path to both agency and adulthood are lengthening, adulting has turned into more of an ongoing struggle than a seamless progression.

In this chapter, we address how we grow with our kids as they pursue their *relational* adulting by navigating friendships, romantic interests, and social communities. In chapter 8, we will explore how we can encourage our kids' *vocational* adulting through their service and career choices. For both chapters, we operate on the adulting assumptions that as our kids mature from learner to explorer to focuser, they will grow in their desire and capacity to take responsibility for themselves and make independent decisions that enhance their life aspirations.

## Adulting Insights

### Learners and Their Adulting Relationships

In our national interviews, mothers and fathers felt most disconnected from their kids when they found themselves competing for their attention. That competition intensifies in adolescence as our learners develop two social worlds—one with family and one

## Kids with Special Needs

It's important for us to name that each child's journey into the adolescent and emerging adult years is filled with variation, opportunities, and challenges. Kids with special needs or who are differently abled experience these transitions in complex ways—sometimes just like other kids, sometimes not. Parents, too, find they sometimes can relate to other parents in the same life stage, and other times feel isolated as they attempt to support the developmental realities of their kids. If you're a parent navigating these complex waters, you've probably already spent years seeking out expert resources and supportive communities. Many churches are becoming aware and are better equipped to walk with you and support your child and family. We encourage you to reach out to your church leadership to educate them in ways they can support you and others in your faith community. Every child deserves the support of a loving community, and our faith communities are blessed by every child.

with peers. As young people grow older and seek more adulting relationships, these two worlds overlap less.[2] Perhaps the tension that we and our learners feel is the start of these overlapping worlds pulling apart. This phenomenon evokes new stressors, desires, and decisions for all family members.

## RELATIONAL STRESSORS

According to a report issued by the School of Public Health at Johns Hopkins University, teenage stress often stems from the accumulation of busy schedules, school pressures, family climate, and peer expectations surrounding friendship, conflict, dating, and social norms.[3] Many of these stressors are directly or indirectly relational as our learners negotiate peer opportunities, peer acceptance, or peer tensions.

Growing with our kids in the midst of these stressors requires work on our part, as our kids' relational spaces are different from when we were their ages. We interviewed a married couple from the Midwest who articulated a common parental sentiment: "Regarding relationship and relational choices, our kids are twenty steps ahead of us. We need to learn because we don't always know what's out there."

While we likely have gone through a breakup, we probably haven't broken up over a text message.

---

The racial and ethnic backgrounds of adolescents and emerging adults influence their family interactions in a variety of ways. For example, while white young people tend to emphasize independence and self-interest in their family relationships, young people with other ethnic identities (examples from research include Korean, Mexican, and Armenian cultural backgrounds) are more apt to emphasize family interdependence and the welfare of the whole family.[1]

1. Jean Phinney et al., "Autonomy and Relatedness in Adolescent-Parent Disagreements," *Journal of Adolescent Research* 20, no. 1 (2005): 8–39.

---

While we can relate to feeling left out as a teenager or young adult, we didn't have to see pictures on social media of events we were not invited to.

While we may have felt desire or pressure to remove our clothing and experiment sexually, we didn't deal with the possibility or even expectation of sending or receiving nude images as part of that relational dance.

While we were distracted when studying, we didn't have the consistent pinging of text messages demanding our attention.

While we experienced the (almost) inevitable awkwardness of growing up and growing pains, as one of the parents we interviewed empathetically described, "We haven't had our whole lives posted online, on display for the world to see."

## RELATIONAL DESIRES

Part of why relationships are stressful for our learners is because they care so much. Your 16-year-old's hunger for relationships is qualitatively different from when they were 12. Developmental psychologist Jeffrey Arnett explains that one of the most distinctive differences between childhood friendships and adolescent friendships is that learners are more intentional in their pursuit of intimacy and more skilled in their attempts to understand others and share more of themselves.[4]

Most adolescents choose friends who share their interests, use technology in similar ways, and are commensurate in their openness to risky activities.[5] In fact, Arnett argues that "friend influence" is a more accurate phrase than "peer pressure." Friends are emotionally and socially valued more than peers your learner may or may not know. When your learner comments that "everybody is doing it," they are more likely referring to their own friends and not their entire school. Friend influence also proves to have both positive and negative effects on risk-taking. It is more likely that your child will gravitate toward those they perceive as similar to them than that they are succumbing to the influence of the "bad kids."[6]

I (Steve) remember a painful period for our daughter Elise when her group of friends started making choices that didn't sit well with her. At the time, she was a 14-year-old ferociously loyal friend who felt stuck. We saw her friends distance themselves from her. We witnessed her pain and loneliness. And we knew we couldn't fix the problem for her. She also didn't want to bad-mouth her friends, so she told us only bits and pieces of what was going on. Eventually she opened up to us, and I vividly remember one night when I held her as her tears soaked my shirt, feeling helpless to take away her pain.

She and I decided to pray for new friends, which at the moment was not trite but a desperate crying out to God from us both. Elise needed friends and we were asking God to deliver. We still remember that night, and while her journey toward new friends wasn't easy, she did find better high school friends, many of whom remain friends today. While scenarios like this do not always work out so positively for the Argue family, we've often referred back to that prayer and, in Elise's eyes, God's miracle.

## RELATIONAL BUNKERS OF SAFETY AND ISOLATION

Chap Clark highlights that adolescents choose to spend so much time with their friends not only because they *want* to but also because they feel they *have* to. His ethnographic research on high school campuses identified adolescent "clusters," meaning groups of four to ten adolescents who band tighter to protect themselves from the overwhelming pressures placed upon them, often by adults. These relational spaces preserve expectations, loyalties, and values in their friendships while also serving as a bunker from society's pressures. These bunkers are located in what Clark calls "the world beneath,"[7] meaning the safe, peer-only domains where adolescents seek support and advice from their friends along with protection from adult expectations.

> ### *Growing With in Real Time:*
> ### Drinking, drugs, and friendships
>
> When it comes to learners, we agree with Chap Clark that parents make a mistake when they assume that drinking and substance usage is about the alcohol and drugs. For learners, parties are often more about social interaction. Clark emphasizes that for high schoolers, "Parties are not about the party, but about the longing for community."[1] Parents must address drug and alcohol use with our learner kids and, when necessary, find help for substance abuse. But it's also important to dialogue with them about the deeper friendship longings that may be driving casual or frequent substance use.
>
> Research on substance use (which includes alcohol, cigarettes, and drugs) indicates that adolescent rates of usage start rising at age 15 and peak in the early twenties. While substance use among adolescents and emerging adults has declined since the 1970s, your teenager or young adult is exposed to social pressures and substance availability. This insight only reinforces Clark's advice that as our kids inhabit learner and explorer life stages, parents are wise to have more conversations with them about substance use—not fewer.[2]
>
> ---
>
> 1. Chap Clark, *Hurt 2.0: Inside the World of Today's Teenagers* (Grand Rapids: Baker Books, 2011), 159–61.
> 2. Jeffrey Jensen Arnett, *Adolescence and Emerging Adulthood*, 6th ed. (Upper Saddle River, NJ: Pearson, 2017), 389–92.

While we celebrate the benefits of strong peer friendships, a social support structure void of adults leaves learners vulnerable to their friends' inexperience and thin on the social capital that supportive adults can provide. There have been seasons when my (Steve's) daughters have made choices on their own without involving my wife or me. While we have applauded these adulting moments, at times we have needed to step in because we could tell they were in over their heads. Often, when we asked them, "Why didn't you ask us for help?" they would explain that they were trying to act responsibly. As we described in chapter 4, learners are trying to negotiate the path from dependence on to independence from to eventual interdependence with their parents. The art of Growing With parenting is encouraging our learners' growing autonomy while nurturing new, interdependent ways of relating with them that remind them we are still accessible.

### ROMANTIC RELATIONSHIPS: "HANGING OUT" MORE THAN "GOING OUT"

If your learner insists that "everyone's dating," the data doesn't support that claim. Only 14 percent of 13- to 17-year-olds describe themselves as currently being in relationship with a boyfriend, girlfriend, or significant other they consider serious. An additional 16 percent of teens surveyed are not currently dating but have had some sort of romantic relationship (whether serious or otherwise) in the past, and 5 percent are currently in relationships but do not consider them serious. The remaining almost two-thirds of teens indicate that they have never been in a romantic relationship of any kind.[8] High schoolers today are more likely to spend time together in informal, mixed-gender groups than formal one-on-one dating situations.

If learners are not really dating, what exactly are they doing together? Let's not assume the best or the worst but ensure we check our assumptions while remembering that dating-ish relationships are new to them too. In order to support their relational adulting, help your learner think through and keep you informed about:

Where they're going and what they're doing. (What's the plan? Details please!)

Who's going. (Are they your regular friends? Any new friends?)

What they will do if . . . (How will you respond if someone brings alcohol, tries to kiss you, offers you drugs, asks you to text them a nude picture of yourself?)

What's going on internally. (You seem more happy/sad/depressed/worried lately. What's up?)

## ONLINE RELATIONAL EXPERIENCES: MORE THAN VIRTUAL

We have already noted that most adolescents and emerging adults are digital natives living in a world where online access has always been part of their lives. Thus, the way young people approach technology is often quite different than for us older digital immigrants. As parents navigating the new world of technology, Kara and I think it is helpful for you to remember the following:[9]

*Learners make online friends.* While making new friends online may seem foreign to parents, 57 percent of learners describe doing so. Boys (61 percent) are more likely to make friends online than girls (52 percent), largely because of multiplayer gaming.

*Learners experience online connection and support.* Of those who are social media users, 83 percent report that they feel more

> "My two sons have been 'gamers' since early high school. They are actually very good and have been ranked in some major gaming competitions. Gaming is not like when we grew up with Atari. I will never be able to challenge my sons or even keep up, so that creates a huge relational gap between their interests and my abilities! What I have done is try to take time to learn, engage, dialogue, and support the interests of my teenagers and emerging adults by showing interest in their passions. Though I don't play the games with them, I have found ways to share articles that reference their favorite games and also offered to buy tickets to attend the world champion gaming finals together. It hasn't been easy to learn about their games, and it's even harder to grasp gaming lingo, but it's been fun to try and worth it to gain that shared connection."
> —Henry, a New York parent of one learner and one explorer

connected with their friends' lives and 70 percent feel more connected to their friends' feelings.

*Learners believe online activity can hurt relationships.* A majority (88 percent) believe that people share too much online, and just over half have witnessed people posting events to which they were not invited. These experiences can leave our kids feeling more aware of their social world but also more uncomfortable and more left out.

*Learners feel the pressure of online interaction.* A significant minority feel pressure to post and to "like" others' posts (40 percent). Some (21 percent) feel worse about their own lives when they see online posts of their friends.

*Learners experience online conflicts and unfriending.* Sixty-eight percent say they have experienced online "drama," including everything from misunderstandings to bullying. Over half (58 percent) of learners say they have unfriended or unfollowed online friends, while almost that many (45 percent) have blocked an ex-friend. Blocking or unfriending is higher for girls (63 percent) than boys (53 percent).

*Learners encounter pornography with detrimental effects.* Those learners who consume pornography may develop unrealistic values and beliefs and start sexual experimentation earlier. In addition, pornography affects adolescents' self-concept since both boys and girls often feel (rightly so) they cannot live up to the unrealistic images portrayed in this material. Adolescents who use pornography report decreased self-confidence, lower social integration, higher conduct problems, higher depressive symptoms, and decreased emotional bonding with parents.[10]

So now you may be more anxious. Or slightly comforted (because you thought it was even worse). Perhaps you're jotting down these statistics to quote over dinner tonight.

Instead of following these instincts, log this data to help you talk with your teenagers about their online activities and relationships when the time and mood are right. Which probably isn't over tonight's egg rolls.

The intrusion of racism into learners' lives is coming in new forms through the technology of gaming, computers, and smartphones. Racial prejudice is often experienced by teens through direct and indirect anonymous online posts, and this discrimination leads to depression, anxiety, lower academic motivation, and other problematic behaviors.

Yet at the same time, many people of color experience great support through groups and individual relationships initiated and cultivated through social media since it gives them a space to share both frustrating and encouraging experiences.[1]

1. Beverly Daniel Tatum, *"Why Are All the Black Kids Sitting Together in the Cafeteria?" and Other Conversations About Race* (New York: Basic Books, 2003), 141–42; Jason Chan, "Racial Identity in Online Spaces: Social Media's Impact on Students of Color," *Journal of Student Affairs Research and Practice* 54, no. 2 (2017): 163–74.

Try to approach online relational interaction in the same way you would attempt to get to know your learner's friendships—with interest and a desire to know the friends who are important to them. Explore reasons your learner wants to use their computer in their room by themselves and have their phone with them at dinner, and decide together if that's appropriate and wise.

As we journey through our learners' adulting, keep in mind that the key is not only *what* we talk about with them but also *how often* we talk about it. The vast majority of parents (up to 95 percent according to one study) seem adept at initial conversations with our adolescents about their media activity. The challenge is that only 36 percent of us are having these conversations frequently.[11] More regular conversations about their (and our) online activity may be an easy and crucial Growing With step.

## TALKING ABOUT SEX BEYOND THE "SEX TALK"

According to the most current data on younger teen relationships, most adolescents are not sexually active. Yet teenage sexual activity increases as adolescents get older. While a quarter of boys and girls disclose having sexual intercourse by their 16th birthday, two-thirds report that they have had sex by 18.[12]

As with all peer relationships, parents play a critical role in helping learners navigate sexual activity and possibilities. A meta-analysis of over 30 years of data from 52 studies and over 25,000 adolescents confirms that talking with kids about sex in general, and kids' sexual behaviors specifically, makes a difference.[13]

Similar to the need for ongoing conversations regarding our learners' online activity, we believe the "sex talk" isn't a single talk but a series of conversations. When each of our learner kids was in fifth grade, Dave and I (Kara) gave them a book about sexual purity geared for teenagers. As parents, we read a few chapters at a time, underlining what we wanted to talk about with our learner. Our child would then read those few chapters, and the three of us would gather to discuss what had been underlined, as well as any other questions that emerged. In order to make talking with our teenagers about sex as normal as possible, we held those conversations in all different places and at various times. Sitting on their bed as we tucked them in. In the family room after watching our favorite cooking show together. In the kitchen as one of us finished cleaning up after dinner. In the minivan as we drove home from church. We wanted to send the message to each of our learners that there is no single place or time to talk about our sexual desires and choices. Any time and any place is fair game.

If you've had "the talk" (or lots of such talks) with your kids, please don't think that's enough and you're now done. If you haven't had "the talk," please don't believe the lie that you've

For those of you wondering, later in this chapter we share insights and ideas for parents growing with a child who expresses same-sex attraction or identifies as LGBTQ.

already missed the chance to talk with your adolescent about their sexual activity. Also, based on your racial or ethnic background, this topic of conversation might be approached more directly or indirectly. Whatever the context, it is unlikely that we can outsource addressing this topic to other adults or other institutions. During our national interviews, one mother of two older teenagers on the East Coast named a common parenting experience: "I found our church hesitant to address the topic of sexuality and sex before marriage. I think that so many kids just have no idea how to talk about this subject, and are just not being given the tools to have this conversation."

## Explorers and Their Adulting Relationships

### EXPLORERS' FRIENDSHIPS

One of the unique friendship dynamics facing explorers stepping away from high school is that, often for the first time, they have the opportunity and challenge of making new friends while simultaneously trying to preserve former friendships. Seeking new friends can prove difficult, as illustrated in one study of college freshmen ten weeks into their first semester away from home. These new explorers were still more invested in maintaining friendships from home and had delayed making friendships at school.[14] In this world of online connections, your explorer may be more inclined to stay in touch with old friends than invest the energy (and risk) it takes to forge new community.

While that may be your explorer kid's tendency, it often doesn't serve them well long term. Psychologist Meg Jay advises young people in their twenties to become disciplined in making new

> "So how do I encourage my kids in the midst of waiting for the right relationship? How do I encourage them when they confide, 'I am all alone and I fear I will never find anybody'?" —Michael, a West Coast father of a learner and an explorer

friends. She observed that emerging adults who stalled in their relational and vocational goals did not branch out, only maintained the same small group of friends, and missed out not only on new conversations but also new opportunities.[15] Encouraging our explorers to relationally extend their friend groups seems to inspire new ideas and foster new possibilities.

Jerome, one of the dads we interviewed, shared how his son, Kenneth, went to college with one of his close friends from youth group. While they didn't choose to be roommates, they ended up living on the same dorm floor. Instead of growing closer, Kenneth experienced this friendship growing apart as his friend leaned heavily into drinking and partying. Jerome was proud about Kenneth's decision to build friendships differently, but it was hard to see him losing a significant high school relationship.

The effect of losing that friendship was so powerful that Kenneth chose to take the academic spring quarter off and transferred to another school the following fall. Jerome confessed how much expectation he had for his son to "finish college in four years" and how he feared that his son would acquire more debt or not finish college at all. Jerome realized that he had to walk with Kenneth rather than try to force his own dreams on his son. He also admitted that even the good friendship choices his son makes can still have painful outcomes that are agonizing to watch.

## HOOKING UP, SWIPING UP, AND BREAKING UP

Three unique experiences surface in our explorers' romantic relationships, the first of which is how common it is to "hook up." This very ambiguous term can mean everything from making out to intercourse. Often related to alcohol use, it can happen with strangers or "friends with benefits."[16]

Some explorers express regret as they reflect on the emotional complications that come with sex. Having studied young adults' sexuality, Smith and his research team conclude, "Not far beneath the surface appearance of happy, liberated emerging adult sexual adventure and pleasure lies a world of hurt, insecurity, confusion, inequality, shame, and regret."[17] This regret seems especially prevalent for young women who face the additional complication of being more physically vulnerable in sexual relationships.[18]

The second unique experience for explorers' romantic relationships is how they are fueled more by a click or a swipe than face-to-face contact. Online dating increases as young people get older. Reports suggest that one-fourth to one-third of explorers' long-term relationships begin online. While traditional dating may be in decline, some argue that online dating serves as an important precursor, especially given that 66 percent of those who meet online go on a date together.[19]

> For more on the delay of marriage for today's young people, flip back to the sidebar titled "Why Are Young Adults Getting Married Later Than Previous Generations?" in chapter 1.

Third, since relational stakes are higher than in adolescent relationships, more explorers experience breakups as devastating. Women especially reveal more feelings of loss and emotional and physical distress. Men, on the other hand, seem to be less impacted by breakups and downplay being emotionally affected by sexual encounters. Many women admit that it may have been wiser to wait until they were older to become sexually active. The pain that permeates their breakups reflects the reality that those in their twenties often feel they need to hold off on marriage but still long for intimacy.[20]

## COMING OUT

Emerging adults' growing self-discovery sometimes raises new questions about their sexual orientation. Given less peer pressure, fewer family expectations, and a cultural acceptance of same-sex attraction and orientation, more young people are coming out as lesbian, gay, bisexual, transgender, or queer/questioning (LGBTQ), and are doing so at younger ages.[21] Of all Americans, 4.4 percent

## Growing With in Real Time:
### Your sons and social pressures[1]

Studies show that males report more risk-taking behavior than females. These activities include sports that have a higher degree of danger (e.g., rock climbing, surfing, or jet skiing) or behaviors such as reckless driving, risky sexual practices, and substance use. Thus, there is a higher mortality for emerging adult men than women.[2]

Christian Smith and his colleagues suggest that social pressures for men to be "tough" and "daring" still endure, which may directly or indirectly encourage emerging adult men to act out, often to the detriment of themselves and others.[3] For instance, colleges have had to address too-common instances of males sexually assaulting women and fraternities crossing the line with hazing initiation rites.

As he attempts to negotiate the conflicting societal messages about manhood, don't assume your son will just figure it out on his own. Young men need a variety of older voices in their lives who encourage and inspire them to become thoughtful and responsible.

Ask your son more than task or accomplishment questions. Talk with him about his dreams, desires, pressures, and fears. Take time (more than once!) to discuss risk-taking behaviors by asking him to walk through his plans with another person or role-play scenarios. Hold him accountable for his actions and don't make excuses for any behavior that may harm himself or others.

1. Adapted from Steven Argue and Kara Powell, *Eighteen Plus* (Atlanta: Orange Books, 2018).
2. Jerika C. Norona, Teresa M. Preddy, and Deborah P. Welsh, "How Gender Shapes Emerging Adulthood," in *The Oxford Handbook of Emerging Adulthood*, ed. Jeffrey Arnett (New York: Oxford University Press, 2015), 62–86.
3. Christian Smith et al., *Lost in Transition: The Dark Side of Emerging Adulthood* (New York: Oxford University Press, 2011), 187–92.

of women and 3.7 percent of men identify as LGBTQ, and 18- to 36-year-olds represent the largest proportion of that group.[22] While there is some indication that the average age is dropping when individuals reveal same-sex tendencies (i.e., "come out"), at this point it seems to be hovering around an average age of 20.[23] Also, while the percentage of LGBTQ is relatively small compared to the overall US population, studies report that 87 percent of Americans know someone who is gay, with 30 percent knowing someone who is transgender.[24]

Some young people are more likely to come out to close friends before their parents for fear that their parents may reject them, ignore them, or perhaps even disown them (if not literally, perhaps emotionally).[25] For other young people, coming to terms themselves with their own sexual identity is just as challenging. Justin Lee describes his own experience of admitting what he knew *about* himself *to* himself:

> Even after realizing it was true, it was a long time before I could bring myself to breathe the word aloud.
>
> I sat up late at night, after everyone else had gone to bed, trying to come to grips with what this word meant for my life. In my softest whisper, paranoid about being overhead by anyone, I tried to muster up enough courage to say to myself those two words: "I'm gay."
>
> "I'm . . ." A pause. A deep breath.
>
> "I'm . . ."

Steve and I recognize that there are a variety of opinions and theological approaches to questions swirling around same-sex attraction, activity, and identity. Our purpose here is not to promote any particular theological stance toward same-sex relationships but rather to help you grow with and provide relational support to adulting young people—both inside and outside your family—who identify as LGBTQ.

But the "g" word would never come. It was dark and frightening. I knew it was true, but I couldn't bring myself to say it, not even in a barely audible whisper alone in my room at night.[26]

Once parents are told, they often must work through their own processing of their child's disclosure. As we mentioned in chapter 2, we often have to adjust our vision for our child's future. For many parents, this reframing process follows a cycle of grief and involves denial, anger at themselves or others, bargaining with God or their child, bouts of depression, and eventual acceptance of their child's disclosure as a starting point for new conversations about their identity and their relationships.[27]

### SEXUAL ASSAULT

Studies from the US Department of Justice relay that women ages 18–24 experience higher rates of rape and sexual assault than other age groups. Also, female nonstudents were 1.2 times more likely to be sexually assaulted than their college student counterparts.[28] Seven out of ten rapes are attempted by someone the victim knows. Ninety percent of rape victims are female and 10 percent are male.[29] As our explorers enter new social situations, groups, and dating relationships, wise parents keep conversations open to help navigate our alarming climate and empower our kids to be part of the solution.

For more information about sexual assault for all generations, call the National Sexual Assault Hotline at 1-800-656-HOPE (4673), or visit their website, https://www.rainn.org.

### Focusers and Their Adulting Relationships

Relational commitments and behaviors blur as our growing kids enter their mid to late twenties and become increasingly autonomous. Our focuser sons and daughters are beginning to approach that psychologically powerful marker of age 30, which raises big adulting questions about their long-term relationships.

## LIVING TOGETHER AND GETTING MARRIED

Most emerging adults admit that they would like to be married by age 30, and that often does happen.[30] But before they tie the knot, many focusers end up with relational loose ends. Estimates are that 60–70 percent live together, with cohabitation often starting as early as 21 for women and 23 for men.[31] Couples cohabit out of deep feelings for one another or a desire for an increased commitment, as well as for pragmatic reasons such as to save money or to raise a child.

Those who are "serial cohabitors" (meaning they experience several cohabiting relationships) exhibit higher risks of divorce, lower marital satisfaction, higher levels of domestic violence, and lower levels of communication with their partners. When it comes to "sliding versus deciding," couples who make intentional decisions about their relationship status, rather than sliding into a live-in relationship, are more likely to flourish in their relationships and describe having happy marriages later.[32]

## DEBT AND GETTING MARRIED

As of 2012, the average young person left college (having graduated or not) with $25,000 of debt.[33] In 2016 this number climbed to over $30,000—a rapid increase rate. This means that every former college student will pay around $300 per month over the next 10 years to eliminate their loans.[34] Those financial burdens become anchors in our focusers' adulting relationships. Twenty percent of emerging adults report delaying marriage because of college debt. Furthermore, marrying a focuser with debt places additional strain on young marriages.

As is obvious from the above insights about learners, explorers, and focusers, relational adulting is complex and young people need to know we understand that. Before we consider "Adulting Ideas," perhaps this is a perfect moment to personally commit to:

- Learning more about your child's online gaming interests, habits, and friends.
- Having an honest conversation with your child about their (and your) social media use.
- Telling your child that you're aware of how ambiguous dating is and that you just want them to know you're here for them.
- Confessing that sometimes the physical and online worlds that they are discovering make you feel anxious.
- Being warmer to their significant other.
- Praying for your child (and their friends).

## Adulting Ideas

### How Teacher Parents Can Encourage Learners' Relational Adulting

#### GARAGE CONVERSATIONS

As our learners grew through their high school season, Jen and I (Steve) found ourselves meeting in a strange room in our house—the garage. Typically, one of our daughters would propose an outing with her friends, ask to have "everyone" over, or even a more outlandish request like, "We want to go snowshoeing in the forest about an hour away. I know it's snowing, but can I take the car?" Jen and I have discovered that we have different thresholds for our daughters' requests, and so we often need a pre-decision meeting for just the two of us—which usually ends up happening in the garage—to ensure we're on the same page.

Our hope was that our garage-based decisions to approve or reject their requests emerged from our desire to grow our relationship with them and to prepare them for their own friendships. Decisions made out of fatigue, control, or pitting the "yes" parent against the "no" parent only made our family relationships confusing.

Our kids need clarity from us to help them navigate their often-unclear friendships. So whether it's your actual garage, another room in your home, or a phone call when you are traveling, look for a place where you can talk privately with your spouse, family member, or a friend to get needed input and perspective.

## TELL ME I NEED TO COME HOME

Often our learners find themselves in new situations they don't feel prepared to handle. They may walk into a party where kids are drinking alcohol or be surrounded by peers who don't treat each other well. Sometimes our kids get asked to events they aren't sure about. In the Argue family, we learned that these scenarios are too tricky to figure out in the moment; we have to plan ahead.

Our girls devised a simple code to help them get out of tough situations. We would agree ahead of time that if they called and asked if they could go to a particular event or stay longer at a party, we would tell them no. We had a code (typically a word or phrase) for when they would (pretend to) protest our decision, but we would remain firm. Our plan gave our daughters a gracious "out" when they were in a tough spot, felt peer pressure, or were just plain tired. If they determined that they *really* wanted to stay, they would call us from a more private location and we would revise our plan.

As parents, we often help our learners by being the ones they can "blame" to get out of tough spots. When they come home, we then have the opportunity to debrief the situation and perhaps help them be more prepared next time.

## NO ONE'S LEFT OUT

As our learner kids get older, they often have closer friends and their friend groups can feel more exclusive. While that's developmentally normal, given the self-centeredness of teenagers, their groups can easily morph into cliques that become hurtful and destructive. One family we know held to a simple mantra when their sons planned gatherings or outings: "No one's left out." The parents encouraged their boys to err on the side of inviting rather than excluding, which made their friend groups more accepting, fluid, and fun. Once, one of the popular kids in one of their son's grades confided that he wished he could be in the son's friend group because it was more fun and less stressful. Their son told him that he was welcome, but sadly this friend was unable to break free from the peer pressure of his more exclusive group.

### KID SPACE AND FULL FRIDGE

As our kids entered high school, we (the Argue family) wanted to elevate our commitment for our home to be a safe and welcoming place for all. We saved money and renovated a room in the house dedicated for them to hang out in, complete with comfy old furniture and a refrigerator perpetually stocked with simple (and inexpensive) snacks and drinks.

We learned from our kids (and from their friends' parents) that most of their friends didn't seem to enjoy having friends over. They were worried that their friends might feel bored. Hosting friends is a life skill, so we encouraged our girls to invite friends over any time. They knew there was always space and that we'd provide food. We also found that we needed to give them some ideas about what they might do with friends and how to be a good host. Some of our learners' best memories stem from when they've had friends over to watch movies, hold sleepovers, or get ready for prom.

For those of us in smaller homes without a room that can be renovated as a hospitable space for our learners, we can achieve the same effect by vacating from the kitchen or living room so that our learners can have a place for their friends. As parents, we do not need to be financially well-off to host this space. We just have to be flexible.

## YOU LIKE YOUR FRIENDS—WE WANT TO LIKE THEM TOO

Many parents have told us they have a goal of getting to know their kids' friends. As their learner kids solidified their friend groups, parents tried to ask their kids about their friends. Not only did those conversations help parents learn about their kids' social life, they also helped kids articulate what they appreciate most about their friendships. So consider asking questions like:

- What do you like most about Amy? What would you guess she likes about you?

- How are you similar to Paolo? How are you different from him?

- How does Kenzie's life inspire you?

- Tell us about Danielle's family. How is her family similar to or different from our family?

## SETTING A SPECIFIC AGE FOR DATING . . . OR NOT

Jen and I (Steve) told our daughters that they couldn't date until they were 16. We reasoned that in high school, upperclassmen may be interested in dating our daughters, and we were not too keen on them dating or being driven around town by teenage boys. We thought our daughters would push back on this rule, but we actually found they used it to their advantage. If they wanted to gently let down interested boys, they could evoke the "terrible" rule that their parents inflicted upon them. Our parameter also encouraged them to go out in groups and slow down romantic coupling, which can get complicated and stressful.

Dave and I (Kara) have a different philosophy. We haven't given a specific minimum age for our learner kids' dating. (If we did, my protective husband would be inclined to choose age 32, and I've told him that is unrealistic.) While some of our kids' major

*"Each of our sons started dating at different ages—the youngest in tenth grade and the two older in college. My wife had a great idea and volunteered to have a 'talk' with each of our boys. This was more than the 'sex talk.' It was important for her to help them understand how to treat women respectfully with grace, honor, and as image bearers of God. My sons have been impacted by their mom's reminders to treat women as peers and equals. I've seen our sons enjoy healthy friendship with girls and our conversations about their romantic interests seem more natural." —Justin, a Pennsylvania parent of one learner and two explorers*

milestones have happened at the same age (for instance, both girls got their ears pierced at age 10, and all three of our kids could stay up until 9:00 p.m. beginning at age 11), there is no universal Powell family age for dating. It's not dependent upon a birthday but rather their emotional and relational maturity, as well as who they want to date.

Nathan had his first girlfriend at age 15. She was from church, I had been her small group leader in middle school, and I've been friends with her parents longer than Dave and I have been married. So we felt fine with the two of them hanging out at an ice rink for two hours. We likely would have felt differently if we hadn't known her.

Steve and I offer our different philosophies on high school dating not to start a debate (that wouldn't really be fair, because obviously I'm right). Rather, we offer our two different parental approaches to our kids' adulting relationships—both of which were guided by the same desires to balance protection with independence—as illustrative of how every family needs to figure out what works for them. We know young people in general, and we know the young people who are our offspring specifically, but we don't know *your* young people. So please make the decisions that make the most sense for your family.

## How Guide Parents Can Encourage Explorers' Relational Adulting

Because our explorer kids have moved out or branched out, parents recognize that our contact with their relational adulting tends to be more episodic than continual. But every moment we connect with our kids, whether in person or through technology, gives guide parents opportunities to grow with our kids.

### ALWAYS ROOM AT THE TABLE (AND ON THE COUCH)

In the explorer stage, my (Steve's) kids' holidays, breaks, and vacations do not always line up with our work schedules or their siblings' breaks. For instance, Thanksgiving is often a hard time for explorer kids to make it home due to expensive flights and a short vacation. So we have appreciated it when other parents have taken in our college-aged kids and given them a home away from home. We also have discovered that Thanksgiving works better for our explorers if we view it as an "open invitation" holiday. If our girls come home, they can bring whomever they want. Sometimes I long for the holidays like they used to be—just the five of us. But I have found that these open gatherings are great chances to meet our kids' friends. Somehow our girls still have managed to give a little extra attention to their parents too!

While Jen and I have full lives and we're not waiting around for our kids and their friends to pop over, we've learned to welcome these moments with our kids and their friends and turn them into memories. Parents who want to serve as guides for their explorers can ask questions like:

- What traditions might we need to hold loosely in order to make room for our kids' friends who need a meal or a place to stay?

- How welcoming is our home? What's one step we can take to ensure our kids' friends feel more at home? One answer in the Argue home is that Jen buys extra toothbrushes and even puts names on them for our regular visitors. That small and inexpensive gesture makes our guests feel more at home.

## TOO HARSH (OR "I WOULDN'T EVEN LET JESUS DATE YOU")

Getting to know our girls' significant others has been a learning curve for me (Steve). The shift from our kids being learners to explorers not only raises the relational stakes for them but affects parents as well. We face weightier questions about our kids' romantic interests, and I find myself holding stronger opinions as the stakes seem higher.

Last summer, one of my daughters started dating a new boyfriend. He was in town, and she invited him to stay at our place in order to get to know us. The day before he came, while my daughter and I were sitting outside, I asked her how I was doing with meeting her boyfriends. She walked right through the conversational door I had opened and shared that she felt like I had been harsh and cold toward another young man she had dated the previous year.

Her critique was both surprising and painful. But what I appreciated was her honest feedback. Perhaps my anxiety about her dating was perceived by her as coldness. I told her that no boy will measure up to my expectations and that I would probably have issues even if Jesus dated her—which is my problem, not hers. Ever since, she has reminded me of how ridiculous that sounded, and she keeps encouraging me to give her boyfriends a chance.

After the last boyfriend visited, I asked her how I did. Her feedback was important to me and for my own parenting.

Model a Growing With posture with your adulting explorers by:

- Asking them how you're doing with their significant other and how you could improve.

- Looking for ways to meet your explorer's significant other in lower-stakes environments. Instead of starting with Thanksgiving dinner, can you first meet for coffee?

- Observing how their partner interacts with your family, as well as how your kid behaves around you with their partner. Are they acting like themselves? Later, when it's just the two of you, what feedback can you offer them about what you noticed and what that might say about their relationship? Take the opportunity to ask your kid to process how well they thought their significant other fit with the family.

## MENTORS, NOT ENEMIES

While our daughters have called me out for being too cold or intimidating with their boyfriends, there have been a few instances when the relationship has developed to the point where it's time for me to talk to a boyfriend one-on-one.

This is no laughing matter. For me. For my daughters. And certainly not for their boyfriends.

Because we are committed to our daughters, we have expectations about how they should be treated. So when we perceive a boyfriend isn't measuring up, I have taken initiative to talk with him. I admit that I have often approached these meetings ready to let the boys have it. But after talking with them, I've recognized that they're trying to navigate their own adulting journeys. Some come from great families and supportive parents, and others stem from more toxic and disruptive family contexts. In either extreme and everything in between, I have learned that a young man needs an older man in his life who challenges him but also believes in him. I can either threaten him into behaving differently, or I can tell him that I believe he can aspire to be a young man who puts my daughter's best interests ahead of his own. In those moments, they need me to be a mentor, not an enemy. As you seek to guide your explorer child and those who become particularly close to them, ask yourself:

- Does your child and their significant other know your expectations? If not, how and when can you better communicate those?

- Are you willing to hope for them to have a successful relationship, or will you only be a barrier? What practical steps can you take to live out your answer?

- In what ways can you mentor your explorer kid's partner through your words and actions?

## COMING OUT, STEPPING CLOSER

For those parents wanting to grow with our LGBTQ kids and friends, we offer a few starting points:

*Tell them you love them.* What your kid needs desperately is love. Many parents withhold love when their child comes out because they are afraid their child may mistake empathy for approval. Withdrawing your love will certainly drive a wedge between you, and possibly between them and God as well.[35]

*Show them you'll walk with them.* No matter our understanding of our and others' sexual identities, we are perpetually considering what our sexuality means for our lives. Perhaps more than any other age group, explorers need others to be sounding boards—reflecting their ideas and helping them refine their identities. Be courageous and walk with them, even if it is new territory for you. Remember that *all* of us are in-process, and at our core we are defined as being made in the image of God. It's often valuable to involve trained professionals (such as psychologists, pastors, and counselors) to help us and our family more fully experience the intimacy we seek with both God and each other as we navigate the complexities of kids coming out.

*Check your assumptions.* Through my (Steve's) work as a pastor serving brothers and sisters in our community who feel same-sex attraction, I have found that many parents and adults have strong opinions on LGBTQ persons and how they ought to live their lives. I have also discovered that few have solid reasoning for their positions. In a representative survey conducted in our previous church, most of our faith community wanted to be welcoming of all while also admitting that they really were not clear on Scriptural teachings about faith and sexuality.

I have also talked with many parents who feel stuck because they felt so sure of their position until their child came out. Whether we are parents of gay kids or parents of straight kids with gay friends, let's reject calling sexuality an "issue" and recognize that all young people need adults to be with them in what is often a lonely and hurtful adulting journey. Let's consider what it means for us to engage others thoughtfully, compassionately, and generously. Anything less brings pain and division, which are antithetical to the core message of the gospel.

## How Resourcer Parents Can Encourage Focusers' Relational Adulting

By their focuser stage, our kids have begun to solidify their relational tendencies and decisions. They are likely making life decisions about marriage and parenthood. As resourcer parents, we must again adjust to their new relationships and be families that grow with them.

### GETTING MARRIED

I (Steve) talk with many graduate students at Fuller Seminary who find love and decide they want to get married. Frequently, I'll hear them say that they'd like to skip the wedding and just elope. Often these sentiments surface because the wedding planning has become too complicated or expensive, or because parents (and sometimes grandparents and extended relatives) are becoming too stressed-out. We have many friends who have offered their engaged children money to elope because it's cheaper than a full-fledged wedding!

Every family has different wedding expectations, but as ministers who officiate weddings, both Kara and I remind the engaged couple to prepare for the marriage more than the wedding. We hope you're nodding along, because the same principle holds true for us as parents. Let's resist putting so much energy into the wedding ceremony that we lose sight of what is more important—our hope that our kids are walking into marriage as healthy people, a healthy couple, and in many cultures, a healthy joining of two families.

Let us also be healthy parents (and in-laws). A recently married focuser confessed to us that one of the more stressful parts of getting married was instantly having more family. Her spouse's family is great, but she is figuring out how to create a family bond

## Growing With in Real Time:
## What if we don't like their significant other and then they get engaged/married?

We parents may dislike our maturing kid's significant other, and the reality of their partner becoming a member of the family can strain our relationship with our kid. In these seasons, we likely need to express our opinions carefully without trying to sabotage the relationship, as our kid's partner may turn into our long-term son- or daughter-in-law. Parents may consider the following suggestions:

- *Ask yourself: Is my dislike or unease for my kid's partner justified?* Do I have grounds for worry, or am I being overly suspicious, protective, or involved?
- *Check your assumptions.* Before addressing your concerns with your kid, talk with your spouse, a friend, or someone who knows your kid well. Practice how you might raise your concerns with your son or daughter.
- *Have a conversation (not in the heat of the moment).* Invite your son or daughter to coffee or lunch to talk with them about their relationship. Seek to understand why they are committed to this person. Respectfully share what you've observed. Try to avoid being accusatory, but ask questions to help you better understand their partner.

with people who are still strangers (and whose names, especially when it comes to aunts and uncles, she can't always remember). As resourcer parents, be sensitive to your focuser's marriage and look for ways to grow your new relationship with them as a couple by:

- Talking about the process of becoming one as much as about planning the wedding.
- Reaching out to the new in-law parents to learn more about your son/daughter-in-law's family, and if their cultural

> - *Spend more time together.* Go to dinner with them as a couple, attend an event together, or just have them over. Look for ways to interact with them to get to know them as a couple and for your kid to see their partner engage in your family setting.
> - *Share your concerns.* After you've tried the above suggestions, if you still have concerns, talk with your child about what you are observing. Encourage them to see a pastor or go through premarital counseling before they commit to marriage.
> - *Encourage your kid to ask their friends to share their honest opinions about their significant other.* Invite your child to see if other people who love and care about them have the same observations you do.[1]
> - *Intervene when necessary.* If their partner shows signs of being abusive, struggles with addiction, or displays inconsistent behaviors, you may need to voice concerns more directly. Offer to connect them with, and if possible to pay for, a therapist. If necessary, help them consider options for helping their partner find treatment; in the case of abuse, serious interventions (such as a restraining order) may be required.

---

1. This is one of many good and practical ideas for your young adult children from *Welcome to Adulting* by Jonathan Pokluda with Kevin McConaghy (Grand Rapids: Baker Books, 2018), 143.

background is different, committing to learning and listening even more.

- Having honest conversations about family traditions and holiday attendance expectations.

- Looking for new benefits to be gained even while feeling the sacrifices that are almost inevitable as your young person begins a fresh life with their new spouse.

## LIVING TOGETHER

While many of us may oppose cohabitation based on our understanding of Scripture, the reality is that many of our focuser kids will nonetheless end up living with a partner before marriage. Similar to our Growing With response to our focusers' other decisions, let's not default back to our past teacher or guide roles but instead evolve into a resourcer role. If their goal is to eventually move toward a committed marriage relationship, then let's do our best to help them with that journey.

- Be honest with your focuser about your perspective on their living with a partner. Remind them that though they are free to choose their adulting path, part of adulting is recognizing that their decisions affect others. Ask them to give you time to learn how to navigate this relational dynamic that now affects your family.

- Seek ways to get to know their partner. Ignoring them or protesting them won't make the situation better—for them or for you.

- Ask them about their long-term plans. If they choose to live together, continue to encourage them to think about their relational goals. Remember that relational goals need intentional deciding not passive sliding.

- Be available to them when they seek you out for advice.

* Be ready to celebrate their marriage goals or grieve their breakup. These are high-stakes moments where your focuser kid needs your presence more than your "I told you so."

Doorbells may or may not ring. Boyfriends and girlfriends may be something we pray for or something we dread. We might long for our adulting kids to have more friends, or maybe we wish they had fewer. In the midst of this variety of family situations, our teenagers and emerging adults will come in and out of that front door by themselves, with friends, and with romantic others. Every time that door swings open, we have the opportunity either to welcome them home or to bless them as they venture out.

## Practical Questions to Grow With My Child

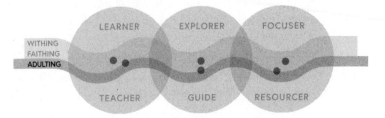

1. How optimistic and confident are you that your learner, explorer, or focuser is working toward their interests, goals, and values?

1·······································································5·······································································10
Worried                    Seeing progress                Very encouraged

2. We often are tempted to be too optimistic or pessimistic about our kids' present and future lives. In this moment, without judgment, how would you describe your child's interests, goals, and values?

3. After reading this chapter, what information, quote, or story inspired your thinking or gave you a fresh perspective on your learner, explorer, or focuser's adulting and relationships?

4. If your child is a learner or perhaps a young explorer, how might you engage in ongoing, constructive conversations about their social media use and online behaviors?

5. What are ways you can work toward getting to know your learner, explorer, or focuser's romantic interest? What might make this challenging for you?

6. Growing With parenting requires you to make room for your kid's friendships and relationships. Where might you need to be more flexible with your expectations/traditions as well as perhaps more direct about what is really important to you?

7. What might be a next step for you to consider as you support your child's relational adulting? What other adults might be able to encourage you or offer you wisdom?

# 8. Vocational Adulting

*Shaping Our World through Service and Career*

Rebecca is a 29-year-old I (Kara) have known and walked alongside for 17 years. Recently, she and I met for coffee so she could bring me up to speed on her plans for graduate school. To my delight, she was planning to pursue a master's degree in occupational therapy and was moving out of state to attend a graduate school that specialized in helping refugees.

Rebecca's choice brought me chills.

But Rebecca was on the verge of tears.

Eyes moist, she explained, "I can't believe I'm 29 and I'm just now figuring out the career God has for me. I feel so late and left behind."

I listened for a few more minutes, and then I recapped for her the statistics about this generation of young people that we shared in chapter 1. "Rebecca, your generation is taking five years or longer to figure out life. Trust me. I've studied this. For young adults today, 28 is the new 18."

Now the tears started to come. Right there in the middle of our neighborhood coffeehouse. Rebecca offered between sobs, "No one ever told me this. No one ever told me I wasn't lame or abnormal."

Need a refresher on the reasons why 28 is the new 18? Check out chapter 1.

And my heart broke.

Upon graduating from a prestigious four-year university, Rebecca had worked and volunteered at multiple local nonprofits, searching for her vocational home and calling. What Rebecca—and Rebecca's parents—thought would take a year or two had taken seven years. But that extended search had made a difference. Rebecca was now confident about her career calling and committed to using her skills and voice to serve and advocate for refugees as they entered the US workforce. Rebecca hadn't been wandering or stalling; she was adulting.

## Service and Career: Two Vocational Adulting Opportunities to Shape the World

In the last chapter, we highlighted the importance of adulting, meaning *a child's growth in agency as they embrace opportunities to shape the world around them*, specifically in their relationships. In this chapter, we transition from relational adulting to vocational adulting. Committed in our mission to "form global leaders for Kingdom vocations," we at Fuller Seminary define vocation as "identity in Christ, embodied in a specific context, expressed in service to God's mission." As described by theologian Frederick Buechner, vocation is "the place where your deep gladness and the world's deep hunger meet."[1]

Two of the primary vocational channels that help learners, explorers, and focusers make our world a better place are *service* and *career*. Both service and career reflect God's universal call on each person to use our resources (our skills, time, energy, and finances) to further God's work in our world. Both aim to restore the peace

We recognize that vocational choices are often a privilege, meaning that some in our society (especially those who are marginalized or of lower socioeconomic status) often lack certain decision-making power and opportunities in their career trajectory, and may overtly face job discrimination due to a combination of systemic organizational barriers. This can make work a context that may or may not carry a sense of personal fulfillment or seem the result of calling. Our own kids or other young people we know who experience work this way may find deeper fulfillment in serving through church, family, or neighborhood involvement.

(or *shalom*) that God intends for all people and relationships. Put more simply, both share the same end goal of righting wrongs.

In the midst of these similarities, your learner, explorer, or focuser likely thinks of the two differently. They consider their present or future job as their career—whether that be as a stay-at-home parent, a white-collar professional, a blue-collar laborer, or a uniformed soldier or sailor. In contrast, they view service as the difference they make *outside their career*—often by volunteering in church, nonprofits, faith-based ministries, or local philanthropies.

In a world that puts more and more pressure on young people to know what they want to do before they even really know themselves, we think service is often an important step in helping our kids identify their career calling. That's what happened to Rebecca. It was her volunteer work at nonprofits in Los Angeles that revealed her deep burden for refugees. Her career calling emerged as she experimented with service.

In Rebecca's initial pursuit of service and her eventual pursuit of a career, she needed patient, wise adults—her two parents and a handful of other mentors—to help her identify God's vocational call on her life and to support her during her longer-than-expected adulting journey.

## Adulting Insights: Research Related to Your Child's Service

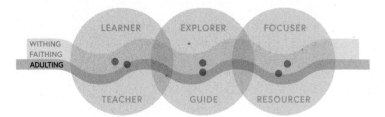

Every day, often through social media, our young people are exposed to the best and worst of our world. This section showcases research insights that capture how, when, and where young people typically serve—and how Growing With parents not only fuel our kids' service but also roll up our sleeves and get involved.

### The Good News: Young People Are Already Changing the World around Them

We at the Fuller Youth Institute embarked on four years of research on Growing Young churches with the primary goal of understanding how churches are changing teenagers and young adults.

We accomplished that goal, but along the way we identified an important corollary. Churches are definitely shaping young people, but the reverse is just as true: *young people are also shaping churches.*

When we asked pastors, congregational leaders, and parents to describe what teenagers and young adults add to churches, the term we heard more than any other was *vitality.*

Adulting young people add more passion.

More innovation.

More creativity.

And sometimes even more money. While teenagers and young adults are often not themselves huge financial givers or tithers (to put it mildly), their energy can attract older adults with more resources, who in turn faithfully support the ministries of the church.

### Serving Together: A Starting Point and a Launching Pad

Perhaps your learner, explorer, or focuser is already bringing vitality to a church or nonprofit through their involvement and ideas. That's terrific, but if your family is like most, you aren't around while they serve. Maybe the members of your family are serving *individually* through church and other philanthropies, but your family is not serving *together*.

While more challenging for your family schedule, recent research reveals that serving together—doing the same activity at the same time in the same place—can become a springboard for families, especially families of learners, to have rich Growing With conversations about serving and adulting that wouldn't happen otherwise.[2] This was confirmed in our interviews with parents growing with their learner teenagers. Despite juggling busy schedules and a host of priorities, over half of the families we studied are serving together.

Saundra, a mother of explorers and focusers, told about shopping with her two children years ago. During their errands, they encountered a cashier at a grocery store lamenting that it was her son's birthday and she didn't have the money to buy him the gaming device he really wanted. Saundra recalled, "As we left the store, I asked our kids, 'Should we take the money we were going

"For the last 18 months, our family has had a seven-year-old child of an addict we know living with us. That's been stressful for our kids. But it's also been growing for them. At first, we were frustrated because we didn't get more help from other friends, but we've realized why people give up on addicts and their families. It's not convenient. Helping other people is inconvenient." —Myesha, an Illinois mom of one learner and three explorers to use on something fun for our own family and buy a gaming device for this mom to give to her son?'"

Saundra's three sons immediately responded, "Yes." So the family made a quick run to Walmart, bought the gaming device, and headed back to the grocery store. Saundra gave the bag to her kids and stayed in the car. She wanted them to experience how it felt to give such a special gift to a stranger.

From that point on, her kids were quick to look for ways to serve strangers—whether it was helping a senior adult load groceries or buying a sandwich for a teenager sitting on the curb of the 7–Eleven. Saundra summarized one of their family's mottos: "If God is meeting our needs, we ask ourselves, 'How can we meet somebody else's?'"

### Serving "Together" Even When You're Not in the Same Room

For some families, serving together is infeasible. Your child may live 3,000 miles away. Or they may live three yards away but roll their eyes when you ask if they want to serve with you at the nearest hospital or public school.

Our interviews with Growing With families yielded two suggestions for parents who can't serve at the same place at the same time as their kids:[3]

1. *Model* service to your adulting learner, explorer, or focuser through your attitude and actions.
2. *Encourage* your child to find a cause they care about and serve on their own.

One Massachusetts dad who is growing with his high school and college students has seen the power of these two steps in his family's financial stewardship. The dad described, "We have always been very transparent with our kids about how we contribute to the church, and why we think it is important. Our kids care deeply about our church's local and global impact, so at our church's last stewardship campaign, they made their own pledges. And it wasn't, 'Hey Dad, I haven't yet made my pledge, can you loan me ten bucks?' It was, 'Dad, I'm going to pledge $200,' and they figured out how to honor that pledge with their own money."

### Learners: Lots of Service but Not Lasting Service

According to one national survey of 12- to 18-year-olds, 55 percent of teenagers are serving, contributing more than 1.3 billion hours of service annually. That is almost twice the adult volunteer rate of 29 percent. (Read that sentence again, adults!)[4]

That's the good news. But here's the bad news. While learners are serving a lot, it's not clear their service leaves a lasting impression on them. Of the more than two million US teenagers who participate in mission trips every year, five out of six report that those trips don't leave a long-term mark on their lives.[5] More specifically:[6]

- The data is unclear about whether service trips cause participants to give more money to help alleviate poverty once they return home.
- Service trips do not seem to dampen participants' materialistic appetites.
- While there has been explosive growth in the number of young people and adults participating in short-term mission trips, that increase has *not* translated into similarly explosive growth in the number of career missionaries.

Wait. So should you not put down a deposit on your daughter's mission trip?

Should you just tell your stepson to get a real summer job this year?

Not necessarily! In the "Adulting Ideas" section later in this chapter, we give some practical suggestions to help your learner's service experience yield the spiritual and overall ROI (return on investment) we all hope for.

## Explorers: Struggling Somewhere between Busy and Complicated

While explorers are old enough to periodically be in the driver's seat of your family's service, they often end up in the back seat, or never quite make their way into the vehicle at all. One study of age cohorts conducted by the US Bureau of Labor found that volunteer rates were lowest among 20- to 24-year-olds, with about 18.4 percent reporting they serve.[7]

Some of the barriers that keep our college-aged young adults from serving are internal, such as their perception that they aren't capable of nor have adequate resources for helping others right now. They believe those capacities will come when they are older, so it makes sense to wait until later to serve.[8]

In addition, compared with teenagers who follow household rules and thirtysomethings who often have households of their own, twentysomethings tend to have more latitude to decide about their own schedules, living situations, and relationships. Consequently, according to Jeffrey Arnett, "There is no time in life that is more self-focused than emerging adulthood."[9]

Yet before we point a finger at explorers in general, or more specifically at the explorer in our own family, let's remember that

Explorers feel a unique tension between being optimistic about their own prospects and simultaneously pessimistic about our world's. While 96 percent of 18- to 24-year-olds believe they will get to where they want to be in life, this same age group is also highly likely to believe the world is full of perils and the future of our country is grim.[1]

1. Jeffrey J. Arnett, *Emerging Adulthood: The Winding Road from the Late Teens Through the Twenties* (New York: Oxford University Press, 2004), 223, 227.

some of the barriers preventing philanthropic service stem from what they have seen modeled in adults. Including us.

Perhaps their consumerism mirrors our own drive to achieve the "middle-class dream" of a family, nice car, and comfortable house.[10]

Maybe their embrace of individualism and the consequent belief that it's up to each individual to answer how (if at all) they want to serve others—on their own time and their own terms—reflect our attitudes and actions at home.[11]

Our intent in sharing how our kids mirror the good, bad, and ugly in us isn't to make any of us feel judged. Instead, it's to help us each stop and look at our own perspectives and practices before we judge those of the nearest explorer.

### Focusers: Benefiting from Rolling Up Their Sleeves and Serving Others

When service data is not confined just to 18- to 23-year-olds but expanded to all adulting twentysomethings (and even thirtysomethings), a more encouraging picture of their service emerges. According to the Nielsen Company, 57 percent of Millennials (those born from 1980 to 2000) engage in volunteerism, more than any other age group. The top three causes young adults care about are

For young adults, serving and encountering others beyond their "normal tribe" raises "vital, transforming questions that unsettle examined assumptions, foster adaptive learning, and spur the formation of commitment to the common good."[1] Perhaps that's partly why 90 percent of Peace Corps volunteers later say they would make the same decision to serve if they had it to do over again.[2]

1. Sharon Daloz Parks, *Big Questions, Worthy Dreams: Mentoring Young Adults in Their Search for Meaning, Purpose, and Faith*, 2nd ed. (San Francisco: Jossey-Bass, 2011), 181.
2. Jeffrey Jensen Arnett and Elizabeth Fishel, *When Will My Grown-Up Kid Grow Up?* (New York: Workman, 2013), 192.

education, poverty, and the environment.[12] Given these passions, it's not surprising that more young adults than ever are looking for first jobs in community service programs like Teach for America, Habitat for Humanity, Engineers without Borders, International Justice Mission, and AmeriCorps.[13]

## Adulting Insights: Research Related to Your Child's Career

For our young people, vocational adulting involves not just service but also expanding (and at times narrowing) career choices. Our kids' career roller coasters give us a new ride to grow with our kids—if we are willing to climb on board.

### Parents' Struggle and Support during the Career Highs and Lows

When we asked parents which areas of their adolescents' and young adults' lives require the most support, the top two answers were "major life decisions" and "career, vocation, or work-related decisions." Four times as many Growing With parents found the career process to be "hard" compared with those who labeled it as "easy."

For their part, our adulting young people often feel like they are stuck in a pit of career stress. They know they are supposed to be exploring new career options, but often the daily pressure to pay the bills leads them to jobs that are dissatisfying in the present and unlikely to lead to a dream job in the future. Sometimes our explorers and focusers who had particular career intentions in the preceding life stage realize that those past inclinations no longer fit them, so they feel like they are starting over vocationally. It takes longer to figure out a vocational call than today's twentysomethings expect, which leads young people (and their parents) to fret that they will never land a "real job" that is meaningful, stable, and financially sensible.[14]

In the midst of the career stress and pressure felt by kids and parents alike, the Growing With parents we interviewed try to

Parents in immigrant families often experience additional vocational challenges as they attempt to raise their kids in a culture different from what they experienced as teenagers or young adults. As a result, children may be more familiar with the new culture's vocational values and norms, meaning parents often feel a need to rely on their children's perspectives for living in a new context. For families and cultures with strong parental hierarchies, this may feel counterintuitive and challenging.[1]

1. Norma J. Perez-Brena, Kimberly A. Updegraff, and Adriana J. Umaña-Taylor, "Transmission of Cultural Values among Mexican-Origin Parents and Their Adolescent and Emerging Adult Offspring," *Family Process* 54, no. 2 (June 2015): 234–35.

support their learners, explorers, and focusers by taking two primary steps:

1. Offering affirmation and encouragement
2. Asking helpful questions

One Georgia mom of learners and explorers discovered the importance of these two steps by doing the opposite. Since first grade, Tasha has said she wants to be a teacher. Her mom has been worried about this goal because she sees teachers struggle financially from paycheck to paycheck. Tasha is now in college and is going to graduate with some debt, so her mom started verbalizing her concerns more frequently. Finally, Tasha stopped her mom, looked her in the eye, and said, "Mom, God told me I'm going to be a teacher when I was seven years old. Will you please stop trying to tell me to do something different?" According to Tasha's mom, "That pretty much made me be quiet."

### Learners' Initial Vocational Experiments

As with many paths crisscrossing your teenager's life, their career steps take the form of experiments that typically lurch—and at times stumble—forward haphazardly. Often as your child enters high school, they branch out into new academic disciplines or extracurricular activities. Your former math whiz kid might lose interest in geometry and instead immerse themselves in ceramics. Your basketball player gearing up for a fall tournament might also choose to audition for their school's winter musical. While these adolescent experiments may not last more than a year and may not lead directly to a long-term calling, they often contribute to your adulting child's unfolding grasp of career possibilities in unexpected and powerful ways.[15]

I (Steve) recall that when our middle daughter entered high school, she was introduced to so many new activities. Elise was excited, but Jen and I could tell that she was having trouble figuring out how to choose and prioritize the best activities for her. I thought I was helping when I asked her, "What activities and clubs do you want to join?" Elise answered, "All of them."

While her answer was impractical, it was honest. Her instinct made sense to her: "If I can't choose, I'll just do them all." I learned that growing with Elise involved the added step of helping her find a healthy balance between investing in a few things and doing everything. In fact, many families find that empowering their adulting learners to pursue one interest outside the classroom may be enough in certain seasons.

Some need limits.

Others need encouragement to step out.

None of our learners can do it all.

### Explorers and Focusers: Experimenting or Floundering?

Depending on who you talk with and what you read, twentysomethings are either deadbeats dragging down our entire economic system or innovative geniuses representing the hope for Western civilization. We may gravitate toward one side or the other of this debate, but research paints a compelling picture that most young people are simply trying to survive in an increasingly competitive world.

## ECONOMIC EMPLOYMENT REALITIES

While our culture often points a finger of shame at our underemployed adulting young people, the underlying causes for their vocational and career upheaval are diverse and often beyond their control.

- National or regional economic challenges affect all generations, but are more likely to disrupt younger workers' job trajectories.

- Various industries are increasing their use of temporary and part-time employees, and some Boomers are staying in the workforce longer, making it more challenging to find long-term or full-time positions.[16]

- Technology often enables workers to be more efficient, so one or two workers can now accomplish what previously required 10 or more employees. While often encouraging for a company's bottom line, that sort of automation is discouraging for young people searching for work in an economy that requires fewer laborers.[17]

- Since 1981, college costs have increased five times faster than family income. Currently, 40 percent of four-year college students and almost 75 percent of part-time students work in order to contribute to their tuition and living expenses. In 1970, only 10 percent of full-time students worked 20–34 hours per week; now that number is 17 percent.[18]

This economic environment has upended traditional pathways for explorers and focusers seeking employment. Facing empty kitchen cupboards in their apartments and rent due at the end of the month, the average 22-year-old has held more than four different jobs in the last four years.[19] One Gallup study of twenty-somethings found that more than one-third were unemployed, underemployed, or living "gig to gig," meaning they were making do with part-time work, juggling several interim jobs, freelancing, or starting their own business.[20] If you're like the two of us, you know explorers and focusers who work full time while also supplementing that income with one or more "side hustles."

## VOCATIONAL (HOLY) DISCONTENT

At times, our explorers' and focusers' job transitions are due to their own limitations and flaws, such as their poor understanding about their own strengths, or their lack of information about the job market, available career options, and training requirements.[21] Perhaps our kids suffer from a lack of "grit," meaning a lack of commitment and perseverance, without which it's tough to pursue a vocational goal, especially after failing the day before.[22] Or maybe our kids have swallowed the "30 is the new 20" mythology; instead of investing in their careers, they avoid vocational decisions, squander career opportunities, and coast.[23]

But at other times, even when explorers' and focusers' job-hopping stems largely from their own choosing, the motivations that drive their transitions are admirable, such as:

- Emerging adults' refusal to settle for a "McJob" that doesn't reflect their core identity and passions, instead holding out for a job that truly fits who they are. In one poll of 18- to 29-year-olds, 80 percent reported that enjoying their job was more important than making a lot of money, but 61 percent said they had not been able to find the type of job they wanted.[24]

- Their desire to have more of a personal life and make work less central than other age cohorts. One study comparing young people in 1982 with young people more recently shows significant decreases in their agreement with statements such as "The most important things that happen in life involve work" and "Work is something people should get involved in most of the time."[25]

* Having experienced the blessing of more career and training options than previous generations, today's explorers and focusers are reticent to make vocational decisions that narrow their short- and long-term options.

While others accuse explorers and focusers of floundering or drifting, we prefer to view them as *experimenters*. We agree with a fleet of career counselors who view indecisiveness as a normative phase in career development that is most often temporary and eventually resolved. Indeed, most adulting explorers and focusers report finding careers that are both satisfying and long-term by their late twenties.[26] And those ultimate vocations often are a better fit for our children since they have spent several years considering options and analyzing their own strengths and weaknesses.

That's easy to say, but when it's *your* 26-year-old cobbling together various part-time jobs while living in your guest room, it's tougher to take comfort in such so-called "normalcy." While there is no guarantee for our kids (or us) that their experiments will eventually lead to the career promised land, some of the encouraging signs of young adults' vocational adulting are when they maintain:

* A commitment to pinpointing what they are learning about themselves and their vocational choices and preferences in the midst of their career pits and peaks.[27]

* An openness to talking about their career options (or lack thereof).[28]

* A list of short- and long-term vocational goals. One study that followed nearly 500 young adults from college into their midthirties found that increased goal-setting in their

## *Growing With in Real Time:*
## Your daughter's pressure to "do it all"[1]

Currently, a greater share of emerging adult women hold bachelor's degrees than their male counterparts. Among those ages 18 to 33, women are 6 percent more likely than men to have finished at least a bachelor's degree (27 percent for explorer women versus 21 percent for explorer men) and 71 percent are employed.[2] Female emerging adults experience more opportunities in multiple career fields and have more career choices than women even a few decades ago, despite often facing hiring and wage discrepancies and at times overt discrimination.

The challenge, however, is that women feel the (internal and/or external) pressure to "do it all." Your daughter's quest to balance aspirations of career and family can heighten her feelings of inadequacy, stress, and guilt.[3] Emerging adult women report being optimistic about maintaining balance, but also contemplate this vocational tension earlier and more deliberately than men.[4]

Regardless of your gender or your own career choices, grow with your daughter or stepdaughter by being available to talk about her tensions and dreams. Celebrate her opportunities and normalize her conflicting aspirations. Help her connect with other women you know who are a few steps ahead in navigating this tightrope. In a world where emerging adult women feel increasing and conflicting demands, you and others you know can be a needed safety net.

---

1. Adapted from Steven Argue and Kara Powell, *Eighteen Plus* (Atlanta: Orange Books, 2018).

2. Richard Fry, Ruth Igielnik, and Eileen Patten, "How Millennials Today Compare with Their Grandparents 50 Years Ago," Pew Research Center, March 16, 2018, http://www.pew research.org/fact-tank/2015/03/19/how-millennials-compare-with-their-grandparents/.

3. Jeffrey Jensen Arnett, *Emerging Adulthood*, 2nd ed. (New York: Oxford University Press, 2014), 149.

4. Stacey R. Friedman and Carol S. Weissbrod, "Work and Family Commitment and Decision-Making Status among Emerging Adults," *Sex Roles* 53, no. 5 (September 2005): 317–25, doi:10.1007/s11199-005-6755-2.

twenties led to greater purpose, mastery, and well-being in their thirties.[29]

- A willingness to meet older adults to learn about career fields.
- A good use of their time, whether or not they are employed full time.

### Growing With in Real Time:
### How can you grow with your adulting child while they serve in the military?

**An interview with Jordan Henricks, a Fuller Seminary alumnus and active duty army chaplain in the special operations community**

*Jordan, how does military service help clarify young people's vocational goals?*

Basic training, or the two to three months of intense training that is the launch to military service, is the premier goal-setting crash course in the world. For most, simply completing basic training becomes a major goal.

After basic training, the military helps its young people develop and accomplish vocational goals by fostering an environment of continual personal growth. Soldiers are required to better them-selves physically and mentally every day, which often overflows into all areas of a person's life.

*How does being in the military strengthen a person's faith, and how might it erode it?*

The military is a gruff environment—with lots of coarse lan-guage and a lack of some of the niceties we are used to in our culture. Often enlisted men and women have a hard time discern-ing how to best love God and love their neighbor since the culture is so different from what they are used to. But the discipline of military culture often translates into a new commitment to spiri-tual disciplines that can strengthen faith.

Plus, the saying that there are "no atheists in foxholes" is true. During basic training, when recruits are scared and over-

### Parents Are Also Invited to Grow during This Vocational Adulting Season

Right as our kids are navigating their own quarterlife career transitions and choices, we parents are often hip deep in our own midlife job shifts. While many of us are hitting the peak of our job satisfaction and expertise, others are losing our jobs or retiring early. Now that our kids' college tuition bills have been largely paid,

whelmed, they are more interested in attending chapel and talking about God. In my role as chaplain, I've seen countless examples of God deepening a young person's faith because of the storms they face.

*What advice would you offer to parents who want to encourage their military kids' adulting when they are away from home?*

The biggest mistake I see parents make is that they try to fix things for their kids. Sometimes parents who have received texts or emails from their military kids describing the challenges of military service even try to contact the military to try to make their child's life easier. That just ends up embarrassing the kid, and the parents too.

*So what can parents do to better support their child?*

Listen to your kid's hardships. Affirm that they are indeed hard. It is no fun to have a drill sergeant yell at you. But also ask them about some of the exciting opportunities they are experiencing. Let your child know that you believe in them and you know they are capable of overcoming the obstacles they face.

*How can parents best grow themselves as their kids are in the military?*

Your son or daughter is learning so much. They are learning a new language, new culture, new tasks, and new skills. This is a season of learning, learning, learning. Now is a great time for you to invest in some learning too. Learn a new skill yourself. Integrate a new spiritual discipline or habit into your life. Your child is growing and they want to see you grow also.

some of us are even reinventing ourselves in an "encore career," pursuing a long-deferred dream we have postponed for the good of our family's financial stability.[30] Others find that just as their own kids leave the nest, their aging parents require care and perhaps also financial support. Even though we have more vocational mileage than our kids, we are still adulting and navigating the new twists and turns that come our way.

In the midst of this winding vocational road, our kids' choices reveal our hidden anxieties and unresolved disappointments. Some of us wish we could redo our twenties so we'd be in a different spot today. Deep down, we hoped our kids would follow in our career footsteps. Or maybe we secretly envy our child for having the courage and faith to pursue the riskier career that we wish we had pursued. Parents thrilled that their kids are the first in their family to go to college are ecstatic about their kids' accomplishments, but may also be anxious about their own inability to fully empathize with and support them.

Our own career challenges and changes give us a prime laboratory to grow with our adulting learner, explorer, or focuser. We can model how to face vocational regret and anxiety with determination and honesty. We can be an example of how to persevere even when our own initial online applications and job interviews don't pan out as we hoped. We can empathize with the good, bad, and ugly of the career journeys that we experience alongside our adulting kids.

I (Steve) once hiked a mountain ridge with a friend, and we came over a crest and saw a wandering river below. We mused that if we created that river, it would be straight, efficient, clean. Yet in the twists and turns of this river, life sprang up at every bend. In our own vocational journeys, perhaps the "wrong turns" aren't detours but opportunities for life and growth—opportunities that will be even more meaningful as we share them with our adulting kids.

## Adulting Ideas: Enabling Your Child's Adulting through Their Service

*Helping Your Family Serve Others*

The earlier your family jumps into the adventure of service, the better. Many of you have been serving together with your families since your children were toddlers. When your kid has a free Saturday morning or is home for Christmas break, it feels normal to volunteer together at the local recycling center or at your church campus.

If serving together isn't yet part of your family's identity, try these baby steps to help your learner, explorer, or focuser understand how service can shape the world around them.

### IF YOUR CHILD LIVES AT HOME

- Occasionally or regularly, eat a rice and beans dinner to empathize with what much of the world eats. Let your family know that the money you save on this simple meal will be donated to people in need.

- As you come across folks in your community who work at local nonprofits, invite them over for dinner so your family is exposed to them and their work.

- Keep granola bars or gift certificates for local restaurants in your car to give to adults and children who ask you for money.

> *"When our two kids were teenagers, we would go to restaurants and pick out one family and pay for their bill. One time, we decided to cover the bill of a sweet old couple, which blew away our waitress. When it was time to pay our bill, the waitress said, 'Oh, it's been paid. The family next to you heard what you did, and they were so touched by it that they offered to cover your tab.'"*
> —Anya, a California mother of one learner and one explorer

Or better yet, when you are approached for food, walk as a family with that individual to the nearest restaurant and ask to hear their story over a sandwich.

- During dinner or during a short conversation in your child's room, share an email or social media update from a missionary or a philanthropy your family supports so they appreciate how your family is already making a difference.

> For an expanded list of ideas to help your family dive into service, see Kara's book *The Sticky Faith Guide for Your Family.*

- Talk about your own financial giving, which is all the more important in this era of online banking. As one Colorado mom of three reflected, "I grew up Catholic and we saw my dad put the envelope in the collection every week. Now when giving is electronic, our kids have no idea this is a priority to us. My husband and I feel like we have to explain to our kids that we give online and that it's a big priority for us."

## IF YOUR CHILD DOESN'T LIVE AT HOME

- Donate a portion (note that we suggest *a portion* and not 100 percent) of what you would normally give your child for their birthday or Christmas to a nonprofit they care about.

> "Helping our kids recognize they are called to serve and make a difference in our world is not always about seeing a big finish. Often it is the smaller things. The things that might seem inconsequential can actually have the biggest impact. We might not be able to see that impact, but we have to trust how Christ works in that." —Andrea, a mother of a learner and an explorer

- Forward them emails or texts you receive from leaders and organizations your family supports so they can celebrate the impact of that investment.

- Discuss justice topics that are important to your kids. Identify a first step they can take to get involved, as well as a few ways they want you to be part of their cause.

## View Service as a Process, Not an Event

Whether we are serving together as a family or our kids are serving on their own, we are more likely to be transformed when we no longer consider a Tuesday evening visit to a senior center as a mere three-hour activity but rather as a 24-hour journey. Instead of thinking of a weekend house-building trip as a two-day event, we view it as a two-week adventure.

That mindset is possible when you think of service as a three-step process: before, during, and after.[31]

*Before:* A lasting service experience starts when we help our learner, explorer, or focuser properly *prepare* for the sometimes menial and often mind-blowing service experiences awaiting them.

*During:* Enhance the adulting that can emerge from service by helping your young person *reflect* on their experience.

*After:* Deepen the impression of service by helping your child *connect* the dots between the public school building they painted in a nearby city and the homeless woman they pass every day on their way to class.

Recently, Dave and I (Kara) had the chance to take our three kids, two of whom were teenage learners at the time, to Brazil with Compassion International. To maximize the adulting this trip offered our kids, we treated this six-day trip as a six-week process.

Beforehand, Dave and I downloaded key insights about Brazilian culture and history. With a bag of York Peppermint Patties to motivate our kids to stay focused, we spent an hour sitting on

> "When our kids were teenagers, we took them on our first family short-term mission trip. Our kids got to hear me discuss how I arrived at my faith. Plus they got to express their faith to people their age who had no idea who Jesus was. I think we would have been okay without that trip, but that trip really solidified our family unity and our sense of family faith." —Marcos, a Texas dad of one learner and one explorer

a picnic blanket at a nearby park and learning the highlights of Brazil's past and people.

We also received the names, ages, and interests of the families and children we were going to visit. That information, along with pictures of the young children we would be meeting, helped nudge us to pray for our soon-to-be friends.

A month before the trip, each of our kids asked an adult to meet with them for coffee to help them process how they were feeling, what they were looking forward to, and what they were anxious about.

When we returned home from Brazil, Nathan, Krista, and Jessica each got together with that same mentor. They shared what they learned about themselves and how God used their unique interests (Nathan's love of sports, Krista's love of organizing people to play games, Jessica's love of photography) to build relationships with Brazilians of all ages.

Since we were able to sponsor a child we met through Compassion, we now keep in touch with and regularly pray for 11-year-old Ticiane. Every Christmas and at Ticiane's birthday, our kids pool their money for a special gift to let Ticiane know they are thinking of her.

In part as a result of the trip, Nathan began tutoring lower-income elementary school kids for an hour each week. Krista commits a week each summer and multiple afternoons during the school year to volunteer at a neighborhood educational center and at our church. Too young to serve as a volunteer in local nonprofits, Jessica serves every summer in our church's vacation Bible school. Because we treated our trip to Brazil as a process and not an event, we were able to grow with our kids, and the seeds planted there continue to bear fruit in our family.

This before/during/after approach applies not just to global philanthropy but also to service you do in your own neighborhood. Last Tuesday night, Krista and I volunteered for 90 minutes at a shelter for homeless families located 10 minutes from our home.

During our short drive there, I asked Krista a few key questions: Why are the families we are going to meet living in this shelter? What do you hope happens while we're there?

On the way home, I gave Krista a few minutes on her phone so she could catch up with friends she hadn't texted in 90 minutes (which can feel like an eternity to her and her friends). Then I asked her to put the phone away and I shared about the pregnant resident I met who peppered me with questions about nearby hospitals and doctors. We talked about our favorite parts of the evening, highlights of the conversations we had with the children and parents, how it was different than she expected, and how we hope to do it again next month.

## Adulting Ideas: Empowering Your Child's Adulting through Their Career

### *Become a Key Chain Parent*

In our research on Growing Young churches, we found that the leaders who best mobilize young people in their gifts and callings are those who show what we came to call "key chain leadership." Key chain leaders are regularly looking for ways to hand keys to the church over to young people. Not necessarily literal keys, but rather keys that represent new authority, power, and access that expand young people's experiences and opportunities in their congregations and communities.

We believe that a parallel process of "key chain parenting" is just as vital in our families. The good news is that our adulting kids are ready for those keys; they are divinely gifted with unique skills and a unique vocational calling to offer the world. The bad news is that only 55 percent of young people who can identify their passions and skills receive adult support to develop and showcase them.[32]

That's unfortunate because in all three stages of learner, explorer, and focuser, our kids benefit from an adult who identifies and hands over keys. As our kids unlock vocational possibilities, they need a parent or a trusted adult to affirm what works, thereby empowering them to open new doors toward their future career and calling.

### Handing the Right Keys to Your Child

In the learner stage, key chain parents reflect on their child's preferred academic disciplines or talents emerging in extracurricular activities. A quick glimpse at 17-year-old Nathan's report card makes it pretty obvious to him (and anyone else) that he excels in math and science (like his engineering dad). What has been less obvious to Nathan is that he is also a gifted teacher. Whether he's helping his grandmother with her cell phone or his sisters with their math, Dave and I (Kara) have shared with him that he has the patience of Job and the teaching instinct of Socrates. We have told him that we don't know if teaching will play in to his career calling, but it's a key that we hope he continues to use to unlock the potential of others.

Based on what we see as Krista's interests and strengths, we have helped her pinpoint some of her keys: speech and debate, playing with little kids, designing images on her laptop, and editing videos. Oh, and coming up with great ideas and enlisting people in executing them. Dave and I aren't sure what career recipe will emerge from those ingredients, but we are glad we have paid attention to her hobbies and joys so we can imagine her future with her. We look forward to doing the same with Jessica when she hits high school.

When kids reach the explorer stage, key chain parents remind their kids of dreams they may have forgotten. Your 21-year-old might not remember their intention three years ago to take as many literature classes in college as possible, or to spend a year abroad to understand microeconomic forces in the developing world. As parents, we remember the lyrics to our kids' past dreams and sing them back to them when the timing is right.

Sometimes the songs we sing back to our kids are new songs for us as parents. My (Steve's) oldest two kids have very different career goals. Elise is pursuing business. I was a finance and marketing major and worked in the business world, so as she talks with us about potential post-college careers, I have numerous opinions and examples.

My eldest daughter, Kara, is an accomplished artist. Since graduating with her bachelor's in fine arts, she has tried to navigate non-art work for life's daily expenses while also developing her art career. I'm embarrassed to say I used to swoop in with lots of advice on how Kara should market her art and get ahead in her field. Typically this was met with resistance from her and frustration from me. But then after a serious conversation between us, I realized that I was trying to give business career advice to an artist! I have not stopped trying to help her navigate her art career, but I am learning how to understand her field and career goals before superimposing my experiences on her. It is a new tune for me and a more encouraging one for her.

In all three stages of learner, explorer, and focuser, identifying keys does *not* mean prescribing a career for them. Their career is *theirs*, not ours. Often when we see passions or proclivities in our children, our best step is to pray. As one Midwest couple with children who are now young adults and beyond recalled, "When our oldest son was really little, we had a feeling that he was going to become a pastor, but we always thought it was not our place to

---

### Growing With in Real Time:
### Vocational mistakes to avoid

Based on others' interviews with emerging adults, parents, and career counselors, we advise Growing With parents to avoid these common vocational mistakes:[1]

- Making negative comments about the job prospects in your adulting child's potential or chosen field.
- Urging your learner, explorer, or focuser to choose a field that pays well but that they hate.
- Using financial support as a way to control your child's decisions.
- Highlighting the exciting career options your friends' children are pursuing.

---

1. Some items on this list are adapted from Jeffrey Arnett and Elizabeth Fishel, *When Will My Grown-Up Kid Grow Up?* (New York: Workman, 2013), 195–96, 279.

---

tell him that. If God wanted him to be a pastor, God would need to speak that to his heart. So we never told him, but we prayed about it. Sure enough, God did call him to ministry. It's hard to hold your tongue at times and sit back and watch your kids struggle a bit, but God is faithful."

### Reframe All Work as "Holy"

"I'm so sick of speakers at chapel inviting us to be pastors." This frustrated junior at a large Christian college continued, "Most of us are going to be engineers, nurses, teachers, or accountants. I'm tired of speakers making us feel like those jobs don't matter as much as being a pastor or missionary."

Contrary to the message this adulting explorer was hearing at his college chapel, we believe that every career provides opportunities for ministry. Sure, there are some (like both of us) who are called into full-time ministry as a career. But every vocation has the potential to be ministry. Any and every job gives our kids the opportunity to worship God, love and serve others, use their gifts to create new solutions, and point our world to the God who loves them more than they can imagine. As one Florida dad we interviewed regularly reminds his three sons, "I do not care what you do for a living. What I care about is that you live your life for God's purposes. Frankly, that is where fulfillment, significance, purpose, and joy lie."

*Teaching your learners.* Give your learners a taste of your own attempts to live for God's purposes. Make sure your kids know not just *what* you do (which may require a visit to your job site for them to truly grasp how you spend your time) but *why* you do it and *how* you try to minister to others through high quality work and relationships.

*Guiding your explorers and resourcing your focusers.* As your twentysomething children move into the explorer and focuser stages, it's time to invite them to peer behind the curtain of your job experiences to understand how God continues to grow you through the highs and lows of your vocational trajectory. The boss who seemed to favor others. The layoff you didn't expect. The promotion or raise you deserved but didn't receive. As you discuss these common job situations and experiences with your emerging adults—sharing your mistakes as well as how God both protected and guided you—they gain a bigger vision of what it means to love and serve God in all jobs and all seasons. Sharing these stories also gives your kids a front-row seat into how you are still adulting too.

> "We try to help our kids avoid judging possible jobs based on what's the best career opportunity or what makes the most money. The question is, 'What do you see God calling you to?'"
> —Wendy, a mom of a learner and a focuser

One very blunt dad we interviewed confessed, "Along the way, I have sometimes whined about my job. I've told my kids that sometimes supporting a family and working kind of stinks. But in the midst of those challenges, here's what I'm learning or what I am growing into. I think that's helping my kids understand that a job isn't just a place to make money. It's also a place to grow and give back."

### Growing With Your Learner as They Prepare for Life after High School

You grab your keys and head to your car for a 15-minute drive to the nearest shopping mall with your high school junior or senior. As you back down your driveway, you think, "Oh good, this will give us a chance to talk about life after high school."

Your child sitting next to you thinks, "Oh no, now he's going to want to talk to me about life after high school."

Both Steve and I have realized (often through our mistakes) that planning with our learners about their future can be a season of great family success or great family strife. If you want to grow with your child in these early vocational and college choices about life after high school, try the following.

*Create a system that works for your learner to keep track of deadlines.* If your learner has the option of attending college, junior and senior years bring a quantum leap to the application, scholarship, and test deadlines that your family needs to track. Before shifting the burden of responsibility for all those deadlines to your learner (which we recommend), help them develop an organizational calendar and a system that works for them. It doesn't matter if it's a spreadsheet or a stack of sticky notes; what's most important is that it works for your teenager.

*Visit where you can.* As much as budget and schedule allow, visit potential schools with your child. Take tours, talk to current students, and visit a class or two. Countless families of learners have found it was the campus visit that was the clincher. Plus all those visits give you time over meals, in the car, and maybe even on planes to talk with your learner about the major and college experience that will best prepare them for their possible future vocation.

*Remember there is no single perfect job or school for your child.* Admittedly, all the unknowns after high school can be stressful. But don't add an unnecessary cloud of anxiety to your family's ecosystem by believing the lie that there's only one great job or one great school for your learner. That puts too much pressure on the decision of one (often unpredictable) college admissions committee or one (potentially arbitrary) employer. Most high school graduates have lots of good options, any one of which sets them up to succeed in their twenties and beyond.

*Be interpreters of their interests.* Learners will often answer "I don't know" to questions about their future work aspirations or possible undergraduate majors. As parents, pay attention to what they're interested in and help them see where their interests and gifts connect with real jobs. For example: Does he love babysitting? Perhaps he would be a great elementary teacher. Is she always looking for excuses to get outside? There are some exciting jobs in forestry, marine biology, or mountain guiding. Does she find herself taking appliances apart to discover how they work? Engineers or mechanics do that every day. Does he continually ask "why"? Maybe he would be a great reporter or writer.

*Enjoy the ride.* My (Kara's) personality is rather type A (or at times, more like type A+). Before diving into the college experience with our oldest, I feared that I would put too much pressure on him—and myself—to work every possible angle to enhance his college application and thus expand his college options. But early in Nathan's junior year, I felt like God reminded me of this reality: I only get to go through this college experience with Nathan once. After that nudge, when I felt my inner anxiety—and my subsequent tendency to place undue pressure on my child—rise,

### Growing With in Real Time:
## 12 skills your learner needs before they move away from home

Tacos. Pasta with sausage. Tuna casserole.

These are the simple dinners Nathan and I (Kara) cooked together to help him get ready for college.

During high school, Nathan's strengths were more in the "eating large quantities" category than in actual meal preparation. Looking ahead to life after high school, Dave and I knew that needed to change.

Whether you have a few weeks or a few years before your learner leaves home, Steve and I invite you to make sure your child knows how to

- Do laundry (including their bedsheets!)
- Clean the dishes and do basic housecleaning
- Use an ATM machine, conduct banking online, and exchange money on Venmo or PayPal
- Manage a budget
- Perform basic first aid
- Hang a picture (a skill that many college freshmen lack but almost all need)
- Make healthy eating choices at a school cafeteria
- Grocery shop with a budget
- Cook a few simple meals
- Change a tire and understand routine car maintenance
- Use Uber, Lyft, or other means of public transportation
- Identify one adult they can call or text in a crisis

If time is short, don't skimp on the last one. Moving into the explorer stage means your learner will face new choices and new temptations. They will need the wise input of an adult mentor to help them make the right choices, as well as to comfort them if (or maybe more accurately *when*) they make a decision they regret.

I reminded myself that we'll never get to go through this again, so let's enjoy the ride!

*Rest in God's plan.* As a mom of three learners, one explorer, and one focuser summarized, "The most helpful prayer that God has led me to pray with sincerity is, 'I trust you.' I can almost mark the season when that went from being something I knew in my head to something that was a genuine anchor for me. God has our son covered. We are given responsibility but we are not ultimately responsible."

## Bobblehead Parenting with Your Explorers and Focusers

Serving as a guide to our explorers and a resourcer to our focusers often means avoiding overreacting to our children's shifting career decisions. One mother of a young adult who delayed going to college referred to her philosophy of parenting as "bobblehead parenting." As she summarized, "Our 20-year-old son is thinking about going to a four-year college to get his bachelor's degree. But that changes almost weekly. I never know what plan is going to stick. So I now just sort of shake my head 'yes' and 'okay' to whatever his plan is this week. I call it 'bobblehead parenting.'" Responding more calmly and somewhere in the range between neutral and positive is making this Growing With mom more approachable and a better sounding board.

Nodding along with your kids—at least for a few moments or a short season—buys you and them time to process while keeping the channels of dialogue open in those moments when you most need them to remain open. Like when your daughter tells you she is leaving a secure job. Or when your son announces that he is changing majors, which means it will take him another 12 months—and another year of tuition—to finish his degree. In those moments, nodding along helps you to do the following:

Take a breath.

Be curious and open to their ideas.

Listen and hear them out without cutting them short.

Catch the deeper longing that lies beneath their crazy idea.

Stay connected relationally and avoid overreacting.

Walk through their plan with them to see the possibilities and hurdles.

Remember that your adulting kids are growing to appreciate your feedback, not depend on your permission.

### Knowing How Best to Help Your Explorers and Focusers in Their Job Search . . . and When to Step Aside

Based on their interviews with career counselors who specialize in working with young people, Jeffrey Arnett and Elizabeth Fishel provide the following practical vocational suggestions for parents of twentysomethings.[33]

*Remember: It's their job search, not yours.* The same tendency that may have led you during your high school senior's application process to tell others, "*We're* applying to college" can lead you to think "*We're* searching for a job." The reality is that *you* are not going to be hired; your child is.

*Offer a menu of possible choices of help, and let young people pick what works best.* Instead of trying to guess what your child wants from you, offer a host of options—ranging from reviewing a résumé and brainstorming potential contacts to role-playing an interview and helping set six- and twelve-month goals—and let them choose from the menu.

*Assist in creating a jobs advisory network.* Since up to 60–70 percent of job possibilities come through networking rather than listed openings, one of the primary channels of support for explorers and focusers is helping them build a network of contacts and advisors. You can help them brainstorm relatives, teachers, coaches, former supervisors, neighbors, and church members they can contact (note that it's your kids initiating the contact, not you) for advice and potential connections.

As one mother of a learner and an explorer we interviewed reminisced, "Our daughter met with a female CEO of a psychological hospital who started with a bachelor's degree in psychology. My daughter was utterly blown away that she started with this degree and went on to such a major accomplishment. My daughter was also surprised at the turns and twists in this successful professional's career journey. She realized that life and our vocations are not always linear."

*Encourage your child to seek internships and volunteer roles to gain experience and connections.* Unpaid or barely paid internships are a primary way for your adulting explorer or focuser to gain real-world work experience during (or instead of) college, over the summers, and after graduation. What they lack in salary they often make up for in your child's ability to get a foot in the door, make contacts, and try on jobs for size. Or you might want to encourage your child to volunteer a few hours or evenings a week for your church or another organization that needs help. Just make sure that while you're supporting unpaid internships, you're not also hinting that your child "make money"—which places your child in an untenable and unwinnable dilemma.

At Fuller, we love helping our students (many of whom are twentysomethings) think about service and career. And we love acronyms. So we've developed a CIQ (central integration question): *At this point in your Christian journey, how do you envision your call to God's mission in the world?* Steve and I applaud this question because the phrase *At this point in your Christian journey* implies evolution and growth.

This question, as well as this phrase, is a regular part of our curriculum.

It captures the tears and relief of Rebecca, whom we described at the beginning of this chapter.

And it names what we sense in our families as we watch our kids navigate their vocational adulting and, if we're honest, discern our own unfolding call to both service and career.

## Practical Questions to Grow With Your Child

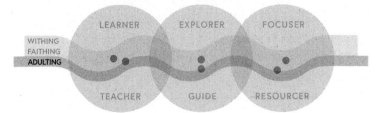

1. On a scale of 1 to 10 (with 1 being "we stink at this" and 10 being "we rock at this"), rate your family on the adulting research insights presented in this chapter.

   Our family serves together (or I model and encourage service) on a regular basis.

   1 ............................................... 5 ............................................... 10

   I view service as a before, during, and after process.

   1 ............................................... 5 ............................................... 10

   I am a key chain parent who identifies and hands over keys to my learner, explorer, or focuser.

   1 ............................................... 5 ............................................... 10

   I frame all careers as "holy."

   1 ............................................... 5 ............................................... 10

   I share with my children about my own ongoing vocational adulting.

   1 ............................................... 5 ............................................... 10

2. What insight, idea, illustration, or story in this chapter is most relevant to your family today?

3. How have your attitudes and actions already helped your learner, explorer, or focuser shape their world through their service and career?

4. What is your child learning about service and career from your own attitudes and actions? How do you feel about your answer?

5. Given your answers to the previous questions, what one or two changes might you want to make in your family?

# Conclusion

## *Growing With from Here On*

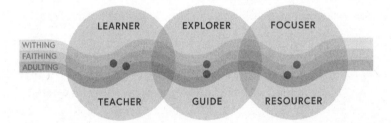

If you're like us, your antenna is perpetually searching for useful resources and strategic insights that will help you keep up and parent just a little bit better. Heaven knows we will take any advantage we can get!

But all the effort we pour into parenting leaves us emotionally drained, exposes our (sometimes) thin skin, and exasperates any relational raw nerves in our families.

We can empathize with your dreams and your fatigue. We hope this book encourages you to keep at the great parenting you are already doing. We trust it inspires you to see your growing kids through fresh perspectives that motivate you to risk trying new parenting approaches.

And we hope that this conversation not only changes your parenting but also changes you. In fact, it must.

## Symptoms

If you take seriously what this book suggests, you will contract
Growing With symptoms. You will likely know you are Growing
With your kids when:

*You develop an increasing awareness and urgency to address
your own growth areas as much as your kids'.* Growing With
parenting calls you to be honest about your place in your family's
relational ecosystem and for you to consider where you may need
to grow, change, forgive, let go, celebrate, or mourn. Increasingly,
you are giving yourself permission to be human even when your
presence in your growing kids' lives reveals the best and worst of
you. You refuse to hide your humanity, and you no longer let your
true self become invisible when your parenting becomes hard or
self-revealing.

*You recognize that your parenting will raise as many questions
as it offers answers.* Growing With parents reject the notion that
parenting is about "faking it until you make it." Instead, we admit
we have limitations. We cannot know everything, control every
situation, or give sage-like answers to every question. Not only
can we not deliver parenting perfection, but our kids do not want
that from us anyway!

On the one hand, this brings relief as you rest in knowing you
do not have to know or do it all. From another angle, you come to
realize that what is being asked of you is even harder. What your
growing kids want is for you to be curious, to be open, to struggle,
to wait, to search, and to discover *with* them. You are becoming
more comfortable with the answer "I don't know," realizing that
the "answer" is in the process and in the relationship.

*You anticipate parenting a different kid tomorrow than the one
you are parenting today.* Growing With parents admit that while
we might benefit from past parenting wins or sting from parenting
misses, each day starts with new possibility. We stay on our toes,
knowing that our previous successful parenting methods may not

# Four Options to Move from Parenting Alone to Parenting Together

As you wrap up this book, you might be feeling rather overwhelmed by your parenting inadequacies. You may fear that your kid is the only one who gets stuck adulting, questions their faithing, or rejects your attempts to grow with them. We've emphasized that the new terrain our teens and young adults are trying to navigate is new territory for parents as well. Parents—all kinds of parents—can feel alone as they attempt to get their bearings and do their best.

Often, formal communities like churches or schools offer great venues to connect parents with their parenting peers. We encourage you to engage in these opportunities. In this sidebar, we offer a few additional approaches that can help you take your own steps from feeling isolated toward cultivating peer parenting groups and friendships.

### Option #1: Stop competing and start connecting

Sometimes it is hard to connect with other parents because we spend too much of our energy comparing our kids with their kids and assessing each other's parenting styles. Resist these impulses and find another parent or group of parents where you can admit that you're all in this parenting life stage together. Commit to meeting and taking steps toward trusting each other with your ups and downs as parents. Start with what you have in common—your love for your kids and your desire to be the best parents you can. Let's reject the parenting perfectionism that divides us and embrace ways to be there for each other.

### Option #2: Make a start and end date

We find that many parents feel overbooked, are cautious about committing to "one more thing," and are especially fearful that if they join a group they can never leave it. Instead of committing to a never-ending schedule of gatherings, we encourage parents to try meeting consistently four to six times over a defined period. Try meeting in a rhythm that works with your friends—once a week, twice a month, or once a month—with a clear understanding that this group will *start* and *end*. At the end of that period, some parents may find they really resonate with a few others from the group and they may want to keep meeting on their own. But even if not, you've built relational roots that can be nurtured in other ways.

### Option #3: Connect over shared interests then commit to real conversations

I (Steve) admit that it is hard for me to join one more group. One summer, I met a dad whose daughter ran cross-country with my daughter. At one meet, we got to talking and realized that we both shared our daughters' passion for endurance running. We started meeting a couple times a month to train together. When you do longer runs, you have plenty of time to talk—which led to deeper conversations about parenting our daughters. We shared different situations that were going on in their lives, tested our theories with each other, shared our joys and fears of being dads of daughters, and confessed our imperfections. You may not love running, but connect your interests with another parent who shares those interests and become parenting conversation partners.

### Option #4: Be mutual friends and mentors

Find a friend with whom you can share your parenting journey. Make it a priority to chat by phone or over coffee. In addition, consider whether or not your friend can be an adult friend to your child who is available if your kid wants to talk with another adult (who should promise not to be an informant back to you). In fact, Jen and I (Steve) have tried to do this with another family and their kids, and our kids refer to the other parents as "their second parents." Pretty cool.

work in the present. We have courage that yesterday's fails do not disqualify us from being the best parents we can be today. Tomorrow your kid will be different and so will you. You are becoming more courageous as you refuse to hide behind yesterday's parenting track records and trust God to help you be the parent your kids need now. You have the grit to try, and you refuse to believe the lies that you can't.

## Momentum

Perhaps this book has renewed or evoked something new in your parenting outlook. We encourage you to honor that thoughtful inspiration by not letting it remain dormant. To turn that inspiration into Growing With momentum, consider the following:

*Go back through this book and review your underlining and notes.* What struck you as most important or intriguing? Do you see any recurring themes? What might your own reactions be prompting you to name or address? Perhaps you want to journal your thoughts, talk with a spouse, or share with a close friend. Name what is stirring inside of you. Let it speak to you.

*Connect with other Growing With parents.* One of the most powerful steps to help you maintain momentum is to find a handful of other parents in your life stage. Together you can normalize your experiences, empathize with each other's successes and challenges, and lean on one another for support and collective wisdom. Let these Growing With themes provide a springboard for your conversations.

*Celebrate.* You are smart and a good parent. (We parents need to remind each other!) We are convinced that there are insights and ideas in this book that you are already doing and even doing better. Take a moment and gratefully ponder these wins. Thank God for the good things you are already doing as a parent.

## Hope

Whether you are pondering your parenting wins, planning your next steps, or gauging your Growing With symptoms, we are convinced that your best parenting is not motivated by fear or shame but springs from hope.

We believe God gave you your kids.

We believe you love your kids.

We believe you want to be the best parents you can be.

We want that for our parenting too.

May any inspiration sparked from the pages of this book spill over into our conversations and our families with hope, possibility, and growth.

> *Our prayer for Growing With parents:*
>
> *Jesus, we thank you that in the midst of the ups and downs of parenting, we can place our hope in you. We are grateful for how you use parenting to prune us and shape us more and more into your image. Please help us abide in you so that we may bear great fruit in our families and in our world. Thank you that you love our kids even more than we do. Thank you that you want the very best for them and for us. Please help us rest in your powerful grace that continues to transform us all. Amen.*

# Appendix

## Growing Young Families Project

### Research Goals

The goal of the Fuller Youth Institute's Growing Young Families Project was to build upon findings from the Churches Engaging Young People Project (described in detail in *Growing Young: Six Essential Strategies to Help Young People Discover and Love Your Church*) and to investigate how parents understand and describe their relationship with their children and the church as their children grow in their faith and participate in churches. Accordingly, two primary questions motivated this study: (1) How do parents stay connected to and support their children's faith journeys as they grow older? and (2) How do parents and churches jointly support children's faith journeys?

For more on the research methodology of the Growing Young Families Project, including the questions asked in interviews and focus groups, as well as a full explanation of the initial Growing Young Project, please visit fulleryouthinstitute.org/growingwith.

## Participants

Representatives from FYI contacted 181 leaders from churches that had participated or were currently participating in a Sticky Faith or Growing Young cohort coordinated by FYI. Leaders were asked to nominate one to five parents and provide their names, contact information, number and ages of children, and an explanation of why they were nominating that individual.

Fifty-two leaders responded by nominating a total of 148 parents (either individuals or sets of parents). Of these 148 parents, 44 were selected to participate, were contacted by a member of the research team, and completed a 60-minute semi-structured phone interview during May and June 2017 that explored various topics, including their maturing child's faith, church involvement, service, career, and relational intimacy with family and friends. Further demographic information concerning these participants is below:

### State Distribution

| | | | |
|---|---|---|---|
| Alabama | 1 | Massachusetts | 2 |
| California | 11 | Minnesota | 3 |
| Colorado | 3 | Mississippi | 2 |
| Connecticut | 2 | Ohio | 1 |
| Florida | 4 | Pennsylvania | 1 |
| Georgia | 1 | Texas | 5 |
| Indiana | 4 | Washington | 1 |
| Iowa | 2 | Wisconsin | 1 |

### Gender

Female/male couple   14
Female   23
Male   7

## Marital Status

Divorced   3

Divorced and remarried   1

Married   36

Widowed   1

No marital status reported   3

## Ethnicity

Asian or Pacific Islander   2

Hispanic or Latino   3

White   39

## Subsequent Focus Groups

Given the importance of diversity for the present research, the research team initiated a second phase of data collection involving focus groups that included 7 additional single parents, 7 additional parents of post-college children, 10 additional African American parents, 7 additional Asian American parents, and 4 additional Hispanic or Latino parents. In total, an additional 35 parents participated, yielding 79 total participants for the research project (44 participated in interviews, 35 participated in focus groups).

## Limitations

Though the present study provides insights we believe are valuable to the study of faith formation and young people, limitations of the research design should also be noted. Nominations for participation relied on the perceptions of nominators. Other parents who also matched the criteria noted above but were unknown to the nominator may have been omitted from nominations. The present study also relied on nominators within FYI's network of churches, and future studies may benefit by extending similar research to other contexts. Results of the study are also reliant on what was expressed by participants to interviewers; other important factors may have contributed to their children's faith formation without their awareness.

It is also difficult to identify causal relationships with the design of the present study because various factors noted by parents may influence óne another and other important factors may not have been identified. Future studies may seek to establish causality using experimental designs by introducing interventions that incorporate the factors noted in the present study and may improve the generalizability of the present findings by increasing the sample size as well.

# Notes

### Chapter 1 Growing Up Today

1. Marina Mendonça and Anne Marie Fontaine, "The Role Maturity of Parents of Emerging Adult Children: Validity of a Parental Maturity Measure," *Journal of Adult Development* 21, no. 2 (2014): 116–28.

2. Remember that this is not mere spiritual optimism. The Scriptures perpetually talk about God's faithfulness to forgive us (1 John 1:9), God's desire to transform us (Phil. 1:1–6; 2 Cor. 5:17–21), and our collective hope that Christ dwells in us in order that we might know the fullness of God's love in our lives that often surprises us (Eph. 3:14–21).

3. All names have been changed in stories and quotes. Also, periodically we have smoothed out a few phrases or words in interview quotes to make them more readable and changed minor details in stories we share in order to maintain the anonymity of our interviewees.

4. Susan Y. Euling et al., "Role of Environmental Factors in the Timing of Puberty," *Pediatrics* 21 (February 1, 2008): S167–71.

5. American Psychological Association, "American Psychological Association Survey Shows Teen Stress Rivals That of Adults," February 11, 2014, http://www.apa.org/news/press/releases/2014/02/teen-stress.aspx.

6. American Psychological Association, "2010 Stress in America Report," http://www.apa.org/news/press/releases/stress/2010/key-findings.aspx.

7. Chap Clark, *Hurt 2.0: Inside the World of Today's Teenagers* (Grand Rapids: Baker Academic, 2011), 31.

8. Amanda Lenhart, "Teens, Social Media and Technology Overview 2015," Pew Research Center, April 9, 2015, http://www.pewinternet.org/2015/04/09/teens-social-media-technology-2015/.

9. Common Sense Media, "Fact Sheet: Teens and Smartphones," https://www.commonsensemedia.org/sites/default/files/uploads/pdfs/census_factsheet_teensandsmartphones.pdf.

10. Common Sense Media, "Fact Sheet: Teens and Smartphones."

11. Lenhart, "Teens, Social Media and Technology."

12. Madeleine J. George and Candice L. Odgers, "Seven Fears and the Science of How Mobile Technologies May Be Influencing Adolescents in the Digital Age," *Perspectives on Psychological Science* 10, no. 6 (November 2015): 832–51, doi:10.1177/1745691615596788.

13. Andrew K. Przybylski et al., "Motivational, Emotional, and Behavioral Correlates of Fear of Missing Out," *Computers in Human Behavior* 29, no. 4 (2013): 1841–48.

14. D'Vera Cohn et al., "Barely Half of U.S. Adults Are Married—A Record Low," Pew Research Center, December 14, 2011, http://www.pewsocialtrends.org /2011/12/14/barely-half-of-u-s-adults-are-married-a-record-low/.

15. Jeffrey Jensen Arnett and Elizabeth Fishel, *When Will My Grown-Up Kid Grow Up? Loving and Understanding Your Emerging Adult* (New York: Workman, 2013), 154.

16. Arnett and Fishel, 160.

17. T. J. Matthews and Brady E. Hamilton, "Delayed Childbearing: More Women Are Having Their First Child Later in Life," NCHS Data Brief, no. 21, August 2009, 1, http://www.cdc.gov/nchs/data/databriefs/db21.pdf.

18. Arnett and Fishel, *When Will My Grown-Up Kid Grow Up?*, 2.

19. N. A. Fouad and J. Bynner, "Work Transitions," *American Psychologist* 63, no. 4 (2008): 241–51.

20. "America's Young Adults at 27: Labor Market Activity, Education, and Household Composition: Results from a Longitudinal Survey," Bureau of Labor Statistics, March 26, 2014, http://www.bls.gov/news.release/nlsyth.nr0.htm.

21. Robert Schoeni and Karen Ross, "Material Assistance from Families During the Transition to Adulthood," in *On the Frontiers of Adulthood*, ed. Richard Settersten, Frank Furstenburg, and Ruben Rumbaut (Chicago: University of Chicago Press, 2005), 396–416.

22. Robin Marantz Henig, "What Is It About 20-Somethings?," *New York Times*, August 18, 2010, http://www.nytimes.com/2010/08/22/magazine/22Adult hood-t.html.

23. David P. Setran and Chris A. Kiesling, *Spiritual Formation in Emerging Adulthood: A Practical Theology for College and Young Adult Ministry* (Grand Rapids: Baker Academic, 2013), 2. It's also worth noting, however, that pre–World War II American ideals of adulthood and the time lines for marriage, childbearing, and other markers have varied quite a bit over the centuries. The standard expectations that had emerged by the 1960s were arguably creations of white, middle-class postwar America, particularly expectations of college education and home ownership. See Steven Mintz, *The Prime of Life: A History of Modern Adulthood* (Cambridge, MA: Belknap Harvard Press, 2015). Relatedly, Jeffrey Arnett acknowledges that the phenomenon of emerging adulthood is currently more prevalent in Western contexts, along with Asian industrialized and post-industrial contexts. Arnett anticipates that "it seems possible that by the end of the 21st century emerging adulthood will be a normative period for young people worldwide, although it is likely to vary in length and content both within and between countries." Jeffrey Jensen Arnett, *Emerging Adulthood: The Winding*

*Road from the Late Teens through the Twenties,* 2nd ed. (New York: Oxford University Press, 2014), 24.

24. Arnett, *Emerging Adulthood*, 15.

25. Varda Konstam, *Parenting Your Emerging Adult* (Far Hills, NJ: New Horizon Press, 2013), 26.

26. Mary C. Waters et al., *Coming of Age in America: The Transition to Adulthood in the Twenty-First Century* (Los Angeles: University of California Press, 2011), 192.

27. Gabrielle Bosché, *5 Millennial Myths* (BeReady Media, 2016), 22.

28. Bosché, 16–17.

29. Bosché, 32–33.

30. Meg Jay, *The Defining Decade* (New York: Hachette Book Group, 2012), xiv.

31. Jay, xxvii.

32. These are not three imposed categories. Rather, these domains—relationships, faith/belief, and vocation—are what young people themselves identify as the most important priorities to pursue if they hope to make it in this world. See Arnett, *Emerging Adulthood*, 83–243.

33. We are grateful to Sharon Daloz Parks for first helping us understand faithing as a verb. Her definition is broader than ours—namely, "putting one's heart on that which one trusts as true." Sharon Daloz Parks, *Big Questions, Worthy Dreams: Mentoring Young Adults in Their Search for Meaning, Purpose, and Faith,* 2nd ed. (San Francisco: Jossey-Bass, 2011), 34.

34. Christian Smith and Patricia Snell, *Souls in Transition: The Religious and Spiritual Lives of Emerging Adults* (New York: Oxford University Press, 2009), 150.

35. Arnett, *Emerging Adulthood*, 176.

36. R. Flory and M. Denton, *Disconnected Souls: Religion and Spirituality in the Lives of Emerging Adults* (New York: Oxford University Press, 2018). This forthcoming resource reports on the third wave of the National Study of Youth and Religion regarding the religious and spiritual lives of emerging adults, especially those that we define as focusers (ages 23–29).

37. The exact origin of this phrase is unknown, and while Albert Einstein is allegedly the source of this phrase, no citation has ever been located.

## Chapter 2 Pursuing the Growing With Posture

1. Author and biblical scholar Eugene Peterson reminds us that young people are God's gifts to middle-aged parents. Peterson explains that adolescence (and now emerging adulthood) is a process designed by God to bring young people to adulthood. Simultaneously, this period is designed by the Creator to provide something essential to parents in their own critical time in life. Eugene H. Peterson, *Like Dew Your Youth: Growing Up with Your Teenager* (Grand Rapids: Eerdmans, 1994), 97–98.

2. Carol Dweck defines "growth mindset" as a person's belief that their most basic abilities can be developed through dedication and hard work (versus believing that abilities are "fixed" and can't be significantly improved). Carol S. Dweck, *Mindset: The New Psychology of Success* (New York: Random House, 2006), 174–93.

3. For our more academic readers, we acknowledge that we are oversimplifying the complexity of development. We also acknowledge that development is rarely stage-like, meaning young people do not grow in a linear fashion. Further, we acknowledge that young people are often more developed in certain domains of life than in others. Finally, we recognize that research on race, gender, ethnicity, sexual orientation, and socioeconomic status is essential in understanding the unique perspective of every young person. Our goal is merely to offer a helpful guide for generally understanding stages young people likely encounter and to give language to their experiences.

4. Jeffrey Jensen Arnett, *Adolescence and Emerging Adulthood*, 6th ed. (Upper Saddle River, NJ: Pearson, 2012), 85–87.

5. Arnett, 43–52.

6. D. J. Siegel, *Brainstorm: The Power and Purpose of the Teenage Brain* (New York: Penguin, 2015), 41.

7. Siegel, 35.

8. J. W. Fowler, *Stages of Faith: The Psychology of Human Development and the Quest for Meaning* (San Francisco: Harper & Row, 1981), 31; Kara E. Powell and Chap Clark, *Sticky Faith: Everyday Ideas to Build Lasting Faith in Your Kids* (Grand Rapids: Zondervan, 2011), 143–45.

9. Parks, *Big Questions*, 107–9.

10. Paul Taylor, *Is College Worth It? College Presidents, Public Assess Value, Quality and Mission of Higher Education* (Washington, DC: Pew Research Center, 2011), 65–67.

11. Arnett, *Emerging Adulthood*, 9–11.

12. Arnett, 49–82.

13. Laura M. Padilla-Walker, Madison K. Memmott-Elison, and Larry J. Nelson, "Positive Relationships as an Indicator of Flourishing During Emerging Adulthood," in *Flourishing in Emerging Adulthood: Positive Development during the Third Decade of Life*, ed. Laura M. Padilla-Walker and Larry J. Nelson (New York: Oxford University Press, 2017), 212–36.

14. Steven C. Argue, "Undergraduate Spiritual Struggle and the Quest to Remain Faithful," *Journal of Youth Ministry* 16, no. 1 (2017): 8–29.

15. Georgia T. Chao and Philip D. Gardner, "Healthy Transitions to Work," in Padilla-Walker and Nelson, *Flourishing*, 104–28.

16. "Millennial Careers: 2020 Vision," (Milwaukee: ManpowerGroup, 2016), 6.

17. Wyndol Furman and Jessica K. Winkles, "Transformations in Heterosexual Romantic Relationships across the Transition into Adulthood: 'Meet Me at the Bleachers . . . I Mean the Bar,'" in *Relationship Pathways: From Adolescence to Young Adulthood*, ed. W. Andrew Collins and Brett Paul Laursen (Thousand Oaks, CA: SAGE Publications, Inc., 2012), 191–213; Smith and Snell, *Souls in Transition*, 61–62.

18. Richard D. Putnam and David E. Campbell, *American Grace: How Religion Divides and Unites Us* (New York: Simon & Schuster, 2010), 167–74.

19. Christian Smith et al., *Lost in Transition: The Dark Side of Emerging Adulthood* (New York: Oxford University Press, 2011), 110–47.

20. Padilla-Walker, Memmott-Elison, and Nelson, "Positive Relationships," 212–36. Padilla-Walker and associates acknowledge that, from a life course

perspective, "the trajectories of family members are interdependent and there is a consistent interplay between the individual development of the emerging adult child and his or her family members" (213).

21. Maryellen Weimer, *Learner-Centered Teaching: Five Key Changes to Practice*, 2nd ed. (San Francisco: Jossey-Bass, 2013), 15–16.

22. Weimer, 72–83.

23. Padilla-Walker, Memmott-Elison, and Nelson, "Positive Relationships," 212–36.

24. Arnett, *Emerging Adulthood*, 80–82.

25. Parks, *Big Questions*, 127–34.

26. These two commitments align with the research of Carol Dweck, a leading researcher in motivation and human behavior, who advocates for a "growth mindset paradigm." Dweck, *Mindset*.

27. Jill C. Bradley-Geist and Julie B. Olson-Buchanan, "Helicopter Parents: An Examination of the Correlates of Over-Parenting of College Students," *Education and Training* 56, no. 4 (2014): 314–28.

### Chapter 3 Getting Warmer

1. Vern L. Bengtson, Norella M. Putney, and Susan C. Harris, *Families and Faith: How Religion Is Passed Down across Generations* (New York: Oxford University Press, 2013), 79.

2. Bengtson, Putney, and Harris, 98.

3. Bengtson, Putney, and Harris, 74.

4. Bengtson, Putney, and Harris, 76–79.

5. Bengtson, Putney, and Harris, 74–76.

6. Brené Brown, *Daring Greatly* (New York: Penguin, 2012), 81.

7. Erika M. Manczak, Anita DeLongis, and Edith Chen, "Does Empathy Have a Cost? Diverging Psychological and Physiological Effects within Families," *Health Psychology* 35, no. 3 (March 2016): 211–18.

8. Arnett and Fishel, *When Will My Grown-Up Kid Grow Up?*, 47.

9. Konstam, *Parenting Your Emerging Adult*, 131.

10. Arnett and Fishel, *When Will My Grown-Up Kid Grow Up?*, 51.

11. Arnett, *Emerging Adulthood*, 56.

12. Smith and Snell, *Souls in Transition*, 43–44.

13. Padilla-Walker, Memmott-Elison, and Nelson, "Positive Relationships," 220.

14. Padilla-Walker, Memmott-Elison, and Nelson, 220.

15. Bengtson, Putney, and Harris, *Families and Faith*, 100–101.

16. Bengtson, Putney, and Harris, 100.

17. Padilla-Walker, Memmott-Elison, and Nelson, "Positive Relationships," 222.

18. Bengtson, Putney, and Harris, *Families and Faith*, 104–12.

19. This story is adapted from Kara Powell, *The Sticky Faith Guide for Your Family* (Grand Rapids: Zondervan, 2014), 79–80.

20. Arnett and Fishel, *When Will My Grown-Up Kid Grow Up?*, 44.

21. These birthday and milestone ideas are adapted from Steven Argue and Kara Powell, *Eighteen Plus* (Atlanta: Orange Books, 2018).

22. Steven C. Argue, "Supporting Undergraduate Spirituality: College-Related Factors Evangelical Christian Students Perceive as Affecting Their Working through

Spiritual Struggle While Attending a Public University" (PhD diss., Michigan State University, 2015), 130.

## Chapter 4 Walls of Support

1. Lisa Damour, *Untangled: Guiding Teenage Girls Through the Seven Transitions of Adulthood* (New York: Ballantine Books, 2017), 23.

2. Steven Covey, *The Seven Habits of Highly Effective People* (New York: Simon & Schuster, 1989), 53.

3. American Psychological Association, "Stress in America: Are Teens Adopting Adults' Stress Habits?," February 11, 2014, 4, https://www.apa.org/news/press/releases/stress/2013/stress-report.pdf.

4. APA, "Stress in America," 4.

5. APA, "Stress in America," 4.

6. APA, "Stress in America," 4.

7. APA, "Stress in America," 6.

8. Sociologist Tim Clydesdale coined the term "daily life management" to describe the daily pressures faced by college students. Tim Clydesdale, *The First Year Out* (Chicago: University of Chicago Press, 2007), 2.

9. Arnett and Fishel, *When Will My Grown-Up Kid Grow Up?*, 33–36.

10. American Psychological Association, "Stress in America: Key Findings," 2010, http://www.apa.org/news/press/releases/stress/2010/key-findings.aspx.

11. Interview with Ellen Galinski, "The Teenage Brain," *Frontline*, January 31, 2002, http://www.pbs.org/wgbh/pages/frontline/shows/teenbrain/interviews/galinsky.html.

12. Jeffrey Jensen Arnett and Joseph Schwab, "The Clark University Poll of Parents of Emerging Adults," September 2013, http://www2.clarku.edu/clark-poll-emerging-adults/pdfs/clark-university-poll-parents-emerging-adults.pdf.

13. Padilla-Walker, Memmott-Elison, and Nelson, "Positive Relationships," 218.

14. Scott Cormode, Sticky Faith Cohort, Fuller Theological Seminary, Pasadena, CA, February 25–26, 2016.

15. Arnett and Fishel, *When Will My Grown-Up Kid Grow Up?*, 43.

16. Jeffrey Sparshott, "Congratulations, Class of 2015. You're the Most Indebted Ever (For Now)," *Wall Street Journal*, May 8, 2015, https://blogs.wsj.com/economics/2015/05/08/congratulations-class-of-2015-youre-the-most-indebted-ever-for-now/.

17. Maggie McGrath, "Desperate and in Debt: 30% of Millennials Would Sell an Organ to Get Rid of Student Loans," *Forbes*, September 9, 2015, https://www.forbes.com/sites/maggiemcgrath/2015/09/09/desperate-and-in-debt-30-of-millennials-would-sell-an-organ-to-get-rid-of-student-loans/.

18. Adapted from Arnett and Fishel, *When Will My Grown-Up Kid Grow Up?*, 43.

19. Shaunti Feldhahn, "Everything We Think We Know about Marriage and Divorce Is Wrong," Catalyst, May 6, 2014, http://catalystconference.com/read/everything-we-think-we-know-about-marriage-and-divorce-is-wrong/.

20. The remainder of this section is adapted from Kara Powell, Jake Mulder, and Brad Griffin, *Growing Young: Six Essential Strategies to Help Young People Discover and Love Your Church* (Grand Rapids: Baker Books, 2016), 206–7.

21. Elizabeth Marquardt, *Between Two Worlds: The Inner Lives of Children of Divorce* (New York: Three Rivers Press, 2005), 48, 59, 85.

22. Arnett, *Emerging Adulthood*, 60–61.

23. Marquardt, *Between Two Worlds*, 155.

24. Arnett, *Emerging Adulthood*, 50.

25. Arnett, 54.

26. Arnett and Fishel, *When Will My Grown-Up Kid Grow Up?*, 110.

27. Greg McKeown, *Essentialism: The Disciplined Pursuit of Less* (New York: Crown Business, 2014), 103.

28. Peterson, *Like Dew Your Youth*, 45.

29. Reggie Joiner and Carey Nieuwhof, *Parenting Beyond Your Capacity* (Colorado Springs: David C. Cook, 2010), 101, emphasis added.

30. Arnett and Fishel, *When Will My Grown-Up Kid Grow Up?*, 46.

31. Brown, *Daring Greatly*, 71.

32. Adapted from Arnett and Fishel, *When Will My Grown-Up Kid Grow Up?*, 116.

## Chapter 5 Personal Faithing

1. Bengtson, Putney, and Harris, *Families and Faith*, 184–206.

2. Parks, *Big Questions*, 24–26.

3. James W. Fowler, *Stages of Faith: The Psychology of Human Development and the Quest for Meaning* (San Francisco: HarperSanFrancisco, 1995), 16–39.

4. K. L. Bailey et al., "Spirituality at a Crossroads: A Grounded Theory of Christian Emerging Adults," *Psychology of Religion and Spirituality* 8, no. 2 (2016): 99–109.

5. Parks, *Big Questions*, 53–103.

6. Argue, "Supporting Undergraduate Spirituality," dissertation research field notes, January 2014.

7. Powell, Mulder, and Griffin, *Growing Young*, 126–62.

8. Don Everts, *Jesus with Dirty Feet: A Down-to-Earth Look at Christianity for the Curious and Skeptical* (Downers Grove, IL: InterVarsity, 1999), 21–28.

9. M. Chan, K. M. Tsai, and A. J. Fuligni, "Changes in Religiosity across the Transition to Young Adulthood," *Journal of Youth and Adolescence* 44, no. 8 (2015): 1555–66.

10. T. W. Hall, D. C. Wang, and E. Edwards, "The Spiritual Development of Emerging Adults over the College Years: A 4-Year Longitudinal Investigation," *Psychology of Religion and Spirituality* 8, no. 3 (2016): 206–17.

11. Smith and Snell, *Souls in Transition*, 103–42.

12. Paul Taylor, *The Next America: Boomers, Millennials, and the Looming Generational Showdown* (New York: PublicAffairs, 2014), 163. Generational cohorts are grouped by when populations were born and when they come of age: the Silent generation (born 1928–1945), the Baby Boomer generation (born 1946–1964), Generation X (born 1965–1980), and the Millennial generation (born 1980–2000). These descriptors carry some ambiguity reflected in changing terminology. Those born after 2000 have been called iGen or Generation Z.

13. Thomas E. Bergler, "Mapping the Missional Landscape of Emerging Adulthood," *The Journal of Youth Ministry* 15, no. 2 (Spring 2017): 64–96.

14. Christian Smith and Melinda Lundquist Denton, *Soul Searching: The Religious and Spiritual Lives of American Teenagers* (New York: Oxford University Press, 2005), 30–71.

15. Smith and Snell, *Souls in Transition*, 134.

16. Taylor, *The Next America*, 161–65.

17. Bailey et al., "Spirituality at a Crossroads," 99–109.

18. Argue, "Undergraduate Spiritual Struggle," 18.

19. Bengtson, Putney, and Harris, *Families and Faith*, 54–67.

20. Argue, "Undergraduate Spiritual Struggle," 11.

21. Powell, *Sticky Faith Guide for Your Family*, 131–33.

22. Bengtson, Putney, and Harris, *Families and Faith*, 65.

23. A. Astin, H. Astin, and J. Lindholm, *Cultivating the Spirit: How College Can Enhance Students' Inner Lives* (San Francisco: Jossey-Bass, 2010), 105.

24. Smith and Denton, *Soul Searching*, 131–33.

25. Kenda Creasy Dean, *Almost Christian: What the Faith of Our Teenagers Is Telling the American Church* (New York: Oxford University Press, 2010), 115–17.

26. Larry J. Nelson and Laura M. Padilla-Walker, "Flourishing and Floundering in Emerging Adult College Students," *Emerging Adulthood* 1, no. 1 (2013): 67–78.

27. Kenda Creasy Dean, "How Do We Help Students Practice Their Faith?," *The Collaborative*, Mars Hill Bible Church, 2014.

28. Hall, Wang, and Edwards, "The Spiritual Development of Emerging Adults," 206–17.

29. Read John 10:10, but also recognize that this is the whole redemptive story of God throughout the Christian Scriptures. God is pursuing us and desires to bless us so that we might live as one with God and with each other. With God there is always hope.

## Chapter 6 Faithing Together

1. A quick internet search of articles surfaces titles similar to these examples we have compiled for illustrative purposes.

2. Adults ages 18–29 comprise 16.7 percent of the adult population according to a report from 2015 statistics released by the United States Census Bureau. "Annual estimates of the resident population by single year of age and sex for the United States: April 1, 2010 to July 1, 2015" [Data file], retrieved from https://factfinder.census.gov/bkmk/table/1.0/en/PEP/2015/PEPSYASEX.

Often cited as one of the most up-to-date repositories of data on US churches, the recent National Congregations Study highlights how quickly congregations are aging. Between 1998 and 2007, the number of regular attenders over age 60 in the 2,740 congregations surveyed jumped from 25 percent to 30 percent. During that same short time period, regular attenders younger than 35 dropped from 25 percent to 20 percent. Mark Chaves, Shawna Anderson, and Jason Byassee, "American Congregations at the Beginning of the 21st Century: A National Congregations Study," http://www.soc.duke.edu/natcong/Docs/NCSII_report_final.pdf.

3. Nancy Tatom Ammerman, *Sacred Stories, Spiritual Tribes: Finding Religion in Everyday Life* (New York: Oxford University Press, 2013), 6.

4. Powell and Clark, *Sticky Faith*, 23–24.

5. Powell, Mulder, and Griffin, *Growing Young*, 196–233.

6. Taylor, *The Next America*, 165–69.

7. Taylor, 164.

8. Taylor, 170.

9. Bengtson, Putney, and Harris, *Families and Faith*, 65–67.

10. Powell and Clark, *Sticky Faith*, 83–95.

11. Jean M. Twenge, *iGen: Why Today's Super-Connected Kids Are Growing up Less Rebellious, More Tolerant, Less Happy—and Completely Unprepared for Adulthood (and What This Means for the Rest of Us)* (New York: Atria Books, 2017), 130–32.

12. For starters, see a great resource by our friend and scholar Andrew Root, *Exploding Stars, Dead Dinosaurs, and Zombies: Youth Ministry in the Age of Science* (Minneapolis: Fortress, 2018).

13. Powell and Clark, *Sticky Faith*, 19–20.

14. Argue, "Supporting Undergraduate Spirituality," 130.

15. Smith and Snell, *Souls in Transition*, 112–13.

16. Believing popular but misleading narratives (often perpetuated by movies and novels) exaggerates the animosity between (predominantly evangelical) religious and university contexts and discourages students from finding helpful ways to integrate their faith, learning, and experiences.

17. Jenny Lee, "Religious and College Attendance: Change among Students," *Review of Higher Education* 25 (2002): 369–84.

18. Jeremy E. Uecker, Mark Regnerus, and Margaret L. Vaaler, "Losing My Religion: The Social Sources of Religious Decline in Early Adulthood," *Social Forces* 85, no. 4 (2007): 1667–92.

19. Timothy T. Clydesdale, *The First Year Out: Understanding American Teens after High School* (Chicago: The University of Chicago Press, 2007), 39–41.

20. Smith and Snell, *Souls in Transition*, 75–79.

21. Smith and Snell, 75.

22. Smith and Snell, 76–77.

23. Smith and Snell, 78.

24. Smith and Denton, *Soul Searching*, 89.

25. Powell and Clark, *Sticky Faith*, 167.

26. Chan, Tsai, and Fuligni, "Changes in Religiosity," 1555.

27. Powell and Clark, *Sticky Faith*, 166.

28. Steven Argue, "It's Time to Define the Relationship with Our Emerging Adults," Youth Specialties, September 23, 2014, http://youthspecialties.com/blog/its-time-to-define-the-relationship-with-our-emerging-adults.

29. Parks, *Big Questions*, 165–73.

30. Parks, 191.

31. Sherry Turkle, *Alone Together: Why We Expect More from Technology and Less from Each Other* (New York: Basic Books, 2012), 1–3.

32. Tim Hutchings, *Creating Church Online: Ritual, Community, and New Media* (New York: Routledge, 2017), 220–40.

33. Email conversation with Dave Adamson, October 30, 2017. Used with his permission.

34. Dietrich Bonhoeffer, *Life Together and Prayer Book of the Bible* (Minneapolis: Fortress, 1996), 29.

35. Nancy J. Duff, "Praising God Online," *Theology Today* 70, no. 1 (2013): 22–29.

36. Emma Green, "It's Hard to Go to Church," *The Atlantic*, August 23, 2016, www.theatlantic.com/politics/archive/2016/08/religious-participation -survey/496940/.

37. Turkle, *Alone Together*, 1–20.

38. These ideas are inspired by suggestions in Powell, *Sticky Faith Guide for Your Family*, 99–100.

39. We are grateful for this wise insight inspired from Eugene Peterson's *Like Dew Your Youth*.

## Chapter 7 Relational Adulting

1. A. McCabe and K. T. Dinh, "Agency and Communion, Ineffectiveness and Alienation: Themes in the Life Stories of Latino and Southeast Asian Adolescents," *Imagination, Cognition and Personality* 36, no. 2 (2016): 150–71.

2. W. W. Hartup, "The Social Worlds of Childhood," *American Psychologist* 34 (1979): 944–50.

3. Clea McNeely and Jayne Blanchard, *The Teen Years Explained: A Guide to Healthy Adolescent Development* (Baltimore: Johns Hopkins Bloomberg School of Public Health, 2009), 31–39.

4. Arnett, *Adolescence and Emerging Adulthood*, 215–17.

5. Arnett, 210–22.

6. Arnett, 217–18.

7. Clark, *Hurt 2.0*, 61.

8. Amanda Lenhart et al., *Teens, Technology and Romantic Relationships: From Flirting to Breaking Up, Social Media and Mobile Phones are Woven into Teens Romantic Lives* (Pew Research Center, 2015), 2. Note: 1 percent of young people chose not to report their dating status.

9. Amanda Lenhart et al., *Teens, Technology and Friendships: Video Games, Social Media and Mobile Phones Play an Integral Role in How Teens Meet and Interact with Friends* (Pew Research Center, 2015), 56–68.

10. Eric W. Owens et al., "The Impact of Internet Pornography on Adolescents: A Review of the Research," *Sexual Addiction & Compulsivity* 19, nos. 1–2 (2012): 99–122.

11. Monica Anderson, *Parents, Teens and Digital Monitoring* (Pew Research Center, 2016), 1–33.

12. Lawrence B. Finer and Jesse M. Philbin, *Sexual Initiation, Contraceptive Use, and Pregnancy among Young Adolescents* (New York: Guttmacher Institute, 2013), 1–6.

13. Laura Widman et al., "Parent-Adolescent Sexual Communication and Adolescent Safer Sex Behavior: A Meta-Analysis," *JAMA Pediatrics* 170, no. 1 (2016): 52–61.

14. Carolyn McNamara Barry, Stephanie D. Madsen, and Alyssa DeGrace, "Growing Up with a Little Help from Their Friends in Emerging Adulthood," in

*The Oxford Handbook of Emerging Adulthood*, ed. Jeffrey J. Arnett (Oxford: Oxford University Press, 2016), 215–29.

15. Jay, *Defining Decade*, 84–88.

16. Arnett, *Adolescence and Emerging Adulthood*, 269–70.

17. Smith et al., *Lost in Transition*, 148–49.

18. Smith et al., 148–94.

19. Erin Kramer Holmes et al., "Healthy Transitions to Family Formation," in Padilla-Walker and Nelson, *Flourishing in Emerging Adulthood*, 70–97.

20. Smith et al., *Lost in Transition*, 180–83.

21. Stephen T. Russell, Ryan J. Watson, and Joel A. Muraco, "The Development of Same-Sex Intimate Relationships During Adolescence," in *Relationship Pathways: From Adolescence to Young Adulthood*, ed. W. Andrew Collins and Brett Paul Laursen (Thousand Oaks, CA: SAGE Publications, Inc., 2012), 215–33.

22. Anna Brown, "5 Key Findings About LGBT Americans," Pew Research Center, June 13, 2017, http://www.pewresearch.org/fact-tank/2017/06/13/5-key-findings-about-lgbt-americans/.

23. Paul Taylor, *A Survey of LGBT Americans: Attitudes, Experiences and Values in Changing Times* (Washington, DC: Pew Research Center, 2013), 21–29; Russell, Watson, and Muraco, "The Development of Same-Sex Intimate Relationships," 215–33. We thank Dr. Mark Baker, a Fuller alumnus and therapist in Los Angeles, for his aid in conceptualizing this section.

24. Jessica Hamar Martínez, "Where the Public Stands on Religious Liberty vs. Nondiscrimination," Pew Research Center, September 28, 2016, http://www.pewforum.org/2016/09/28/where-the-public-stands-on-religious-liberty-vs-non discrimination/.

25. Christina R. Peter et al., "Positive Development During Emerging Adulthood for Queer Populations," in Padilla-Walker and Nelson, *Flourishing in Emerging Adulthood*, 586–612.

26. Justin Lee, *Torn: Rescuing the Gospel from the Gays-vs.-Christians Debate* (New York: Jericho Books, 2013), 33.

27. T. W. Harrison, "Adolescent Homosexuality and Concerns Regarding Disclosure," *The Journal of School Health* 73, no. 3 (2003): 107–12; S. Saltzburg, "Narrative Therapy Pathways for Re-Authoring with Parents of Adolescents Coming-Out as Lesbian, Gay, and Bisexual," *Contemporary Family Therapy* 29, nos. 1–2 (2007): 57–69.

28. Sofi Sinozich and Lynn Langton, *Rape and Sexual Assault Victimization among College-Age Females, 1995–2013* (US Department of Justice, December 2014), 1–19.

29. "Sexual Violence Statistics," Rape, Abuse & Incest National Network (RAINN), accessed November 11, 2017, https://www.rainn.org/statistics/victims -sexual-violence.

30. Arnett, *Adolescence and Emerging Adulthood*, 119–21.

31. Holmes et. al., "Healthy Transitions to Family Formation," 70–97.

32. Galena K. Rhoades and Scott M. Stanley, *Before "I Do": What Do Premarital Experiences Have to Do with Marital Quality among Today's Young Adults?* (The University of Virginia: The National Marriage Project, 2014), 1–39, http://nationalmarriageproject.org/blog/resources/before-i-do-2/.

33. Anne Johnson, Tobin Van Ostern, and Abraham White, *The Student Debt Crisis* (Washington, DC: Center for American Progress, 2012), 1–28.

34. Katie Lobosco, "Students Are Graduating with $30,000 in Loans," CNN Money, October 18, 2016, http://money.cnn.com/2016/10/18/pf/college/average -student-loan-debt/index.html.

35. See Richard Allan Beck, *Unclean: Meditations on Purity, Hospitality, and Mortality* (Cambridge, UK: Lutterworth Press, 2012). Beck argues that in Jesus's interaction with the Pharisees in Matthew 9:9–13, his reference to Hosea 6:6 emphasizes that God desires mercy not sacrifice. While both are important, Jesus's priority is mercy. Even though sacrifice draws distinction between religious insiders and outsiders, it submits to mercy and its call to bridge differences for the sake of the relationship. We see this priority in Jesus's own earthly encounters with people.

## Chapter 8 Vocational Adulting

1. Frederick Buechner, *Wishful Thinking* (New York: Harper One, 1993), 118–19.

2. Diana Garland, *Inside Out Families* (Waco: Baylor University Press, 2010), 69.

3. Other research supports these two suggestions, including Patricia S. Herzog, "Multidimensional Perspectives on the Faith and Giving of Youth and Emerging Adults," *Religions* 8, no. 7 (2017): 128.

4. "Youth Helping America: The Role of Social Institutions in Teen Volunteering," Corporation for National and Community Service, November 2005, https:// www.nationalservice.gov/pdf/05_1130_LSA_YHA_SI_factsheet.pdf, 1.

5. Kurt Ver Beek, "The Impact of Short-Term Missions: A Case Study of House Construction in Honduras After Hurricane Mitch," *Missiology* 34, no. 4 (October 2006): 485.

6. Robert J. Priest et al., "Researching the Short-Term Mission Movement," *Missiology* 34, no. 4 (October 2006): 431–50.

7. "Volunteering in the United States News Release," Bureau of Labor Statistics, February 25, 2016, https://www.bls.gov/news.release/volun.htm.

8. Smith and Snell, *Souls in Transition*, 71.

9. Arnett, *Emerging Adulthood*, 12.

10. Smith et al., *Lost in Transition*, 70–86, 93–107.

11. Smith et al., 219–21.

12. "Millennials: Breaking the Myths," Nielsen Company, January 27, 2014, http://www.nielsen.com/us/en/insights/reports/2014/millennials-breaking-the -myths.html.

13. Arnett and Fishel, *When Will My Grown-Up Kid Grow Up?*, 192.

14. Arnett, *Adolescence and Emerging Adulthood*, 328–29.

15. Katherine Turpin, "Adolescence: Vocation in Performance, Passion, and Possibility," in Kathleen A. Cahalan and Bonnie J. Miller-McLemore, eds., *Calling All Years Good: Christian Vocation throughout Life's Seasons* (Grand Rapids: Eerdmans, 2017), 69.

16. Georgia T. Chao and Philip D. Gardner, "Healthy Transitions to Work," in Padilla-Walker and Nelson, *Flourishing in Emerging Adulthood*, 112.

17. Chao and Gardner, "Healthy Transitions to Work," 106.

18. Arnett and Fishel, *When Will My Grown-Up Kid Grow Up?*, 214.

19. "Americans at Age 31: Labor Market Activity, Education and Partner Status Summary," Bureau of Labor Statistics, April 17, 2018, http://www.bls.gov/news.release/nlsyth.nr0.htm.

20. Arnett and Fishel, *When Will My Grown-Up Kid Grow Up?*, 197.

21. Konstam, *Parenting Your Emerging Adult*, 51–52.

22. Angela Duckworth, *Grit: The Power of Passion and Perseverance* (New York: Scribner, 2016), 8.

23. Jay, *Defining Decade*, xvii–xxxi.

24. Arnett and Fishel, *When Will My Grown-Up Kid Grow Up?*, 191.

25. Chao and Gardner, "Healthy Transitions to Work," 109.

26. Konstam, *Parenting Your Emerging Adult*, 130.

27. Konstam, 44.

28. Konstam, 44.

29. Jay, *Defining Decade*, 171.

30. Arnett and Fishel, *When Will My Grown-Up Kid Grow Up?*, 28–29, 188.

31. A major thanks to David Livermore, leader of the Cultural Intelligence Center, and Terry Linhart of Bethel College (Indiana) for collaborating with us in developing this model. See Kara Powell and Brad M. Griffin, *Sticky Faith Service Guide* (Grand Rapids: Zondervan, 2016), 19.

32. Search Institute, *Insights and Evidence in Brief: Finding the Student Spark* 5, no. 1 (November 2010), 1.

33. Arnett and Fishel, *When Will My Grown-Up Kid Grow Up?*, 195–96, 199–202.

**Kara Powell**, PhD, is the executive director of the Fuller Youth Institute and a faculty member at Fuller Theological Seminary. Named by *Christianity Today* as one of "50 Women to Watch," Kara serves as a youth and family strategist for Orange and speaks regularly at parenting and leadership conferences. She is the author or coauthor of a number of books, including *Growing Young, The Sticky Faith Guide for Your Family, Sticky Faith Curriculum, Can I Ask That?, Deep Justice Journeys, Essential Leadership, Deep Justice in a Broken World, Deep Ministry in a Shallow World*, and the *Good Sex Youth Ministry Curriculum*. Kara and her husband, Dave, are regularly inspired by all the learning and laughter that come from growing with their three teenage and young adult children, Nathan, Krista, and Jessica. Twitter: @kpowellfyi

**Steven Argue**, PhD, is an associate professor of youth, family, and culture at Fuller Theological Seminary and an applied research strategist at the Fuller Youth Institute. He has taught undergraduate and graduate youth ministry courses for over a decade; worked in multiple ministry contexts, including the lead pastoral team at Mars Hill Bible Church (Grand Rapids, MI); and serves on the board for the Association of Youth Ministry Educators. Steve researches, speaks, and writes regularly on topics surrounding adolescence, emerging adulthood, faith, and spiritual struggle. He and his wife, Jen, love being parents of their three emerging adult daughters, Kara, Elise, and Lauren. Twitter: @stevenargue

**Fuller Youth Institute**

# Make the church the best place for young people to grow.

---

Here at the Fuller Youth Institute, we transform academic research into practical resources and training for leaders and parents to help unlock young people's potential and unleash them to change the world.

## Join the movement.

f   @fulleryouthinstitute

🐦   @fullerfyi

📷   @fulleryouthinstitute

🌐   fulleryouthinstitute.org

# DR. KARA POWELL

**Finding answers to leaders' and parents' toughest questions about young people.**

Follow Kara to receive blog posts, find out about upcoming resources, and join the conversation at:

## karapowell.com

# DR. STEVEN ARGUE

Read, watch, or listen to more of Steve's research on adolescence, emerging adulthood, and spiritual development by visiting:

## stevenargue.com

f @Steven.Argue    ⬡ @StevenArgue    🐦 @stevenargue